Contempo

Contemporary States and Societies

This series provides lively and accessible introductions to key countries and regions of the world, conceived and designed to meet the needs of today's students. The authors are all experts with specialist knowledge of the country or region concerned and have been chosen also for their ability to communicate clearly to a non-specialist readership. Each text has been specially commissioned for the series and is structured according to a common format.

Published
Contemporary Russia
Edwin Bacon with
Matthew Wyman
Contemporary South Africa (2ed)
Anthony Butler
Contemporary America (3ed)
Russell Duncan
and Joseph Goddard
Contemporary China
Alan Hunter and John Sexton
Contemporary Japan (2ed)
Duncan McCargo
Contemporary Britain (2ed)
John McCormick
Contemporary Latin America (2ed)
Ronaldo Munck

Forthcoming
Contemporary India
Katharine Adeney
and Andrew Wyatt
Contemporary France
Helen Drake
Contemporary Spain
Paul Kennedy
Contemporary Ireland
Eoin O'Malley
Contemporary Asia
John M'Kay

Also planned
Contemporary Germany
Contemporary Italy

Contemporary States and Societies
Series Standing Order
ISBN 978–0–333–75402–3 hardcover
ISBN 978–0–333–80319–6 paperback
(outside North America only)

You can receive future titles in this series as they are published by placing a standing order. Please contact your bookseller or, in the case of difficulty, write to us at the address below with your name and address, the title of the series and the ISBN quoted above.

Customer Services Department, Palgrave Ltd
Houndmills, Basingstoke, Hampshire RG21 6XS, England

Contemporary South Africa

Second Edition

Anthony Butler

First published in 2004
Reprinted four times
Second edition published 2009 by
PALGRAVE MACMILLAN

Palgrave Macmillan in the UK is an imprint of Macmillan Publishers Limited, registered in England, company number 785998, of Houndmills, Basingstoke, Hampshire RG21 6XS.

Palgrave Macmillan in the US is a division of St Martin's Press LLC, 175 Fifth Avenue, New York, NY 10010.

Palgrave Macmillan is the global academic imprint of the above companies and has companies and representatives throughout the world.

Palgrave® and Macmillan® are registered trademarks in the United States, the United Kingdom, Europe and other countries.

ISBN-13: 978–0–230–21766–9 hardback
ISBN-10: 0–230–21766–4 hardback
ISBN-13: 978–0–230–21767–6 paperback
ISBN-10: 0–230–21767–2 paperback

This book is printed on paper suitable for recycling and made from fully managed and sustained forest sources. Logging, pulping and manufacturing processes are expected to conform to the environmental regulations of the country of origin.

A catalogue record for this book is available from the British Library.

A catalog record for this book is available from the Library of Congress.

10 9 8 7 6 5 4 3 2 1
18 17 16 15 14 13 12 11 10 09

Printed and bound in China

For Julia, Anna, and James

Contents

List of Tables, Figures, Maps, and Boxes   x
Preface to the Second Edition   xii
Map of South Africa Today   xiii

Introduction   1

1 Historical Context   5
   South Africa before 1870   5
   The Creation of the State, 1870–1910   12
   Segregation and Early Apartheid, 1910–60   14
   The Rise and Fall of 'high apartheid'   19
   South Africa's 'transition to democracy'   23
   The ANC in Government   31

2 A Rainbow Nation?   33
   The Entrenchment of Apartness under Apartheid   35
   Strength from Diversity?   36
   The Diversity of the Provinces   44
   Conclusions   53

3 The South African Economy   55
   Introduction   55
   Output and Expenditure   55
   Economic Policy   58
   Trade and Internationalization   63
   Investment Flows   65
   Public and Private Sectors   67
   Selected Sectors of the Economy   68
   Labour Relations   73
   Black Economic Empowerment (BEE)   75
   Challenges   80

4   Social Structure and Social Policy   **84**
Human Development in South Africa   84
Explaining Inequality   89
Addressing Poverty and Inequality   91
Public Services and Social Infrastructure   98
Women and Disadvantage   107
Towards a More Equal Future?   109

5   Government   **110**
The Making of a Constitutional Settlement   110
Political Authority under the New Constitution   115
The National Executive   117
The National Legislature   122
The Judiciary   124
The National Sphere   126
Provincial Government   128
Local Government   130
Challenges and Controversies   134

6   Political Life   **139**
The Electoral System   139
The Electorate   140
Party Support and Political Parties   142
The African National Congress   143
Opposition Parties   147
Civil Society   150
One Party Dominance   155
Holding a Dominant Party to Account   158
Internal Pluralism   162
External and Economic Constraints   166
Conclusions   167

7   Culture, Ideas, and Issues   **171**
Professional Cultural Production   171
The Culture of Everyday Life: Urbanization and
  Suburbanization   175
Ideas   180
Issues   183

8   South Africa and the World   **196**
Modern South African International Relations   197
Foreign and Defence Policy from Mandela to Mbeki   202

Foreign Policy for the Twenty-first Century   206
The African Union, Nepad, and Zimbabwe   209
Mechanisms for Foreign Policy Making   211

9   South Africa in the Twenty-first Century   214
The Economy, Human Development, and Welfare   215
Reconciliation, Nation-building, and Democracy   216

Recommended Reading   218
South Africa on the Internet   221
Bibliography   224
Index   235

Tables, Figure, Maps, and Boxes

Maps

0.1	South Africa Today	xiii
1.1	Southern Africa c. 1870	6
1.2	South Africa under Apartheid	21

Figure

3.1	Contribution of various industries to GDP, 2007	57

Tables

2.1	Population by 'race' and mother tongue, 2001	36
2.2	Religious affiliations (estimated 2002)	41
3.1	Economic growth 1994–2007	57
4.1	South African and Brazilian Human Development Index 1975–2005	88
4.2	Unemployment in South Africa, 1993–2007	93
4.3	Social infrastructure and services, 1993–2004	99
4.4	Consolidated national and provincial spending on social services 2008/9	104
5.1	Government functions by sphere	127
6.1	Trends in voter turnout, 1994–2004	142
6.2	National election results 1994, 1999, 2004 and 2009 (per cent)	143
7.1	The changing public agenda 2002 and 2006	184
7.2	Changes in annual crime rates, per 100,000 people	185
8.1	Global annual per capita income growth, 1975–99	207

Boxes

1.1 Key dates in South African history 10
1.2 Three views of 'tribalism' 22
1.3 FW de Klerk 27
1.4 Nelson Mandela 29
2.1 Key facts about South Africa 34
2.2 The Land 40
2.3 HIV/AIDS and population growth 46
2.4 Climate 48
2.5 The Truth and Reconciliation Commission 53
3.1 Trevor Manuel 59
3.2 Key facts about South Africa's economy (2007) 61
4.1 South Africa's Human Development Index, 2005 86
4.2 Land reform 103
5.1 Cyril Ramaphosa 113
5.2 Kgalema Motlanthe 128
6.1 Thabo Mbeki 160
6.2 Jacob Gedleyihlekisa Zuma 163
6.3 Nomzamo Nobandla Winnifred
'Winnie' Madikizela-Mandela 164

Preface to the Second Edition

Twentieth century South Africa was notorious for apartheid, a system of institutionalized racial and ethnic segregation. Apartheid was organized around the enforced classification of a historically complex and diverse South African population as white, Native (later Bantu and then black), Indian, and coloured. These terms have been contested politically by many of those to whom they have been applied. Their use entrenches assumptions about racial difference that have no scientific validity. In this book, where racial terminology is used, the term 'African' refers to those officially classified as Native or black under apartheid. 'Black' refers more widely to all those categorized as black, Indian, and coloured. I capitalize such terms throughout in order to emphasize their problematic nature.

This book reduces and inevitably sometimes simplifies the complex and fast-changing reality of contemporary South Africa in order to produce a manageable but reasonably comprehensive text. I hope readers will forgive inevitable omissions and oversimplifications. In line with the series style, references have been kept to a minimum. Guides at the end of the book direct interested readers towards published and Internet sources of information and analysis on South Africa.

Colin Bundy, Anne Jellema, Samson Muradzikwa, Howard Walker, and three anonymous readers have offered generous advice on particular chapters of the first and this second edition. Cliff Butler's help was invaluable in the preparation of the final manuscript. I am grateful once again to my former colleagues at University of Cape Town for making the Department of Political Studies such a stimulating environment in which to study South Africa's politics and public policy.

Parts of Chapter 6 first appeared in a different form in volume 38 of *Government and Opposition* and many of the themes developed in various chapters were first elaborated on the pages of *Business Day*.

Anthony Butler
Johannesburg

Map 0.1 South Africa Today

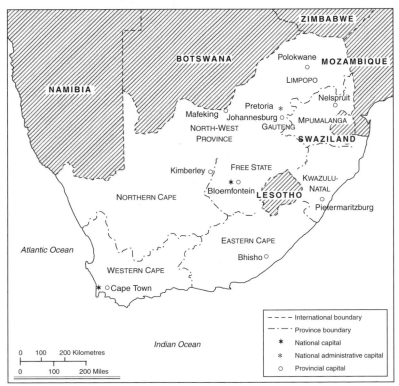

Introduction

South Africa's twentieth century history was dominated by racial segregation and 'apartheid' (or 'apartness'). Only a decade and a half after the country's first non-racial election in 1994, this history of systematic and institutionalized oppression of the country's Black population inevitably still profoundly influences everyday political life.

This historical legacy also influences very varied perceptions of the country's future. Pessimists view the 'new' South Africa's political destiny through the lenses of African decline, seeing the carefully managed 'transition to democracy' as just one more step along the road to the civil war, ethnic division, and one-party rule that has characterized much of post-colonial Africa. Well-wishers see the new South Africa through quite different eyes, as a 'rainbow nation' unshackled by the 'miracle' of transition from the economic and social chains of apartheid. Many of the supporters of the African National Congress (ANC) even see the liberation movement as the glorious locomotive of African renaissance, pulling the continent into a twenty-first century that belongs to Africa.

Nelson Mandela's leadership between 1994 and 1999 helped to calm those who feared that the future promised only tribalism, ungovernability, and civil war. For the anxious White minority, and for international observers, new stereotypes of the 'patient masses' supplanted their once lurid fantasies about ungovernable African youth.

The turbulent politics of apartheid quietly faded away and the urban poor returned to the business of survival. Wider educational and economic opportunities, and 'employment equity' policies within public and private sectors, helped a new Black middle class to emerge. The economy did not boom in the 1990s, but an 'independent' central bank, conservative fiscal policy, revolutionized revenue collection, and an energetic treasury controlled inflation and banished a feared structural deficit. National rituals of racial reconciliation and restitution at the same time created the appearance of a society determined to put its past firmly behind it.

While the doom-mongers' worst fears had not been realized by 1999, however, Mandela's magic was little consolation for the poor. Unemployment sharpened dramatically during the ANC's first term, and poverty became even more deeply entrenched for the poorest quarter of South Africans. Indicators of rural child mortality and life expectancy dismayingly worsened. The extension of public services to the population as a whole, moreover, progressed very unevenly. While the government came close to hitting some tough targets for house building, electrification, and water supplies, critics complained with increasing urgency that ordinary citizens were experiencing insufficient improvement in their living standards.

As a result of a growing population, remorseless urbanization and decreasing household size, backlogs for basic public services remained vast. By 1999, many more South Africans lived in formal housing than ever before but the proportion living in informal housing (such as shacks) had actually increased by half to over 12 per cent. Many water schemes had been completed but the proportion of households with access to clean water scarcely rose. A vast and expensive electrification programme provided electric lighting to almost three quarters of dwellings but failed to eliminate poor people's reliance on dangerous, polluting, and health-destroying household energy sources such as wood, coal, and paraffin (Statistics South Africa 2001).

Mandela left office in 1999 a popular president but his government was widely considered to have failed the test of 'delivery'. The arrival of reputedly technocratic successor Thabo Mbeki, after an active term as deputy president, was for this reason greeted with excitement. Initially, he did not altogether disappoint these hopes. He overhauled the national policy making machinery, clustered government departments to improve the co-ordination of policy, and started to remake municipalities into the developmental agents of the state. At the same time, he strengthened the hand of the formidable Treasury, contained the growth of public debt, and built upon the personnel and policy strengths of Mandela's government. Mbeki's seemingly consistent external strategy created new alliances within and beyond Africa and broke down Pretoria's longstanding isolation on the continent. The 2004 award of the opportunity to stage the 2010 FIFA World Cup in South Africa cemented the new-found confidence of Mbeki's supporters.

Mbeki's administration, however, became increasingly troubled. While citizens were sympathetic towards the government's difficulties in extending public services, the lack of employment opportunities and persistently high levels of crime remained matters of profound dissatisfaction for South Africans of all classes. In this unpromising context, a relentless stream of scandals and challenges buffeted the government from 2001. A major arms procurement package – negotiated during the Mandela presidency but under the auspices of Thabo Mbeki – was hit by accusations of naivety, cost escalation, and high-level corruption. Allegations about the role of Mbeki and his deputy president Jacob Zuma in arms deal corruption dogged his presidency to the very end and ultimately posed a threat to constitutional government.

Inaction and confusion concerning government's response to the HIV/AIDS pandemic led to legal challenges and political protest. The deepening crisis in neighbouring Zimbabwe became a source of growing domestic contention, with Mbeki's 'quiet diplomacy' attacked by the ANC's opponents and closest allies alike. Divisions over economic policy within the 'tripartite alliance' between the ANC, the South African Communist Party (SACP), and the Congress of South African Trade Unions (COSATU) burst into the open, and the alliance was torn by internal division. These many problems were cause for concern in themselves but they also eroded fragile democratic institutions and exposed a crisis of mutual incomprehension between critics and supporters of the ANC leadership.

The Mbeki era ended ignominiously with his ejection from the presidency of the ANC at the end of 2007 and from the state presidency in mid-2008. Constitutionally obliged to vacate the state presidency in 2009, his first defeat at the hands of his ANC deputy Jacob Zuma deprived him of the ability to hand-pick his successor. Immediately after this public humiliation, Mbeki's government tottered under a further series of blows that called his entire legacy into question. A wave of power cuts early in 2008 exposed confusion within government about energy policy. Mbeki's own role in the long-running arms deal fiasco became increasingly hotly debated. The head of the South African Police Service was threatened with prosecution for corruption by the national prosecuting agency. An outbreak of horrific so-called 'xenophobic violence' in May 2008, directed primarily towards foreign nationals but also at South African citizens from the north of the country, left more than sixty people dead and tens of thousands displaced from their homes. Finally, a court judgement concerning Jacob Zuma accepted that it was possible Mbeki had intervened to secure his former deputy's prosecution. In the storm that followed, the ANC leadership decided to 'recall' Mbeki – to insist that he step down – and instructed its members of parliament to choose party centrist Kgalema Motlanthe as state president until the 2009 elections.

The optimism with which most South Africans entered the new millennium has suffered a sharp setback. In a suddenly harsher international climate, the country's economic and political position suddenly seems precarious. Critics ask whether an ANC-dominated executive will continue to collide with the judiciary, damaging fragile political institutions and undermining constitutional supremacy. They worry that negative perceptions will inhibit the investment South Africa needs to grow, and that the emigration of highly educated citizens will exacerbate the country's already desperate shortages of skills. Many citizens are newly concerned that corruption will become a normal part of bureaucratic and economic interaction, while the HIV/AIDS pandemic seems set to generate profound economic and political consequences. The 'miracle' of South Africa's transition to non-racial democracy, in some eyes at least, threatens to turn to ruin.

This book aims to provide a sophisticated introduction to modern South Africa and to clarify the key issues behind such hopes and fears. The first chapter explores the history of this unique country, and sets out the context within which current political and developmental challenges must be understood. Chapter 2 surveys the people of South Africa and their land, exploring the diversity of what Nobel Laureate Desmond Tutu famously called the 'rainbow nation'. The following two chapters look more deeply into the economic and social structures of the country. Chapter 3 details the political economy of the post-apartheid state, the organization and key sectors of the economy and the overall framework for economic policy. Chapter 4 investigates the structure of society, and explores causes of, and potential remedies for, the poverty and inequality that continue to blight national life.

Chapters 5 and 6 turn to governing structures and to South Africa's lively politics, exploring how political institutions function under the new constitution, the nature and quality of political participation, the party system, and the longer term prospects of democracy. Chapter 7 turns to cultural life and to the issues and ideas that animate intellectual interaction. Chapter 8 explores South Africa's foreign relations, as a new force in African politics and a campaigner for continental renaissance. The final chapter appraises the ANC's performance in government to date, and looks ahead to South Africa's prospects in what promises to be an exciting and possibly tumultuous twenty-first century.

1

Historical Context

South Africa is both a new democracy and a developing country. Her people are attempting a difficult experiment in political transformation while managing the economic and social strains that come with poverty, urbanization, and economic development. Like the inhabitants of other developing countries, most South Africans must wage bitter struggles for access to scarce resources in a highly unequal society bequeathed by history.

Yet South Africans often consider themselves to be a special people. Their uniqueness, they believe, derives from their particular history of colonization, racial segregation and triumphal democratization. At the heart of that exceptional history lies 'apartheid' – literally 'apartness' or separation. The inheritance of segregation and apartheid, together with irreconcilable differences over their significance, continue to obstruct efforts to create a sustainable national identity and a coherent and inclusive social order.

South Africa before 1870

South Africa's unique history was decisively shaped by the discovery of diamonds and then gold after 1870, and then by the responses of its imperial power, Britain, to the opportunities and threats these finds presented. Yet, if modern South African history begins with the 'minerals revolutions', the ramifications of these discoveries cannot be understood without first comprehending the complex balance of forces that in the 1870s characterized the area that is today South Africa. Four great historical stories – of the Khoisan peoples, African pastoralists and farmers, 'Boer' European-descended settlers, and British imperialists – are represented in any political map of the 1870s (see Map 1.1).

5

Map 1.1   Southern Africa c. 1870

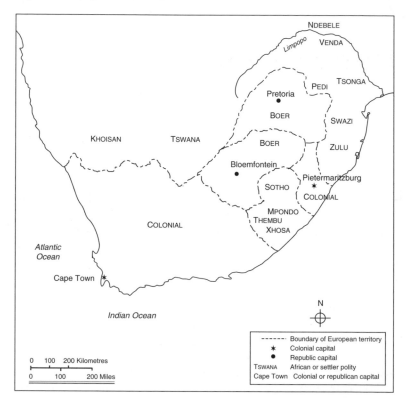

The least widely known history concerns the subjugation of the earliest inhabitants of what was to become South Africa. These hunting and herding societies, known today as Khoikhoi, San, or collectively Khoisan, had been present in the west and northwest since around 1,000 BC. They fared particularly badly during the early period of European settlement – during Dutch East India Company rule from the mid-seventeenth century – as the settlers (and the diseases they brought with them) very rapidly subjugated them in the Cape.

In 1870, within the borders of the yet-to-be created South Africa, three more resilient modes of society, the actors in our three remaining great histories, were engaged in increasingly harsh competition for resources, but with none achieving predominance. The first and most important of these were African peoples whose largest political formations became known in the colonial period as the Xhosa and Zulu. Their resilience in the face of European settlement is evident in the widespread distribution of African polities after 200 years of colonization.

African political kingdoms had been expanding into what is today South Africa from around the Third Century AD. These dynamic African polities had spread by means of a 'migratory drift' or gradual territorial expansion almost to the west of South Africa by the time of European settlement. By the end of the eighteenth century, their population was reaching the limits of the potential of the South African land mass. The economies and social organization of these African societies were centred upon livestock. The effective political units of African pastoralism and farming were hereditary chiefdoms, varying in size from less than 1,000 members to over 50,000. Chiefdoms were not closed entities, but rather included people of different descent groups, migrants from poor regions, and arrivals who had broken away from other chiefdoms. These were not 'tribes', as Thompson (1990: 11) stresses: 'The Western concept of tribalism, which is usually taken to refer to closed populations reproducing fixed cultural characteristics, is not applicable to [these] African farmers'. Rather than closed entities with unique unchanging cultures, he observes, such societies were fluid and politically affiliative in composition. 'People interacted, co-operating and copulating as well as competing and combating, exchanging ideas and practices as well as rejecting them'.

The third extraordinary history concerns the 'Boers' (meaning farmers), primarily descended from the Dutch speaking colonists of the Cape from the early seventeenth century, whose original function had been to supply passing ships of the Dutch East India Company. Initially a fuelling and provisioning station for the ships of the company, the Cape eventually became the springboard for settlers' dynamic, if uncertain, expansion. The experience of these Boer societies was in many respects similar to that of their African contemporaries. Their expansion north and east into the areas occupied by African polities began in the late eighteenth century. Boer settlers achieved advances through a combination of factors: exploitation of divisions in African society, (uneven) co-operation between Whites, the technological superiority of firearms, and the ability to store wealth in a more sophisticated economic system.

New opportunities for Boers were then unexpectedly created by a major transformation in African societies. As a result of a series of devastating conflicts known in Zulu as the Mfecane (crushing) – driven by a centralization of the Zulu kingdom and centring on the region between the mountain escarpment and the Indian Ocean – there was a great dislocation of African farmers across the region. The reasons for this upheaval are contested. Fresh territory for exploitation had become exhausted and competition for land and water supplies grew. Severe droughts in the early nineteenth century triggered a process of concentration of power, and led to the emergence of a new scale of standing armies. The series of major conflicts that ensued dislocated the region's economies, and displaced great numbers of refugees. Some historians argue that foreign trade caused or contributed to Zulu state centralization, with competition to control trade routes spurring militarization. Whatever the dynamics of dislocation, the resulting turmoil presented White settlers with an unprecedented opportunity to colonize seemingly 'empty' and unclaimed land.

Meanwhile, the Cape colony became inhospitable to Boers. Britain, which had taken direct control over the Cape in 1795 to pre-empt French intervention, was introducing cultural and legal changes which damaged their interests and threatened to curtail their hitherto untrammelled power over their labourers. The influence of the ideals of the French Revolution, and evangelical anti-slavery campaigns in England, threatened Boers' customary practices of quasi-slavery. For them, migration to the immediate east was blocked by Xhosa chiefdoms which, in frontier wars, had demonstrated political and military resilience. Many Boers therefore embarked upon what came to be celebrated, a century later, as the 'Great Trek'. In reality this was a series of episodic migrations in the late 1830s totalling about 12,000 persons, half of whom were Khoi servants and former slaves. These 'Trekkers' battled sporadically with African polities, settling firstly in Natal and then (after British annexation of Natal) in the 'highveld' to the north. They secured effective independence from the British since a waning of abolitionist sentiment left London less well disposed to protect African against Trekker. The Boers remained poor and vulnerable, and in quite incomplete control of the territory over which they had claimed the right to rule. But, by 1870, they had established a tenuous presence across great tracts of the African interior.

The final narrative is that of the imperial power, Britain, which increasingly but unevenly predominated over the economy and politics of the coastal regions. These far less numerous British settlers, who complete our survey of pre-1870s polities, were backed by the immense but largely unexercised power of a great empire. London behaved in a characteristically calculating manner, expending few resources on what it viewed as a backwater. The Cape Colony was consolidated as a British possession after 1806 only because of its strategic location on trading routes to India. 'Like the Dutch before them',

Thompson (1990: 53) remarks, 'the British had no vital material interest in South Africa beyond the peninsula. But appended to that strategic prize was a complex, violent, and largely anarchic society, scattered over a vast hinterland'. The limited importance London attached to South Africa was reflected in the small proportion of British overseas capital attracted to it, modest British immigration by comparison with other colonies, and a paucity of manpower and resources. By 1870, the United States had 32 million inhabitants of European origin or descent, and 53,000 miles of railways; Southern Africa as a whole possessed 250,000 White people and around 70 miles of railways. The total value of imports was only £3 million per annum, and exports were even less (Thompson 1990: 53, 108). The biggest town contained only 50,000 inhabitants.

The 'turbulent hinterland' continued to command little attention through the early and mid-nineteenth century. In the face of potential alliances between Sotho and 'Trekker' (migrant Boer), the British were willing to concede Boer independence in the South African Republic (later Transvaal) in 1852. Further Sotho resistance led to a truce between Europeans and to colonial withdrawal (Worden 1994: 16). While the mid-nineteenth century was a time of limited British migration, the 1820 Conservative government, eager to placate domestic critics, funded the migration of 4,000 settlers from the British Isles to the eastern Cape agricultural belt. Rapidly adopting trading and commercial occupations, these migrants remained culturally distinct from Afrikaner settlers, creating a nascent antagonism within the White population that went on to deepen.

'Reform' influences in Britain were not decisive in dividing Whites. Participation in the slave trade was outlawed in 1807 (depriving Cape farmers of easy labour access), and from 1823 minimum standards of food and clothing, and maximum working hours and punishments, were patchily enforced in a spill over from a Caribbean tax on slavery. Further legislation secured the legal position of the Khoikhoi and former slaves, although it could not remove their poverty and economic dependence. As Thompson (1990: 65) puts it, 'the reforms were the reforms of freedom, but the facts were still the facts of exploitation'. The tide of philanthropy, in any event, ebbed in Britain by the mid nineteenth century, and British settlers were increasingly faced with the same conditions as Afrikaners: insecure frontiersmen fighting against Africans for land legally granted to them without the consent of its customary inhabitants. They brought with them the scientistic racism of mid-Victorian Britain, and adapted it adroitly to their new circumstances.

A seeming retreat of British colonial power in the mid-nineteenth century was belied by the establishment of considerable colonial economic influence by the 1850s. While Afrikaners lay beyond the reach of systematic imperial constraint, the colonial heartland was increasingly incorporated into the Empire. Trade was centred on the Cape, and migrant labour had been drawn to the colony from the 1840s. Where Cape interests were threatened, intervention by the imperial power was rapid and effective. Moreover, the very fact of possession brought with it an inescapable if unwanted responsibility to provide a modicum of law and order in the frontier zone. These pressures, mediated through military, evangelical, and commercial interests, resulted in a continuous stream of (to Boers) unwanted interventions by the British authorities.

Many twentieth century histories of South Africa penned by Europeans wrongly viewed the African societies of 1870 as static 'tribes' impacted by dynamic settlers. There was little sign among African societies of the

---

Box 1.1   Key dates in South African history

c. 1000 BC	Khoikhoi herders living in South Africa
c. 300 AD	Bantu-speaking farmers move into South Africa
1652	Dutch East India Company establishes Cape Town settlement
1806	Britain establishes control over Cape Colony
1826–28	Centralized Zulu kingdom conquers neighbours
1834	Slave emancipation
1835–40	Afrikaner 'Great Trek' to interior
1867	First diamonds discovered
1877	Britain annexes Transvaal
1878–9	British defeat Tswana, Zulu, Pedi, commence Transkei annexation
1886	Gold mining begins on the Witwatersrand
1899–1902	British defeat Afrikaners in South African ('Boer') War
1910	Union of South Africa established
1912	South African Native National Congress (later ANC) formed
1914–9	Participation in World War I as part of British empire
1923	*Natives (Urban Areas) Act* formalizes urban segregation
1939–45	Contested participation alongside Allies in World War II
1948	National Party (NP) elected on 'apartheid' slogan
1950	*Group Areas* and *Population Registration* Acts
1960	Police kill 67 demonstrators at Sharpeville
1961	South Africa becomes a Republic

social disintegration that had affected the indigenous peoples of many other colonies. Change within these robust polities was primarily driven by domestic rather than colonial factors, accelerating in the early nine-teenth century with the rise of the Zulu kingdom (Beinart 1994: 16). Africans jostled with vulnerable Afrikaners and isolated colonialists who could command few of the resources of the imperial power. Many Africans, moreover, were using the economic opportunities presented by settlement and trade to their advantage (Bundy 1988).

All of Southern Africa's relatively small 1870s quasi-states were multi-ethnic and multi-lingual. Most of them lacked the bases of political and cultural unity, and limited political self-consciousness was the rule. The history of the polities in the 1870s could never be told as an attempt to master collective destiny. Political leaders were attempting to survive in unforgiving circumstances, and the part-mythical histories through which they justified their claims to rule were themselves ever-changing.

1964	Nelson Mandela and other opposition leaders imprisoned for life
1969	Foundation of South African Students' Organization under Steve Biko
1975–6	Mozambique and Angola become independent
1976–7	Revolt in Soweto followed by national unrest
1976–81	'Independence' conferred upon four of the Bantustans
1980	Zimbabwe independent
1985	Foundation of ANC-aligned union federation Congress of South African Trade Unions (COSATU)
1986	Pass laws repealed
1989	FW de Klerk becomes President
1990	Opposition parties unbanned; Mandela and others released
1991	Repeal of apartheid legislation; formal negotiations begin at Convention for a Democratic South Africa (CODESA)
1994	ANC wins first non-racial election: Mandela becomes president
1996	'Final' constitution is adopted and ratified
1999	ANC wins second national election: Thabo Mbeki is president
2000	HIV/AIDS policy controversy deepens
2004	ANC wins third national election; Mbeki secures second term
2007	Polokwane conference evicts Mbeki from ANC presidency
2008	Xenophobic violence erupts

The Creation of the State, 1870–1910

Post-1870 South Africa was marked by a new speed and magnitude of social change and the populations of the area were driven by a common series of impersonal forces. The roots of this upheaval lay in discoveries of diamonds and gold, and in the responses of the British colonial power to these discoveries. Four massive processes marked the transformation of South Africa over this period: war, unification, economic development, and the forging of a migrant working class.

Diamonds were discovered in 1867, attracting foreign investment, initiating modern capitalism in South Africa, and creating unprecedented demand for labour. By 1871, 75,000 people had flocked to the diamond fields, and development created labour shortages not just in the mines, but also on the farms, in new industries, on the railways and in public works. Diamonds were soon overtaken by gold, discovered in 1886 on the Witwatersrand ('white waters reef'), and soon to transform the entire southern African region. While the metal ore was of low quality and difficult to extract, potential gold wealth was vast, and the metal was central to the liquidity and stability of the then gold-based international economy. Its effective and immediate exploitation was for these reasons a British strategic imperative. In order to accomplish this, the imperial power required a massive input of cheap domestic and skilled foreign labour, together with the infrastructure, regulation, and stability that only a complex and unified modern state could provide.

The demands for stability and for labour led the imperial power to break the resistance of African polities through military force. Then, at great cost, they subdued the Afrikaners in the South African or Boer War of 1899–1902. Unification was the ultimate goal of war. Far from merely representing a legalistic or constitutional device, unification was a comprehensive process of state creation. British power built the machinery of state control through which it could enforce contracts, secure transport links, regulate labour and business, and ensure strategic security across the area of contemporary South Africa as a whole. By so doing it ensured that the mineral wealth of South Africa could be exploited safely by British-based conglomerates.

Economic development in the new urban areas, the third key process of change, was signalled by the extraordinary growth of Johannesburg and the Witwatersrand region, and by the wholesale transformation of the economic geography of South Africa. Johannesburg did not exist in 1880. By 1911 it contained 240,000 inhabitants, and the Witwatersrand as a whole held twice that number. Cape Town, by contrast, contained less than 200,000 people and was to become thereafter something of an economic backwater. The new urban areas were a maelstrom of diversity that encompassed low-waged miners and highly paid immigrants, and a plethora of races and classes. The state carefully managed the influx of African labour, using already embedded practices and ideologies. Britain's High Commissioner Milner viewed native reserves, urban 'influx' control, and the manipulation of chiefs as necessary instruments to keep Africans in check in the colonial economy. Social Darwinism helped justify segregationist policies, and further ideological support was provided by new racial doctrines from the United States.

The fourth major process of change in South Africa lay in part beyond the towns. South Africa developed a system of 'migrant labour' that was to mark its later twentieth century history – the cyclical and often annual movement of able bodied young African labourers into and out of the core urban economy. Migrant labour in South Africa began on the sugar fields of Natal which depended upon labourers from Mozambique. Later cyclical migrancy became a generalized domestic and sub-continental cheap labour system, feeding the country's mining, commercial, and agricultural sectors. Ultimately it became the backbone of the industrial and commercial systems of apartheid as a whole. The mine owners' preference for such migrant labour, primarily because it was cheap, initially coincided with some Africans' own interests. Young male urban labourers – nine out of every ten of the 1910 Black population of Johannesburg was male – provided money for chiefs and for fathers. Only gradually (and in large measure through systematic and deliberate government action) did money become necessary for survival in rural South Africa, and migrant labour correspondingly become a necessity for survival. By the 1920s, 30–40 per cent of active men in rural areas were away at work at any given time.

While white supremacy and segregation predated and shaped this period of transformation, the impersonal forces of market, imperial power, and capital were the primary driving agents of change. The 1910 *Act of Union* formalized the new state's existence and cemented its political structures. It served, moreover, to entrench the privileged interests of Whites by means of a racialised political machinery. Whites secured a virtual monopoly of electoral power, with a property franchise retained in the Cape colony alone. This period of South African history laid the economic, political, and institutional foundations of segregation and apartheid.

Segregation and Early Apartheid, 1910–60

The decade after 1910 saw continued English dominance and deepening racial segregation under the auspices of a political alliance between Afrikaner agriculture, White mine owners, and those dependent on them (Terreblanche and Nattrass 1990). During post-unification reconstruction, labour supply remained at the heart of government policy. Native reserves, 'influx controls', and compliant 'traditional authorities', became reliable policy instruments for a state supporting mining and agricultural capital. The African population was increasingly pervasively regulated where it remained on the land, and further forged into a working class through the migrant labour system.

The *Natives Land Act* of 1913 allocated 87 per cent of land to Whites and moved to prohibit native land purchase and non-labour based tenancies. The 1923 *Urban Areas Act* created legal tools to entrench further the practices of segregation and 'influx control' – the coercive management of migration to work in the cities, increasingly by means of the complex system of accumulated 'pass laws' that regulated the movement of Africans in designated European areas. Initially a partly discretionary process through which cash income supplemented rural economic activity, influx control eventually became unavoidable as taxes, dispossession, and population growth squeezed rural populations. The Chamber of Mines used chiefs, traders, and criminals to recruit young, male workers, and from 1910 became increasingly cost-focused and geographically ambitious in recruitment. By 1920, a centralized labour migration system managed more than 200,000 workers, a number that was to grow in later years, reaching a peak of 430,000 migrants in 1961.

Open class conflict meanwhile intensified in White South Africa between 1907 and 1933, a period of economic nationalism and struggle between mining capital and White workers. The 1922 Rand Revolt, in which Afrikaans- and English-speaking Whites fought against capitalism but also against Blacks, was crushed only by considerable military firepower and at the cost of over 200 lives. The government of 1924, which combined Hertzog's NP with the Labour Party, oversaw the foundations of an Afrikaner welfare state. The emergence of Afrikaner nationalism, itself a creature of social dislocation, served as a bridge across regional and class divides.

From 1933–48, South Africa emerged from the depression into a second industrial revolution. On the back of a rise in the gold price which followed the collapse of the Gold Standard, and further bolstered by increased demand for manufactured exports as the North prepared for global war, the economy grew rapidly with English interests spreading out from their heartland in the gold-mining economy. General economic affluence, fuelled by gold and the export boom, helped to fund government welfare and agricultural support programmes. The period also, however, saw the growth of DF Malan's 'purified' NP, with dreams of more complete racial segregation. White unity, furthermore, was shattered over the issue of participation on the side of the Allies in World War II. After the 'fusion government' was formed in 1934, the breakaway NP had managed to mobilize Afrikaners nationally by deploying cultural and educational organizations, Afrikaner unions, and business groups. Farmers, civil servants, teachers, and poor Whites turned increasingly towards the Nationalists.

The mid- to late-1930s marked a first high-point of segregation. Legislation passed in 1936 consolidated the native reserves and removed propertied Africans from the Cape voter roll. This was also a low point of Black resistance. The African National Congress (ANC), elitist, isolated from labour and radical protest since its foundation in 1913, continued on its ineffectual way. Indian and Coloured political movements organized around particularist or local concerns. Political resistance was largely expressed within churches and through widespread non-compliance with the law. Politics for Africans was a defensive process: the use of forms of traditional authority and religious belief to defend land rights and grazing, and to advance localized interests in urban situations.

The wartime economic bonanza of 1939–48 saw a relaxation of segregation and an inexorable urbanization. White and Black alike were drawn to the towns, but the change in Africans' situation was striking. Between 1936 and 1946, their numbers in urban areas grew from 139,000 to 390,000, and for the first time many of these were women. The presence of Africans in the urban economy was expressed politically in a number of ways. Black trade unions blossomed, higher-skilled jobs were opened to Africans, and colour bars in many sectors floated upwards. The formal structures of African politics – notably the ANC Youth League from 1944 – began to organize deliberately integrative protests to draw together the opponents of segregation. The South African Communist Party arranged anti-pass campaigns in 1943–4. Bus boycotts became a major instrument of protest, strikes escalated across the war years, and thereafter the turmoil continued into the peace as the younger generation of activists, led by

Nelson Mandela and Oliver Tambo, galvanized the ANC into action, catalysing strikes and politically motivated land occupations on the Rand.

1948 is a significant date in modern South African history: the year in which the Afrikaner 'National Party' won the first of many election victories under the slogan of 'apartheid'. The NP was to remain in power until the first universal franchise election of 1994. Continuities between pre-war segregation and post-war 'apartheid', however, were far more striking than the discontinuities. Only in the 1960s, with the second phase of apartheid, did Afrikaner power exert itself to produce the unprecedented social deformation of high apartheid. Why, then, has 1948 so often been taken to be the key date in South African twentieth century political history?

First, the general election of 1948 represented a decisive triumph for a new and non-conciliatory generation of Afrikaner politicians in the NP. This victory was a slender one and represented no massive swing in White (or even Afrikaner) sentiment. Defeated Prime Minister Jan Smuts lost much Afrikaner support because of 'swamping' fears associated with Black urbanization and the presence of Africans in jobs formerly reserved for (war-mobilized) Whites. Local issues made a major impact in Natal, where anti-Indian land restrictions played a central role. In the Transvaal and Orange Free State, doubts among farmers about labour supply and the intentions of the United Party (UP) led to a swing to Malan's NP, despite the latter's Cape origins and core support. Four tenths of Afrikaners voted for the UP, and the NP relied on the votes of 20 per cent of English speakers to achieve their overall 39 per cent (Beinart 1994: chapter 5). Once again, fortune smiled on the NP. While the UP and Labour won 53 per cent between them, the NP secured narrow victories in more heavily weighted rural and peri-urban constituencies. The pivotal 1948 election victory was therefore fortuitous, turning on minority and protest voters. The changed electoral coalitions that secured long-term NP power came earlier and later. Afrikaner nationalism was already cross-class and inter-regional force that could potentially unify labour and agriculture around the policy of segregation. Afrikaner control over the White electorate as a whole was still to be established.

The second reason for the predominance of 1948 as the key date in twentieth century South African historical writing was a slogan: 'apartheid' (or apartness). The term first rose to prominence in the NP's electoral campaign of 1948 and became a common figure of speech across White South Africa in that year. The apartheid of 1948 was not, however, the apartheid of the 1960s. This would be to read history backwards. The slogan 'apartheid', along with the fears of Black urbanization and job competition to which it drew attention, was an important asset of the NP in its marginal minority win in 1948. Its power lay in its very ambiguity. NP supporters agreed that Africans should continue to be excluded from political power and that White supremacy should be maintained. Beyond this, however, apartheid provided a means of papering over great differences. Should Afrikaners strive for total segregation, with the replacement of African labour by White labour (by birth or migration), as many intellectuals, clerics, teachers argued? Or should businessmen and agriculturalists continue to have access to Black labour in a pragmatic and moderated form of segregation? Appealing to new voters, those demobilized from the military, and building cross-class and cross-regional support from a diverse electorate, the slogan 'apartheid' was an accidental success of political rhetoric.

A third reason for the significance attached to 1948 is a body of repugnant legislation enacted by the NP immediately after its first electoral victory. This legislation included the *Population Registration Act,* which enforced the classification of people into four strict racial categories: White, Coloured, Indian/Asiatic, and Native (later Bantu or African). This fourfold classification provided a basis for the systematic social and economic engineering of 'high apartheid' that was to come. In the first period of NP rule, however, the focus was on symbolically important aspects of life as much as upon the economics of the labour market. 'Mixed marriages' were prohibited in 1949, and in 1950 all sexual contact between Whites and other South Africans was prohibited in an *Immorality Act.* Residential segregation was another focus of legislative activity, with the *Group Areas Act* of 1950 applying residential segregation by race comprehensively across the country. The *Reservation of Separate Amenities Act* of 1953 segregated transport, cinemas, restaurants, and sporting facilities, and later acts enforced segregation in schools, colleges, and universities. Unlike much of the law that succeeded it, 'petty' apartheid legislation was not designed to reshape South Africa's structures of economic opportunity but was distinguished by its undisguised racial malevolence.

Three factors in combination – the electoral win of the NP, the significance that the term apartheid later accrued, and the repugnancy of early NP legislation – made 1948 a year of seemingly unprecedented importance. The myth of 1948 as a great break in South African history has been manifest in the notion that apartheid was a 'Grand Plan', unfolded by NP leaders in the 30 years following 1948. The idea of a grand plan became established because of its attractiveness to both liberals and Afrikaners. The former used the notion to condemn Afrikaners as fanatical imposers of a systematic oppression. The latter overemphasized their control over events and concealed the messy reality of oppression behind the moral perfectionism of a project. Scholars, however, have shown that NP policy represented a pragmatic continuation of pre-1948 government strategy – albeit an intensification of it – and a reactive series of responses by the party.

Not merely in the economic sphere, but more generally across the fields of social policy, apartheid in the 1950s represented a series of ad hoc attempts to resolve embedded problems. In urban areas, nationalists wanted to re-establish control over Black population growth, and embarked on a 'stabilization' strategy of squatter camp destruction, the 'purification' of White areas, and the construction of racially (and later also sometimes ethnically) segregated satellite 'townships' adjacent to the major 'European' cities. The complex system of 'pass laws' that had been used to control the movements of African workers since the late-nineteenth century (and still earlier in the Cape) was bolstered by the creation of a dedicated system for the prosecution and 'deportation' of 'offenders'.

In rural areas, the messy compromises of re-tribalisation were formalized through the *Bantu Authorities Act* of 1951 into a distinct realm of African politics with an associated 'traditional' system of administration and authority (Bonner et al 1993: 15–21).

As Deborah Posel (1991) has shown, the steady consolidation represented by the policies of the 1948 government's legislation does not imply a great degree of planning or control. Proponents of the NP's ability to plan systematically point to the government commissioned *Sauer Report* of 1947. This document gave substance to the slogan of apartheid while uniting the farmers of the Transvaal, Orange Free State, and the Cape, with White labour and the Afrikaner petty bourgeoisie. Posel demonstrates, however, that this report reproduced divergencies within Afrikanerdom rather than settling them. The total segregationist aspirations of intellectuals and petty bourgeois Afrikaners were irreconcilable with the practical designs of prosperous Afrikaner industrialists and financiers. The effort to accommodate them led to an 'ambiguous combination of purist and "practical" recommendations', leaving the 1948 government without a 'compelling, unambiguous, and uncontested blueprint from which state policies could simply be read off' (Posel 1991: 60).

Not only was there no consistent plan, moreover, there were immediate and inescapable pressures upon NP leaders. Their policies had to satisfy not merely Afrikaner interests but also English capital and the largest opposition controlled local authorities. They also faced the threat of African resistance and the nagging danger of electoral desertion (Posel 1991: 6). They secured their position rapidly and skilfully, first consolidating the electoral dominance of the National Party by abolishing the 'Cape franchise' (which had provided some non-Whites with the vote) and rigging the Namibian constituency contribution. Second, the NP fostered a new moral climate among White electors as a whole. The blatant and systematic racism of 1950s legislation, combined with population classification, made possible the conception of quite distinct social lives being created for distinct racial and ethnic groups. Third, it sidelined English-speaking bureaucrats and advanced Afrikaners, in particular members of the secretive nationalist establishment group, the Broederbond. 'Bond' members became instruments of Afrikaner political dominance, by the mid-1950s occupying key positions in the heartlands of executive power. The Native Affairs Department (NAD), in particular, grew to be a state-within-a-state, within which the policies of the 1960s fomented.

State intervention was a defining theme of 1950s politics. The Nationalists, according to Bonner et al (1993:31), believed that 'most of the problems [the state] confronted in 1948 could be solved effectively by simply expanding the scope and intensity of state intervention on the social, political, and economic fronts'. Even where the NP appeared to be following a new and distinctively statist route, it seems very likely that a UP government would have followed very much the same one, since the structural problems facing the economy would have predisposed any government towards these policies. The Fagan Commission report of 1946 had recommended 'ideally voluntary' labour bureaux and identity documents in its prescriptions for the control of African urbanization (even while admitting that such population movements had to be tolerated). The UP put its name to Fagan's recommendations. Had the UP won that election, 'there is good reason to suppose that the shift into a more statist era would have happened anyway' (Bonner et al 1993: 31).

The Rise and Fall of 'high apartheid'

The governments of the 1950s were in certain respects unexceptional. White supremacy and the exclusion of Africans from participation in formal political activity were the norm in colonial Africa. Apartheid's second phase in the 1960s, by contrast, represented a qualitatively quite distinct period in South African history, bringing a change of direction rather than merely a cumulatively deepening segregation. Mass forced removals of 'incorrectly' located Black people, newly created homelands or Bantustans, and deliberate 're-tribalisation', added up to a quite new scale of social engineering. The reach of the state increased, the policing system intensified, and distinct security and military apparatuses competed to dominate the South African state's executive core (see Chapter 8).

Segregationist doctrine was supplanted by the more dangerous notion 'separate development'. This involved the idea that Africans and others should reside, and enjoy citizenship rights, in distinct ethnic homelands. Whereas White supremacy and segregation had involved an explicit racial hierarchy in legislative and political practice, the NP from 1961 was committed to formal equality between groups understood in ethnic terms. The inspiration for these moves was in part the decolonization movements elsewhere in Africa, and especially the experiences of the former British protectorates of Botswana, Lesotho, and Swaziland, which many Afrikaner political leaders had earlier hoped to incorporate into South Africa in recognition that they were dependent on the Witwatersrand economy. If African nationalists could press for the independence of artificial and arbitrarily defined states, then why could not equally artificial states be granted 'independence' within South Africa itself? 'Separate development' was the key concept in this phase of apartheid. Africans' political rights were transferred ultimately into ten Bantustans, and in 1970 homeland citizenship was forced upon all Africans. In the following decade, four of the homelands were nominally, and without international recognition, declared independent (see Map 1.2).

The doctrine of separate development implied that every South African must be assigned to an ethnic group, nation, or tribe, and that each of these must have its own site of self-government. Ethnic categories were enforced on a largely unwilling Black populace by means of comprehensive social engineering. Communities, and even families, were divided as the bureaucracy of apartheid categorized an entire people in accordance with rules of descent. Consequent population removals, simplified now by a clear classification by race and ethnic group, could adopt a stark brutality. Between 1960 and 1989, there were 3.5 million forced removals of people who were found to be of 'incorrect' ethnicity for their location.

Map 1.2 South Africa under Apartheid

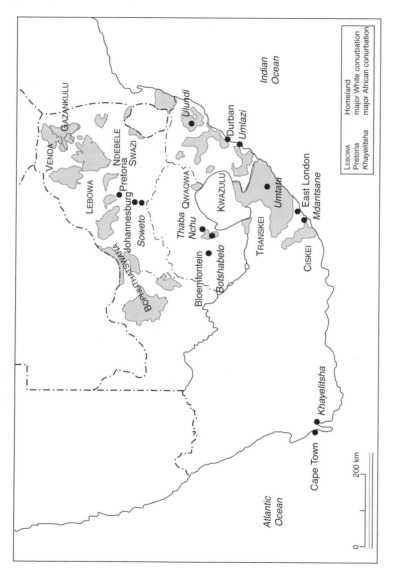

Atlantic
Ocean

Indian
Ocean

Cape Town

Khayelitsha

Bloemfontein

Botshabelo

Thaba
Nchu

QWAQWA

Johannesburg

Soweto

Pretoria

NDEBELE

SWAZI

LEBOWA

VENDA

GAZANKULU

BOPHUTHATSWANA

KWAZULU

Ulundi

Durban

Umlazi

TRANSKEI

Umtata

CISKEI

East London

Mdantsane

LEBOWA   Homeland
Pretoria   major White conurbation
Khayelitsha   major African conurbation

0   200 km

The homelands never came close to acquiring economic self-sufficiency or political legitimacy. As a contribution to their viability, the South African government introduced incentives for business to locate on their borders. The major source of income, however, was always work in the core (now White) economy. Bantustans were justified primarily as political homes for ethnicities, bolstered by systematic 'retribalisation'. Ethnicity or tribalism was established as the principal foundation of homeland self-government, with ethnic affiliation designed to displace South African nationality as the proper basis of African political identification. The official ethnic divisions of 1960s South Africa had plainly been defined by European academics and missionaries who in earlier decades recorded what they took to be permanent 'tribal' languages and cultures. It transpires they were quite mistaken in doing so (see Box 1.2).

Box 1.2   Three views of 'tribalism'

Tribalism has been understood in three ways. A crude 'essentialist' view of African ethnicity saw the warrior 'tribe' as a timeless community with a common essence in shared language, culture, and physical appearance, aspects passed from generation to generation. Such tribes were seen as inherently antagonistic and prone to bouts of warfare. A later 'instrumentalist' view saw the modern tribe as an instrument of colonial rule. Academics, missionaries, and colonial administrators 'invented' tribal practices, conjured pseudo-languages out of dialects, and persuaded a new African elite through missionary education to embrace these invented traditions. Overstretched colonial administrators used tribes to divide and rule, to maintain law and order, to collect taxes, and to extract labour.

Contemporary scholars hold a third and more sophisticated 'constructivist' view, which recognizes that ethnicity could never simply be imposed or invented. Rather it had to be built out of the beliefs and experiences of Africans. Missionaries' teaching of written African languages, they concede, did create the linguistic preconditions for modern tribalism. Native administrators did find tribalist ideas useful in controlling those whom they wished to exploit. According to constructivists, however, local chiefs and currently predominant clans themselves created a-historical 'tribal' justifications for their power, in order to turn their temporary hegemony into permanent rule. The African teachers and intellectuals exposed to the colonisers' interpretations of African history in missionary schools themselves benefited from tribalism as interpreters of tradition for the colonisers and interpreters of colonial practice for 'traditional leaders'. Migrant labourers, for their part, were reliant for survival of networks on support in the hostels and squatter settlements, and discovered in place of origin and nuance of dialect the foundations for systems of mutual trust and support.

Under apartheid, created tribalism was given fresh impetus by a deliberate project of 're-tribalisation'. New groups emerged that found tribalism and the homeland system to be in their interest: the political and bureaucratic elites of the Bantustans. Each Bantustan, destined for political independence, required separate political, judicial, and executive institutions, together with a political elite (often drawn from existing 'traditional leaders') to exercise government. These 'homeland bureaucrats' were joined by a new homeland-based African business class which exploited the withdrawal of White traders and businessmen and took advantage of state investment subsidies.

While Africans' political rights were confined to the Bantustans, 'democratic' elections meanwhile furnished the NP with the legitimacy to entrench its rule. The Broederbond had by 1960 established itself in the heartland of the South African executive and oversaw an ambitious centralization of state powers. The local authorities that had obstructed influx control in the 1950s were easily circumvented by a 1960s central state that had acquired the machinery to run influx control virtually independently of them. African political resistance strengthened the hand of those arguing for new measures, and for the far-reaching revolution of separate development. It was individual acts of defiance of influx control, however, repeated by millions of workers that made the system ultimately unsustainable. Between 1960 and 1970, while the African population in White urban areas fell by over 200,000, the population of the Bantustans grew by almost a million. The extreme overcrowding and impoverishment that resulted in the reserves, and the artificial reduction in available labour in the White urban areas, created a strong incentive for millions of workers to defy the system of influx control.

South Africa's 'transition to democracy'

How did this great structure of high apartheid crumble? What processes explain its demise? How was the 'miracle' of democratic transition negotiated between a racist regime and its 'terrorist' ANC opponent? Long-range international developments profoundly influenced the circumstances within which apartheid collapsed and a democratic settlement was ultimately negotiated. Economic nationalism became decreasingly viable in any country in the 1970s and 1980s as international financial movements and floating exchange rates defeated state defences. The importance of technology transfer and international collaboration for modern industry redoubled these pressures (Goodman and Pauly 1993). Theorists of economic deregulation eventually made inescapable a new neo-classical orthodoxy or 'Washington consensus' fundamentally at odds with the statist and anti-market foundations of apartheid. Domestically, the South African state had long faced a structural crisis. Influx control institutions, never very effective in operation, began to crumble, and urban Black populations to grow rapidly. The effects of South Africa's longstanding productive investment crisis, in which investment barely replaced capital stock, began to kick in sharply.

The economic crisis of the Soviet bloc reduced the interest of the United States and other Western powers in client regimes such as South Africa, while Pretoria was gradually stripped of its buffer regimes to the north by the independence of Angola, Mozambique, Zimbabwe, and Namibia. Many simultaneous experiments around Southern Africa by the 1990s indicate that more general pressures were at work in favour of democratic institutions and practices. The requirements of economic growth, inward investment, and international political legitimacy all pointed the same way. In South Africa, in combination with the stagnation of the economy, the collapse of labour control, and urbanization, these pressures made collaboration between the ANC and the NP government a very great likelihood rather than an unexpected miracle.

While this context pointed towards a negotiated transition, it required decades of organized political opposition to close down the NP's avenues for evasion and delay. The most important single organization in the struggle against apartheid was the ANC. Primarily an exile organization since the 1960s, the liberation movement adopted a two-pronged approach to 'the struggle'. Under its leader, Oliver Tambo, it pursued a diplomatic offensive against the apartheid regime that succeeded in mobilizing a remarkable international consensus between Western powers, the Soviet bloc, and the developing world.

Less successfully, the ANC also engaged in quasi-military operations against the regime, using post-colonial neighbouring states as its bases. Military struggle was mostly unsuccessful as a result of the sophistication of apartheid intelligence agencies and the high degree of penetration of ANC units they achieved. The military wing of the ANC, Umkhonto we Sizwe (MK), may well have propped up the regime by providing a justification for the refusal of the National Party and its allies in London and Washington to 'negotiate with terrorists'.

It was ultimately domestic political conflict that was decisive in bringing the NP to the negotiating table. Young people and students, after a watershed youth revolt that began in Soweto in 1976, were a relentless force for protest and change. The endgame of the fight against apartheid saw extended struggle between an increasingly militarized and oppressive

Afrikaner regime and a powerful mass protest movement – which included organized labour, students, schoolchildren, and community associations – that was able to exert continuous tactical pressure on the regime.

In 1983, a United Democratic Front (UDF) was formed that brought together a wide range of civic, religious, student, and labour bodies in a common platform of anti-apartheid struggle. Independent Black trade unions in the 1980s formed a formidable ANC-aligned Federation (later Congress) of South African Trade Unions (COSATU) that ultimately proved able to bring the economy to a standstill.

Most important of all, however, were localized protests. From 1984, SA saw a progression of localized insurrections, beginning in the Vaal and spilling over into the East Rand, Natal, Eastern Cape, and Free State. These owed virtually nothing to ANC influence. The liberation movement's attempt to capitalize on these uprisings was tactically inept. A minority of astute exiles recognized that domestic 'flashpoints' might best be used to attract new cadres and to shape them into the disciplined underground that the liberation movement so evidently lacked. The dominant view among the exile leadership, however, was that township defence committees could be quickly transformed into 'combat groups' that would challenge the apartheid regime.

As a result of this miscalculation, MK undertook a 'mass' infiltration of 150 poorly equipped and undertrained cadres in 1985–6, an effort that briefly doubled MK presence on the ground before inevitable capture and death at the hands of state security services restored the status quo. At no point could these rashly deployed cadres exercise a 'vanguard' role in community protest.

These battles were made famous internationally by the speech of Nelson Mandela's wife, Winnie Madikizela-Mandela, in support of 'necklacing', murder inflicted using a tyre filled with ignited gasoline. In April 1986, in Munsieville near Krugersdorp, Madikizela-Mandela declared that 'together, hand in hand, with that stick of matches, with our necklace, we shall liberate this country'. The previous year's widely publicized necklacings in KwaNobuhle and Duduza had already provoked Archbishop Desmond Tutu's threat to 'pack my bags, collect my family and leave this beautiful country'. Mandela was demonized in white SA and abroad for her speech.

Most South Africans have since preferred to close their minds to the memory of public burning and accept that necklacing was never ANC policy. By 1992, the liberation movement's information and publicity department was able to state without contradiction that necklacing 'is a barbaric and unacceptable method of execution which the ANC has never condoned'. Nevertheless, there was some equivocation around necklacing in 1985 and 1986, with Oliver Tambo arguing they were 'not happy' with the necklace but would not condemn those driven to use it.

Far from being a potential instigator of 'tactical necklacing', the ANC was an impotent and distant observer. The 14 September 1986 words of then ANC secretary-general Alfred Nzo, in an interview with the London Times, capture the exile leaders' powerlessness perfectly: 'Whatever the people decide to use to eliminate those enemy elements is their decision. If they decide to use necklacing, we support it.'

Necklacing remained a 'punishment' primarily meted out within, and by the members of, local communities. The equivocation of ANC leaders probably testifies to their unwillingness to admit to the limitations of their own power, rather than to any earnest but hypothetical moral deliberation that may have occurred among exiles and prisoners.

As the decade wore on, 'making the country ungovernable' became the tune to which the ANC and domestic anti-apartheid forces increasingly marched. The government responded in 1986 with a State of Emergency that allowed the widespread use of arrests, detentions, and treason trials. Thirty opposition organizations were banned in 1988. Political assassination and torture by the authorities, and the now relentless violence in the townships, were less widely reported in South Africa than abroad as a result of local media restrictions. Although the emergency measures were quite successful in curtailing the opposition's 'ungovernability' strategy, they also provoked further international condemnation and a domestic backlash among Whites.

Meanwhile, ideological shifts among political and economic elites led to the progressive desertion of Afrikaner intellectuals from the NP and to the development of contacts between the ANC in exile and South African business leaders. In the new President from 1989, FW de Klerk, the process of negotiation finally found an adroit and brave Afrikaner tactician. The key parties' arrival at the negotiating table, albeit after a bruising and extended struggle, was ultimately unsurprising, and the prospects of a negotiated settlement would seem to have been bright. There were, after all, few clear ideological divides between the leaders of the NP and the ANC. Both were statist and South African nationalist, pragmatic about economic policy-making and public policy, and each was evidently capable of compromise and sophisticated negotiation. Despite the diverse experiences of exile, imprisonment, and domestic struggle, ANC members showed an almost pathological commitment to organizational accountability and cohesion. The NP had few serious doubts about the reliability and integrity of the military and (with

---

Box 1.3   FW de Klerk

Frederik Willem de Klerk was born in Johannesburg on 18 March 1936, the son of Senator Jan de Klerk, later a minister in the South African government. De Klerk graduated in law from Potchefstroom University in 1958, and practised in Vereeniging in the Transvaal. A gifted analytical thinker, later offered a professorship of administrative law at Potchefstroom, de Klerk rose rapidly through the Transvaal NP becoming member for Vereeniging by the early 1970s. In 1978, Prime Minister Vorster appointed him Minister of Posts and Telecommunications, the first of many ministerial portfolios. Under PW Botha, these included Mineral and Energy Affairs (1980–82), Internal Affairs (1982–85), and National Education and Planning (1984–89). As Minister of Education, he was a supporter of segregated universities but committed to increasing resources for non-whites. A relative centrist in the Party who led moves in 1982 against the extreme right, he was not a natural reformer. In February 1989, de Klerk was elected leader of the NP and in September 1989 he became State President. In his first speech as party leader he called for negotiations about the country's future, and on 2 February 1990 he lifted the ban on the ANC and other banned political organizations, and announced the release of Nelson Mandela. While the ANC's achievement of non-racial democracy had not been de Klerk's goal, he was rewarded with a Nobel Peace Prize in 1993. After South Africa's first universal franchise democratic elections on 27 April 1994, de Klerk was appointed Executive Deputy President in South Africa's Government of National Unity (GNU), a post he held until the NP's June 1996 withdrawal from GNU.

---

some exceptions) the security apparatus. There was little likelihood of state disintegration or coup. Notwithstanding the violent conflict in Natal, moreover, there was little danger of a state destabilising civil war. The means of state coercion remained too overwhelming to permit this possibility.

The negotiation process itself reflected the powerful forces for settlement, with continuity and predictability evident throughout. One insider's account discounts the significance of day-to-day political turmoil, pointing to the immense economic and international pressures that forced even hard-line NP leader Botha to begin contacts with the ANC in mid-1987 (Asmal 1995). FW de Klerk's relaxation of controls on political activity in 1989, after he wrested power from an ailing Botha, seems a natural corollary of this recognition. February 1990 brought de Klerk's decisive legalisation of opposition organizations, multiple unbannings of individuals, and selected releases of detainees. Soon after, government permitted political exiles to return and lifted the State of Emergency that had been imposed in 1986 in an attempt to re-establish government control over the townships. Concentrated and extensive negotiations embarked upon in 1991 ended at Christmas with a reasonably unproblematic statement of joint commitment to negotiation through a Convention for a Democratic South Africa (CODESA). CODESA incorporated 18 political groups which each agreed to the goals of an 'undivided' South Africa, a bill of rights, a multi-party system, constitutional government, a separation of powers, civil liberties, and specified freedoms to be enjoyed by all citizens.

There were wrong turnings and reversals. The year 1992, in particular, was a year of stalemate. The CODESA working party on constitutional principles found itself unable to advance, especially on the size of majorities required to achieve control in the elected constitution-making body. However, even a temporary withdrawal of the ANC was not the dangerous risk that many analysts made it out to be. By March 1993, all 26 negotiating parties were back in public debate in the Multi-Party Negotiating Process. 'Consensus' was the basis upon which talks were built, although this rapidly became established as 'sufficient consensus'. As Johnston has remarked, ANC: NP negotiations were 'helped by the assumption on both sides that "sufficient consensus" meant consensus between themselves' (Johnston et al 1994: 722). As early as April 1993, technical committees were exploring solutions to problems in the fields of violence, discriminatory legislation, the media, the electoral commission, human rights, constitutional issues, and the Transitional Executive Council (or TEC) that was to take over executive functions in the run-up to the first non-racial election. By September, the Constitution of South Africa (known usually as the transitional or interim constitution) had been enacted and legislation on the conduct of a 'free and fair election' had been passed.

The entire process had been enacted by existing institutions – as clear an indication as there could be of the degree of extraordinary control over events achieved by the key negotiating parties. Immense attention to detail was displayed in the drafting of the interim constitution: powers and rules were precisely specified and much of the document read like a detailed contract rather than a framework of general rules. The TEC – the alternative cabinet that was to be the ultimate executive authority in the run-up to the election – was regulated by detailed statutes. Other transitional arrangements were equally carefully defined, including a time-frame that required the final constitution be passed by May 1996, and to be formulated in accordance with 34 'Constitutional Principles' under the oversight of the Constitutional Court. Despite brinkmanship on the

---

Box 1.4   Nelson Mandela

Nelson Mandela was born at Qunu in the eastern Cape on 18 July 1918. His father was chief councillor to Thembuland's acting paramount chief and Mandela himself was groomed for the chieftainship. He started a BA degree at Fort Hare University, from which he was expelled for political activity, and he completed his degree by correspondence from Johannesburg. He helped found the ANC Youth League, and in 1952, by which time he was both Transvaal president of the ANC and deputy national president, Mandela and Oliver Tambo opened the first Black legal firm in the country. After periods of detention and military training, he was convicted and jailed for illegal travel in November 1962. While serving his sentence, he was convicted in the 'Rivonia trial' for sabotage and sentenced to life imprisonment on Robben Island (a prison that was to become a centre for learning and political education). While Mandela was not to be released until Sunday 11 February 1990, in the 1980s he was an increasingly significant interlocutor between the ANC and the regime. After his release, he played a significant role in open negotiations with the ruling NP. He was awarded a Nobel Peace Prize in 1993 and has become recipient of an extraordinary number of honorary degrees and awards. He was inaugurated as the first democratically elected State President of South Africa on 10 May 1994.

---

part of the Inkatha Freedom Party (IFP), the negotiation process was a triumph of political management and elite control. In 1994, a few short years after negotiation began in earnest, Nelson Mandela was President of South Africa.

The chronology and conditions of creation of the final constitution provided a tidy solution to an entrenched difference between the key negotiating parties. While the NP was all along in favour of drafting the full constitution before the first election, the ANC wanted the election to create an assembly with the power to write a constitution from scratch. The inclusion of compulsory respect for Constitutional Principles – together with the safeguards offered by the principle of consensual decision-making, a government of national unity, and the constitutional court – permitted de Klerk to carry his constituency into an agreement that favoured the ANC. The ANC's additional concessions – 'sunset clauses' and pension guarantees for a vast range of state and security force employees – were a blatant and successful bribe to incumbents of state offices. (Guarantees of MPs' pensions were perhaps the most shameless and effective of such measures.) Certain legal-constitutional changes, including the end of the 'parliamentary sovereignty' inherited from British legal thought, rendered less threatening the idea of majority rule. Confidence was cemented by the elevation of the constitution to a new status as supreme law of the land, and by the expanded role of judicial review. A number of 'fundamental rights' were inscribed in the constitution, thus placing them beyond the reach of parliamentary power. Property rights, in particular, were given firm and visible expression.

The negotiators also developed an inclusive formula for parliamentary elections which guaranteed the privileges of parliamentary membership to the elite within even the smallest parties. Inclusion was achieved by means of a broadly proportional electoral system without the cut-off for very low votes that characterizes most such systems. One seat was allocated for every quarter per cent of the vote. In the event, this proved most important in guaranteeing for the very visible Democratic Party and Pan Africanist Congress (PAC) a number of seats in Parliament for their leaders despite their tiny vote shares.

A multi-party executive was guaranteed for a transitional period; fundamental rights were defined; the potential use of emergency powers was restricted; courts with new review powers were set up; and new offices, including the Public Protector, the Human Rights Commissioners, and the Financial and Fiscal Commission were developed. Asmal notes that the 'line between fair and equitable protection of the interests of those not represented in government and the hobbling of a government with a clear popular mandate must be finely drawn' (Asmal 1995: IV) – an issue that has always been at the heart of liberal democratic political thought (see Chapter 6). However, the decisions reached were the product of extended horse-trading rather than of academic deliberation.

In retrospect, the early 1990s negotiations involved less brinkmanship and danger than it seemed. It should have been fairly clear who the central actors would be in South Africa's political drama. Yet, for journalists and academics in South Africa and abroad, the ANC was as unfathomable an organism as the Afrikaner establishment. The mysteries of women's, youth, civic, and church politics defied analysis. ANC-aligned unions, communists, exiles, and former political prisoners seemed comprehensible taken singly, but their sudden throwing together in a new political environment opened bewildering possibilities. The regional peculiarities of Natal (with its Indian Congress and the IFP) and of the Western Cape (with its Coloured politics and its multitude of politicized civic associations) added to the murky stew. Africanism, communism, socialism, Black Consciousness, 'charterism', and the influences of decades in exile:

each left observers bewildered. Out of this confusion emerged the 1994 election, which seemed to be a miracle and the herald of a new era.

The ANC in Government

As a result of the recent challenges and upheavals the ANC has faced, there has been a tendency to underestimate the magnitude of its achievements in government in the decade after 1994. The ANC managed very considerable political and economic challenges associated with profound inequality and social division. It neutralized potential conflicts, defused racial and ethnic tensions, and disciplined potentially antidemocratic leaders. Moreover, it brought consensus to an active membership of former communists, trade unionists, rural traditionalists, religious leaders, and black business entrepreneurs. Five achievements in the decade after 1994 stand out as especially significant.

First, the ANC secured political stability. Political violence was drastically curtailed, and the territorial conflict that characterized the 1994 elections was reduced, in particular in KwaZulu-Natal. Despite its electoral dominance, the ANC mostly avoided the use of non-democratic means to achieve its goals. It maintained public participation in democratic elections, albeit at decreasing levels, and it elaborated an integrated programme of government that helped to contain social conflict and to stabilize the democratic settlement. Its carefully constructed programmes helped to structure citizens' electoral choices, filtered, prioritized and reconciled demands, and neutralized potentially divisive ideological conflict.

Second, the movement's electoral invulnerability allowed it to enforce an unpopular but necessary programme of economic stabilization. The ANC's orthodox or even conservative overall economic policy, the Growth, Employment, and Redistribution (GEAR) framework, increased the prospects of sustainable economic growth (Maphai and Gottschalk 2003). In this way – although at the political cost of placing the burden of adjustment on the shoulders of the poor – it made it more likely that democracy will survive in South Africa (Przeworski et al 2000).

Third, the ANC created a new system of government out of the chaos of the apartheid state. The scale of this achievement – in incorporating former Bantustans, creating new municipalities and provinces, reconfiguring the centre of the state, developing an integrated national planning framework, and moving to medium-term financial planning – has gone largely unrecognized (Picard 2005). The ANC acted energetically to create an institutional framework for good governance, and legislated widely to limit the abuse of public authority by officials.

Fourth, the ANC retained a degree of trust among the poorest citizens, for whom the first decade of democracy brought a deepening of poverty rather than a relief from it (Simkins 2004). The South African electorate has maintained realistic expectations about the pace of change, a realism that has been encouraged by the ANC's ability to rebuild relationships of trust with its constituencies.

Finally, the ANC performed the crucial role of discouraging racial and ethnic conflict. Racial antagonisms are an inevitable product of the country's political and social history. After three centuries of white supremacy, segregation, and apartheid – which culminated in Africans being relocated to Bantustans, restricted to unskilled or semi-skilled work, prohibited from property accumulation, and consigned to a life of labour by 'Bantu Education' – the ANC in government was confronted with a set of daunting, but it hoped not insurmountable, political and policy challenges.

2

A Rainbow Nation?

South Africa's complex history has bequeathed to the present a rich ethnic, racial, linguistic, and religious diversity. According to the country's most recent (2001) census, 79 per cent of the population classify themselves as 'African', 9.6 per cent as 'white', 8.9 per cent as 'coloured' and 2.5 per cent as 'Indian/Asian' (see Table 2.1), using designations directly descended from apartheid's notorious population registration legislation. (The South African government, while no longer supporting routine racial classification of the population, does use racial data to isolate trends, to design policy to bring about historical redress, and to identify the impacts of equity promoting policies.)

The country's diversity, however, transcends the racial categories of apartheid. Around one in five South Africans speaks isiZulu in the home, and only slightly fewer isiXhosa. Other substantial minorities – of between 8 and 14 per cent – embrace Afrikaans, Sepedi, English, Setswana, or Sesotho as their mother tongue. Religious affiliations include a variety of Christian denominations, Islam, Hinduism, Judaism, and traditionalist African systems of belief. Heterogeneous urban, suburban, peri-urban, township, and rural lifestyles reflect a plethora of aesthetic and cultural particularities, in addition to the country's exceptional inequalities of wealth and income. Major cities, and Johannesburg in particular, are rapidly acquiring the cosmopolitan magnificence of the great modern African metropolis.

For some scholars and political leaders, South Africa's 'deeply divided' character is her Achilles heel. For others, such as former Anglican Archbishop of Cape Town and Nobel Peace Prize-winner Desmond Tutu, the potential strength of South Africa lies in her constitution as a 'rainbow nation'. While claiming advantages for diversity, however, Tutu's characterization inadvertently highlights the degree to which the constituent colours of South Africa's rainbow have retained much of the 'apartness' they acquired during the segregationist and apartheid eras (see Box 2.1).

Box 2.1   Key facts about South Africa

Official name:	Republic of South Africa
Regime type:	Constitutional democracy
Executive capital:	Pretoria
Legislative capital:	Cape Town
Currency:	Rand
Land area:	1,219,090 square kilometres
Neighbours:	Namibia, Botswana, Zimbabwe, Mozambique, Swaziland, Lesotho
Resources:	Gold, platinum, diamonds, chromium, manganese, titanium, uranium, copper, silver, zirconium, coal
Gross Domestic Product	US$239.5 billion (2005)
GDP per capita	US$ 11,110 (2006, PPP adjusted)
Population:	47.9 million (2007 estimate)
urbanized:	59.3 per cent (2005)
growth rate:	2.1 per cent (1975–2005) 0.5 per cent (2005–15)
life expectancy:	50.8 (2005)
adult literacy	82.4 per cent (age 15 and older)
infant mortality	55 per 1000 live births (2005)
HIV prevalence	11.1 per cent; 18.8 per cent (15–49 years)
Official languages:	isiZulu, isiXhosa, Afrikaans, English, Sepedi (Sesotho sa Leboa), Sesotho, Setswana, SiSwati, Tshivenda, Xitsonga, IsiNdebele
Provinces:	Gauteng, KwaZulu-Natal, Western Cape, Eastern Cape, Northern Cape, Free State, Mpumalanga, Limpopo, North-West
Major metropolitan areas:	Johannesburg, Cape Town, eThekwini (Durban), Nelson Mandela Metropole (Port Elizabeth), Tshwane (Pretoria), Ekurhuleni (East Rand), Buffalo City (East London), Mangaung (Bloemfontein), and Msunduzi (Pietermaritzburg).

Sources: Adapted from UNDP (2007), Statistics South Africa (2007a).

The Entrenchment of Apartness under Apartheid

Apartheid profoundly deepened and entrenched racial and ethnic division. As we saw in Chapter 1, the entire population was classified by race and by ethnicity according to a political logic devoid of scientific coherence. A still-fluid if segregated 1948 population was fully subsumed under racial categories. Only Whites were accorded full citizenship rights in the Republic of South Africa. Coloured and Asian South Africans were serviced by inferior 'own affairs' administrations, which provided for distinct and segregated public services and limited forms of political participation. Africans were attributed ethnic or tribal identities, with an officially elaborated history, language, and cultural character. Each African ethnic group was allocated a homeland or bantustan within which the population would purportedly develop its distinct nationhood. Africans were systematically 'retribalised', stripped of South African citizenship, their civic and political rights trampled in accordance with the ambitions of the architects of the Bantustans. Hundreds of thousands of people were forcibly removed to their 'correct' locations. The segregation of space and of public amenities was pushed to new extremes.

To some degree, both racial and ethnic categories drew on pre-existing assumptions within South Africa about the nature of social division, especially among Whites. (It is an irony of apartheid that the dark complexions of many of those who defined themselves as 'white' betrayed the pervasive cross racial sex of previous generations.) White supremacist ideology drew upon both the scientific racism of Victorian Britain, brought to South Africa by settlers in the late nineteenth century, and the frontier racism of the Boer settlers. Apartheid helped to make partially fluid conceptions of difference concrete, by forcing those with the same racial and ethnic classification to live, learn, and work together. To be a Coloured South African in the 1960s, for example, was to be labelled a member of a natural population group – one that in fact encompassed a wide variety of classes, languages, religions, and histories. Yet after three decades of forced relocation and residential segregation, Coloured South Africans, while still immensely diverse, were more alike in their self-conceptions than at apartheid's beginning. Designated Africans, for their part, have walked a fine line between pride in distinctive linguistic and cultural heritages, and abhorrence of their distortion and of the malign uses to which they were put under apartheid.

Table 2.1   Population by 'race' and mother tongue, 2001

Race (self-attribution)	% of population
African	79.0
White	9.6
Coloured	8.9
Indian/Asian	2.5
Primary household language	% of population
IsiZulu	23.9
IsiXhosa	17.6
Afrikaans	13.3
Sepedi	9.4
English	9.2
Setswana	9.2
Sesotho	7.9
Xitsonga	4.4
SiSwati	2.7
Tshivenda	2.3
IsiNdebele	1.6
Other	0.5

Source: Adapted from Statistics South Africa 2003.

Strength from Diversity?

South Africa remains a long way from Archbishop Tutu's vision of a rainbow nation comfortable with and strengthened by its own diversity. In the remainder of this chapter, we examine five aspects of the country's heterogeneity – racial and ethnic division, language variety, religion, provincial diversity, and cosmopolitanism. We explore how they contribute or otherwise to the construction of an inclusive and coherent South African society, and how they help or hinder the creation of a common South African nationhood.

Race and ethnicity

We have explored how the country's extended history of white supremacy, segregation and apartheid created, exacerbated and entrenched a variety of racial and ethnic divisions. In urban areas, however, and in particular in the country's industrial heartland of Johannesburg, a cosmopolitan culture and multilingualism survived all attempts to impose apartheid labels. One consequence of the end of apartheid, and later the institution of non-racial democracy has been a less politicized and more creative assertion of pride in ethnicity, nonetheless combined with a vigorous condemnation of racial divisiveness.

One central feature of African National Congress (ANC) opposition to apartheid, moreover, was its ideology of 'non racialism', and its rejection of the implied significance of racial and ethnic labels. Given the dangers that ethnic conflict has posed in Africa, the government has approached all matters ethnic or racial cautiously since 1994. A disciplined political movement, the ANC has been historically intolerant of ethnic politicking at provincial or local level. More visibly since 1999, however, a quasi-Africanist conception of history and of politics has become increasingly prevalent in the movement's leadership, and the doctrine of non-racialism has been somewhat eroded. At times, political debate has been coarsened by the imputation of racial or ethnic motives to political opponents, particularly in the ANC centre's battles against the Inkatha Freedom Party (IFP), the Democratic Party (DP) and its own allies in the South African Communist Party (SACP) and the union movement. Racialisation of conflict has been an inescapable characteristic of postcolonial Southern African politics, most recently in Zimbabwe and Namibia. The roots of such a politics in South Africa lie in an extended history of racial oppression. It is nevertheless fuelled by continuing racist sentiments among many historically advantaged South Africans and by the immense difficulties governments face in dismantling what appears to be a racial hierarchy of affluence and economic opportunity.

Language as a source of division

Critics of the emergence of English as a global language view its unfortunate rise to hegemony in South Africa as only a matter of time. However, the country will remain for many decades a site of multi-faceted multilingualism, even if English seems likely to continue its rise as the language of government and business. The negotiators of South Africa's new political order in the early 1990s did not resolve language issues or debates over the status of ethnic groups with which languages are associated. Instead they designated 11 official languages: isiZulu, isiXhosa, isiNdebele, Sepedi, Sesotho, Setswana, siSwati, Tshivenda, Xitsonga, English, and Afrikaans. The Constitution confers the right to use the language of one's own choice and to learn in that language where this is reasonably practicable. The state's official language policy is to promote and protect linguistic and cultural diversity, and to recognize and promote multilingualism as a national resource.

Constitutionally guaranteed language rights are protected by the Pan South African Language Board (PanSALB) whose purpose is supposedly to promote multilingualism in South Africa. In practice, its role has been primarily to investigate complaints against public or private bodies that have been accused of violating any citizen's language rights. For example, an organization might discriminate against a person on the basis of his or her language, deny the right of association with members of a linguistic community, or deny a person their right to expression within their linguistic community. Complaints have come primarily from Afrikaans speakers and only a relatively small number have to date been processed. The language board has been largely incorporated into the state and its budget is now controlled through the Department of Media, Arts, and Culture. Critics of the board question its willingness or capacity to fulfil its remit by actively promoting multilingualism and the protection of language rights within the society.

The 2001 census indicated that isiZulu is mother tongue of 24 per cent of the population, isiXhosa of 18 per cent, Afrikaans of 13 per cent, and Sepedi, English, Setswana, and Sesotho each of around 8 or 9 per cent (see Table 2.1). Afrikaans and English are very widespread as second languages, and English has increasingly become the language of business, the media, and politics. Nine of the official languages are 'Bantu' languages, representatives of a wider family of languages that stretches across much of sub-Saharan Africa. These languages are unsurpassed in their elegance and integrity of structure. There is very often mutual intelligibility between Bantu languages – for example between most dialects of isiXhosa and isiZulu. Until the formalization of the languages by missionaries in the late nineteenth centuries, these tongues underwent extensive interchanges with one another and with the indigenous languages of the Khoisan and the European settlers. Young Black urban South Africans will often today speak simultaneously in Bantu, Afrikaner, and English languages, seamlessly weaving together vocabulary and grammatical structures.

Afrikaans is a formalized version of a hybrid Dutch and indigenous language patois that emerged among 'Coloureds' in the western Cape across the eighteenth and nineteenth centuries. It was both a creation of, and a vehicle for, the development of Afrikaner nationalism. In the space of just a century, in the 'miracle' of the Afrikaans language, it has developed a comprehensive vocabulary in the natural sciences and applied technologies, an extensive range of philosophical and social scientific concepts and an impressive body of literary and poetic accomplishments.

South African English was the language of the colonial power from the start of the nineteenth century, bolstered by periodic waves of immigration from Britain, most particularly in the later nineteenth and early twentieth centuries. Dominant within national government, and the primary tongue of Whites in the Cape and Natal provinces, it was in addition the language of national government and of the major business corporations that grew out of the gold and diamond industrial revolutions. It has developed to some extent along its own trajectory, while becoming increasingly influenced by developments in American rather than British English.

Most South Africans are multilingual to a greater or lesser degree. African mother tongue speakers are far more likely than others to possess high level multiple language skills, often proficient in two or more secondary Bantu Languages and sometimes also in the English or Afrikaans still so vital for entry into the formal labour market. Afrikaans mother tongue speakers, by contrast, are likely to speak only English as a second tongue. English first-language speakers are those least likely to possess a second language – and where they do so it is usually Afrikaans. Language use thus continues to reflect a history (and continuing reality) in which English and Afrikaans were avenues to economic and social advancement.

Widespread pride in the language and culture of different African language communities is accompanied by a realization that these languages were themselves used as instruments to distinguish one African 'tribe' from another during the apartheid period. Few people wish to see language become once again a source or instrument of division. It is in part for this reason that English is emerging as a *de facto* national language for South Africa's middle classes, its political history excused by its status as a 'global language'.

The problems of mutual cultural accommodation and communication have been most evident at the interfaces between the historically privileged languages of English and Afrikaans and the nine new official languages. (It is no surprise that literature, poetry and the theatre, as we shall see in Chapter 7, have faced extreme obstacles to advance since 1994.) Yet the continuing advantages enjoyed by English and creolized Dutch have profound consequences for the development of a coherent and inclusive social order.

There is much discussion of the blending of cultures in the new South Africa, as groups formerly set against one another by defined ethnicity and race are learning new forms of communication, consensus, and mutual adaption. Cultural defences built to protect group identities, on this view, are crumbling as South Africans learn how to treat one another's cultural practices with respect. Such new interaction is

---

Box 2.2   The Land

Although South Africa is rapidly urbanizing, and her rural population has been in decline for thirty years or more, the land continues to possess a deep emotional resonance for most of her people. The country covers an area of around 1.2 million square kilometres. Two features dominate its landscape: an inland plateau that accounts for the majority of the land area, and a thin strip of coastal lowland upon which historically the population has been concentrated. Between the two rises a Great Escarpment, or set of mountain ranges, reaching in places an elevation of more than 3,000 metres. The interior plateau mostly comprises grassland, shading in the Northwest into the Namib and Kalahari deserts. In the north-east it rises into the Witwatersrand ('White Waters Ridge' in Afrikaans), a gold-bearing rocky formation upon which Johannesburg was built in the great gold rush of the 1880s. In the centre of the country lie the Drakensburg mountains, at the heart of which sits the independent kingdom of Lesotho. The coastal strip, which is sometimes called the 'lowveld', is in places less than 100 kilometres in width.

---

evident in the extraordinary interpenetration of languages in the everyday speech of young Black urban South Africans. Language, however, is not just the most basic instrument for the expression of cultural difference and integration. It is also the most essential precursor for desirable employment. Yet most of the country's population cannot command Afrikaans or English sufficiently well to advance in the formal labour market, and African children are profoundly disadvantaged by their need to acquire scientific and technical vocabularies through English (Alexander and Heugh 2001). While most of the urban Black population speaks several languages, many are most fluent in African tongues which do not serve as economic resources in the way English and Afrikaans continue to do.

Religion

If language continues to be a force for division, religion performs a more equivocal role. South Africa is a highly religious society. Indeed only a small minority of its population has any conception of what it might mean to live without an organized religious tradition. At the same time, there exists a great diversity of religious beliefs and practices, and an

Table 2.2   Religious affiliations (estimated 2002)

Denomination	Members (000s)	% total
Zion Christian Church	4,242	9.71
NG* Churches	3,866	8.85
Catholic	3,757	8.6
Methodist	3,080	7.05
Pentecostal/charismatic	2,416	5.53
Anglican	1,756	4.02
Apostolic Faith Mission	1,232	2.82
Lutheran	1,153	2.64
Other Zionist	2,368	5.82
Other Apostolic	3,857	8.83
Other Christian	5,251	10.62
Subtotal: Christian	*32,978*	*75.49*
Muslim	607	1.39
Hindu	590	1.35
Judaists	74	0.17
African traditional	17	0.04
Other faiths	210	0.48
Subtotal: other religions	*1,503*	*3.44*
No religion	5,089	11.65
Refused/not stated	4,111	9.41
Total population	*43,686*	*100.00*

*Dutch Reformed churches
Source: Adapted from Institute for Missiological and Ecumenical Research, University of Pretoria; reproduced GCIS 2002: 6.

impressive tolerance of and respect for difference. Around 75 or 80 per cent of the population regard themselves as Christians, while there are substantial minorities of Hindus, Muslims, or Jews (see Table 2.2). In addition, there is a substantial body of people who consider themselves 'traditionalists'. This classification is complicated by the fact that most traditional belief systems accommodate a supreme being, and many avowed African Christians also subscribe to some form of traditional belief. 'Ancestors', for many Africans, play a major role in determining the fortunes of the living community of which they remain a part, and it is essential to maintain relations with these ancestors, to talk with them, and sometimes to appease them through rituals.

The largest group of churches in South Africa are the African Independent Churches, descended from so-called 'Ethiopian churches' which themselves emerged as a result of desertions and breakaways from mission-based religion. Primarily Zionist, Apostolic, or Pentecostal, these some 4,000 independent churches have in total more than 10 million members. During the apartheid period, they played a significant, if subdued political role, allowing members to articulate discontent with the racialised order and to reaffirm conceptions of social and political justice systematically disallowed in the wider society. The largest single church in South Africa, the Zion Christian Church (ZCC), typifies their primarily conservative character. It has four million members and is notable for its annual Easter and September pilgrimages to Moria in Limpopo Province where upwards of a million church members gather for religious festivals. It has a prescriptive approach to alcohol, smoking, and promiscuity, and has shunned the formulation of political programmes.

A second significant group of Christian churches are the Dutch Reformed churches, which altogether account for almost 4 million members celebrating primarily in the Afrikaans language. The largest reformed denomination, the Dutch Reformed Church, was closely related politically and ideologically to the Afrikaner nationalist project and in the 1950s and 1960s was sometimes labelled the 'official religion' of the National Party (NP). Towards the end of the apartheid period, the reformed churches became conservative influences on a population that was increasingly questioning the moral coherence and political viability of the apartheid system.

African churches did not engage in open political conflict with the apartheid regime, although they gave strength and cohesion to wider community struggles. Sporadic churchmen's efforts to build an anti-apartheid political project through their religious institutions failed in the 1960s and 1970s. The (primarily Black) Methodist Church campaigned actively against apartheid, and it probably suffered significant desertions in consequence. Attempts by the leadership of the Catholic church to formulate an anti-apartheid consensus provoked factionalism among the religion's four million adherents, and resulted in the emergence of a South African Catholic Defence League to protest against the integration of single-race schools. The financially robust Anglican Church opposed apartheid most consistently and unequivocally but its limited membership and identification with the English establishment militated against its effectiveness. Only through an umbrella organization – the South African Council of Churches – did many of the churches finally begin to engage in systematic protest against apartheid in the 1980s.

The churches retain great but elusive significance in national political life today.

In the run-up to the decisive ANC conference held in Polokwane at the end of 2007, the major protagonists, Thabo Mbeki and Jacob Zuma, felt it prudent to adopt an implausibly pious demeanour. The Full Gospel Church, the eThekwini Community Church, and the Miracles Gospel Church conferred the honorary title of 'pastor' upon Zuma. Meanwhile, Mbeki was invited by His Grace Bishop Barnabas Lekganyane, paramount leader of the ZCC, to attend the church's assembly in Moria, which attracted a staggering 2.5 million believers.

Mbeki recalled Lekganyane's sermon at some length in his ANC newsletter, and used it in support for his own claim to retain the ANC presidency. In Mbeki's emotional recollection, the bishop had concluded with a prayer for the president and his cabinet that they might 'overcome the challenges they have (faced) in fulfilling their mandate to make a better life for all'. Mbeki, perhaps unsurprisingly, concluded that 'Bishop Lekganyane addressed all these important matters as the leader, and on behalf of, the millions of members of the ZCC,' his words suggesting His Grace was delivering a vote of confidence on behalf of his church and its many members in the president and his government.

Such an interpretation of the paramount leader's sermon, however, was misleading. In the apartheid era, ZCC doctrine confused almost all outsiders. Some highlighted what they saw as the church's tolerance for apartheid evils, and accused the ZCC of 'political acquiescence'. Others took the contrary view that the ZCC's rituals and superficial conservatism concealed a robust cultural resistance to colonialism or even a powerful political protest against apartheid.

As Lekganyane explained the crux of the matter more than 20 years ago, ZCC theology demands that 'a man cannot be a follower of God without rendering due respect to the earthly government which He has ordered'. For this reason, 'the president, prime minister, ministers of state, chiefs, and all members of administration, are in authority over you'.

One consequence of this doctrine was that the current bishop's father, His Grace Edward Lekganyane, invited members of the NP to Moria even in the immediate aftermath of the Sharpeville massacre. In 1965, when Bantu affairs minister De Wet Nel visited a conference, Bishop Edward thanked the government for its 'kindness' and 'goodwill'. Barnabas Lekganyane doubtless conferred upon Mbeki the respect due to him as state president. However, this same obligation to a secular authority was evident in April 1985 when Lekganyane invited state president PW Botha to celebrate the 75th Easter Paseka of the ZCC with him. Yet, in 1986, a year after Botha's visit, in a sermon delivered to believers and reported only in the ZCC's official newsletter, the bishop spoke quite unequivo-cally about institutionalized racism: 'The ZCC, and I as a leader, detest apartheid together with all of its discriminatory laws.'

The Zionist obligation to respect secular authority still conceals a wide spectrum of political opinion and a high degree of underlying politi-cal sophistication. Members will not be swayed, and are unlikely to be impressed, by attempts from whatever quarter to mobilize them as recruits in a merely political campaign to advance factional or personal interests.

The Diversity of the Provinces

South Africa under apartheid consisted of four provinces – Cape Province, Natal, Transvaal, and Orange Free State – together with ten designated 'homelands' allocated to African 'nations' in accord-ance with the high apartheid ideology of separate development. In the political settlement reached in 1993, as the country approached its first non-racial franchise election the following year, nine provinces were delineated. This new organization of the provinces involved the incorporation of Bantustans, and the breaking down of some geo-graphically large provinces, notably the Cape, into more appropriate vehicles for service delivery and political accountability. Each of the nine provinces contains a diversity of population, economic activity, and culture.

Wide variations in economic performance, job availability, and pop-ulation structure divide the provinces. Jobs are extremely scarce in the rural provinces and poverty is widespread. Former 'homelands', more-over, act as nurseries for the young and the homes of the old – in Gauteng the dependency ratio (of non-working to working age) is below 50:100 while in Limpopo it is above 100:100. Other than Gauteng, which is by far the most densely populated area in South Africa, population has been most concentrated in the poorest areas of South Africa's interior, espe-cially Bantustans to which Africans were confined by apartheid legisla-tion. Over the past decade, however, the urbanization characteristic of developing countries has accelerated as apartheid era 'displaced urbani-sation' to high-density Bantustan settlements is reversed. At least half the population lives in urban areas (more than 60 per cent using defini-tions of 'urban' that include high-density informal settlements and ex-homeland conurbations). On one widely respected definition, urbanization is expected to rise to 64 per cent by 2015 (UNDP 2007). These figures again disguise considerable regional variation. Gauteng is currently almost entirely urban and the Western Cape's population is more than 90 per cent urbanized, whereas Free State and Northern Cape have 70 per cent urbanization levels. Eastern Cape, KwaZulu Natal, Mpumalanga, Limpopo, and the North-West are between 35 and 45 per cent urbanized (Statistics South Africa 2002a: 8).

The economic heartland of South Africa, Gauteng is the country's most dynamic province and boasts its highest population density on its smallest land area. It accounts for more than a third of South Africa's Gross Domestic Product (GDP) and contains both Johannesburg – Southern Africa's most populous city – and the country's executive capital Pretoria. Its rapidly-growing population of around 9.7 million (Statistics South Africa 2007a) is almost entirely urbanized and contains an unusually high proportion of young and educated South Africans. Johannesburg is the centre of inward migration into South Africa, primarily from elsewhere on the African continent, and the city is highly cosmopolitan. Many of the business headquarters and offices that grew up in Johannesburg have migrated northwards to the area of Sandton, which was the venue for the 2002 World Summit on Sustainable Development. The city centre has become home to businesses and migrants from around Africa.

Like other parts of South Africa, the province continues to exhibit the residential segregation by race that characterized apartheid. In this tiny province, comprising only 1.4 per cent of the country's land area, the republic's most wealthy citizens live in close proximity to some of its poorest. South of the city lies Soweto (South Western Townships), home to around 2 million people, yet not quite a city in itself because of its dependency upon the economy, services and employment possibilities of Johannesburg. All of the townships in the Gauteng are characterized by a very high degree of linguistic and cultural diversity, and the population is of exceptional political sophistication.

South Africa's most populous province, KwaZulu-Natal (or KZN) contains around 10 million people and accounts for about 17 per cent of GDP. It hosts the country's major port of Durban, and it has a diversified and dynamic economy. About 80 per cent of its population are isiZulu speakers, with the remainder primarily mother-tongue speakers of English. Around 9 million South Africans consider themselves Zulu, and KZN is home to the majority of Zulu-speakers. The province uniquely possesses a Zulu monarchy for which special provision has been made in the constitution.

KZN is also the political heartland of the IFP, South Africa's only major ethnic-based political movement. The IFP has a history of conflict

> **Box 2.3   HIV/AIDS and population growth**
>
> In 1976 South Africa contained just 26 million people. The population today, after three decades of rapid growth, is around 48 million. More than half of all South Africans are under the age of 25. If these bald statistics are indicative of the dynamic population growth typical in any developing country, projections for the next decade tell a more gloomy tale. HIV/AIDS is expected to bring this expansion almost to a halt and growth is unlikely to resume until 2015 (UNDP 2007). Because HIV is primarily spread through sexual contact, its incidence is especially high among young adults. For this reason, South Africa's 'dependency ratio' between those of working age and others will worsen sharply. A smaller working population – much of which is suffering HIV/AIDS-related illness – will have to support a heavier burden of young and old dependants.

with the ANC in the province, with the ANC historically tending to represent more urbanized and less traditionalist Zulu-speakers – whether within the province or in Gauteng where a very substantial Zulu-speaking population lives. The leader of the IFP, Mangosuthu Buthelezi, participated in the post-1994 Government of National Unity and served one term as Minister of Home Affairs under Thabo Mbeki. The co-operative relationship between IFP and ANC has contributed to markedly reduced levels of political violence in the province, but the two parties remain locked in a struggle for votes and patronage.

KZN also contains a considerable Indian-descended population of around one million. Many of these South Africans trace their ancestry to indentured sugar plantation labourers, brought to Natal from the south of India in the late nineteenth century, but others were later voluntary migrants from central and northern India. Most of these Indians are English language speakers, although other languages flourish in many households. Around 60 per cent are Hindus with the remainder mostly Muslim or Christian. The experience of classification and segregation in the apartheid period has helped to reduce the significance of class and cultural differentiation among Indians, but it has not led to any major independent political organization. KZN also contains the descendants of a substantial wave of British migrants in the mid-nineteenth century that quickly moved to the larger towns and established a dominance over business and trade. KZN is notable today for its exceptionally high HIV prevalence – estimated by some to be as high as 20 per cent for the provincial population as a whole, or around 30 per cent for adults aged between 20 and 65.

The Western Cape is the third major economic centre of South Africa, accounting for some 15 per cent of GDP despite its population of only around 4.8 million. Around 55 per cent of this population are Afrikaans-speaking with the remainder equally divided between isiXhosa and English speakers. It has a well-diversified economy, with great potential in tourism, and enjoys the lowest unemployment rates in the country at about 17 per cent (Statistics South Africa 2007b). The majority of the Western Cape's population were designated 'coloureds' under apartheid. This category referred to a heterogeneous collection of people brought together by their failure to fit into the 'African' versus 'European' typologies around which apartheid was elaborated. Many Coloured South Africans speak English as a first language or are fully bilingual, although a majority would describe Afrikaans as their mother-tongue. There is a diversity of religious beliefs within the Coloured community.

Some of the Western Cape's coloured citizens trace their ancestry to the Griqua, a society of largely Khoisan and Afrikaner descent with a three century long history of political organization and displacement. Like most Coloured people, this group are Dutch Reformed church adherents and speak primarily Afrikaans. Others, sometimes labelled 'Cape Malays', are Muslims descended variously from Malaysian, Afrikaner, and Khoikhoi peoples, and the various slave populations that passed through the Cape. As with Indian South Africans in KwaZulu-Natal, the common experience of apartheid oppression – combined with the greater economic and political freedom of Coloured than African – created a complex heritage of community self-recognition and pride together with ambivalence about politics. Coloured people in the Western Cape have been among the most militant and determined opponents of apartheid but also delivered to the NP, apartheid's creator, a provincial election victory over the ANC in the 1994 foundational election.

South Africa's remaining six provinces have distinctive characters but each is blighted by high levels of poverty and immense developmental challenges. Eastern Cape is South Africa's poorest but perhaps most beautiful province, its seven million inhabitants – alongside Gauteng's – the country's most politically sophisticated. Its primarily isiXhosa speaking population has the longest history of interaction with settler and colonial powers, and European missionaries and teachers became an established presence over the nineteenth century. As early as the turn of the twentieth century, most of South Africa's

---

Box 2.4   Climate

South Africa has a mostly temperate climate. The interior plateau is characterized by long hours of sunshine and warm days, and cool but rarely cold nights. Summer temperatures are normally in the high 20s or early 30s degrees centigrade. Rainfall occurs primarily in the summer, between November and March. While it varies considerably from region to region, and within the coastal belt, average annual rainfall in the North and East is sufficient at between 478 millimetres (Limpopo) and 844 millimetres (KwaZulu Natal) to support crop production. Rainfall in the West can support only livestock farming. There are some exceptional climatic zones. The area immediately around Cape Town has a Mediterranean climate, with heavy winter rather than summer rainfall; the North West is very dry and includes an area of desert; and the far North and north-east have subtropical conditions with substantially higher summer temperatures than the highveld and Rand.

---

emerging Black professionals, primarily ministers, doctors, and lawyers ('iigqwetha', originally meaning twisters or deceivers in Xhosa), came from the area today occupied by Eastern Cape. (IsiXhosa speakers, notably Nelson Mandela and Thabo Mbeki, have also been prominent in Black politics.) Its economy is heavily dependent on the motor manufacturing sector but it has the potential to develop a substantial tourism industry.

Northern Cape is a vast and sparsely populated semi-arid province whose economy is centred on sheep farming, mining, and fisheries. The Free State, lying at the centre of South Africa, has a population of less than three million primarily Sotho speaking people distributed over almost 130,000 square kilometres. The province's relatively limited income is primarily derived from mining, manufacturing, and agriculture (particularly field crops). The mining industry is the province's biggest employer and the goldfield region of Free State accounts for almost a third of South Africa's gold output. In addition there are productive diamond mines. These industries have fallen upon very hard times, however, and Free State is suffering a crisis of falling incomes and plummeting formal sector employment.

In the North of South Africa lie three geographically smaller provinces: North-West Province, Mpumalanga, and Limpopo (formerly Northern Province). Two thirds of North West's primarily Setswana-speaking population of 3.4 million live in rural areas, and the provincial economy is based on minerals and agriculture. Mpumalanga's 3.5 million population is concentrated on an area of less than 80,000 square kilometres, and contains substantial mother-tongue populations of siSwati, isiZulu, and isiNdebele. The region is famous for its tourist routes and citrus fruits, but its economy is dominated by its coal reserves and it contains the countries biggest power stations (with resultant high levels of air pollution). Limpopo Province, perhaps surpassing even Eastern Cape in its natural beauty, rivals it also in its poverty. More than half of its 5.5 million people are Sepedi speakers – a tongue sometimes known as Sesotho sa Leboa – but the province embraces a variety of languages including Xitsonga and Tshivenda. Limpopo incorporates several troubled apartheid era Bantustans within its borders, and it has experienced difficulties converting its immense economic potential into enhanced welfare for its population. It is likely, however, to be one of South Africa's major sites of economic growth across the next decade.

The system of provincial government, as we shall see in Chapter 6, has served in both political and service delivery roles. While many have been critical of the poor delivery of public services at provincial level – particularly in health and education services managed by provincial administrations – they have performed relatively well as the vehicles for political competition in a polity dominated at national level by the ANC.

Migration and xenophobia

In addition to the variety of populations bequeathed by its history, South Africa also contains a diverse immigrant and refugee population of more recent origin, primarily from elsewhere in Africa. It is difficult accurately to assess the size of this immigrant population. Until recently, estimates were in the range 750,000 to 1 million, or around 2 per cent of the population (Crush and Williams 2001). This corresponded to a much larger population in major trading and economic centres such as Gauteng, where more than 5 per cent of the population were estimated to be foreign born. In recent years, the gradual implosion of the Zimbabwean economy has led to rapidly increased flows of migrants from South Africa's northern neighbour. There have also been business-creating, and so highly visible, immigrant arrivals from Somalia, West Africa, Mozambique, and even East Asia.

Regional instability, in particular in Zimbabwe, presents the possibility of further substantial cross-border migration in future years. On the whole, South Africans have not responded well to the recent increase in immigration. Despite widespread Africanist rhetoric, xenophobia is rampant, and most venomous when directed towards fellow Africans. In Gauteng, where substantial entrepreneurial immigrant communities have purportedly threatened the livelihoods of local street traders and small businesspeople, there have been many reports of violence and intimidation. Immigrants are blamed by South African citizens for unemployment, HIV/AIDS, and crime. Anecdotal evidence suggests that the Home Affairs department has often dealt in an arbitrary manner with refugee and work permit applications from the nationals of other African states.

It was hoped until recently that such tensions would abate over time, as the economic benefits of a new sub-continental commercial community became apparent. After all Johannesburg, already southern Africa's largest city, had become tied by its human networks into the major commercial centres of the continent and had flourished as a result. Foreign-owned business flourished because they were able to offer consumers lower prices and more convenient service. However, violence against foreigners escalated sharply after 2000. In the first three months of 2008, two Somalis were found burnt to death in their Duncan Village shop, migrants were driven out of Soshanguve in Gauteng, shops and shacks belonging to foreigners were destroyed in Laudium, and the campaign of violence against Somali and other foreign shopkeepers in the Western Cape intensified. In March at least seven Zimbabwean, Pakistani, and Somali residents of Atteridge in Gauteng were murdered. The Human Rights Commission was concerned enough to demand new protections for immigrants. African diplomats wrote to the government to demand a response to attacks on nationals.

Then, in the middle of May of 2008, violence exploded on the streets of Johannesburg's townships. In a three-week long orgy of devastation that affected many townships in Gauteng and the Western Cape, more than sixty people were killed and tens of thousands displaced. This wave of devastation marked the definitive end of President Thabo Mbeki's once internationally persuasive grand narrative which portrayed South Africa as a society moving relentlessly forward towards peace, modernity, and development.

Suddenly the smell of the apartheid years was back in the air. The London Times drew this chilling parallel under the headline 'The Shame of Thabo Mbeki', when it claimed that 'harrowing images of a still unidentified burning man recall the nadir of the apartheid era, when black-on-black violence terrorised the townships and suspected collaborators were set alight with petrol-filled tyres'.

Meanwhile, there were fears of an unfolding ethnic dimension to the violence, fuelled by reports of young men from predominantly Zulu-speaking hostels roaming the streets singing Umshini wam' ('Bring me my machine gun' – an old ANC struggle song), seeking out people with dark complexions, and taunting Tsongas, Shangaans, and foreigners alike.

A devastating lack of political leadership was evident throughout the crisis. Leaders of all kinds viewed the xenophobic rage as a natural force too powerful to be contained. As events moved with startling speed and ferocity, the limitations of the South African Police Service as an instrument of public control were also devastatingly confirmed. The police were widely and understandably distrusted by refugees.

For the international media, the violence provided an excuse to resurrect older models of the country's overall trajectory and ultimate destination. For the New York Times, South Africa once again became a powder keg of frustrated hopes and disappointed expectations. 'The attacks on African migrants have increased political instability at a time of power shortages and disaffection over Mbeki's pro-business policies. Soaring food and fuel prices helped push tensions to breaking point.'

The Financial Times, for its part, claimed that violence against vulnerable foreigners can be used to diagnose more profound pathologies within a society. 'In the 14 years since the dawn of black majority rule,' the paper observed, 'inhabitants of SA's townships have exhibited immense patience. The escalating violence against immigrants around Johannesburg should serve as a warning to SA's rulers that this patience has an end.'

In the aftermath of the turmoil, government has offered a number of inconsistent explanations for the violence. Apartheid elements, third forces, socioeconomic factors, and criminal gangs were all advanced and then dismissed as explanations by political leaders and officials. Many commentators argued that long-range socioeconomic factors, such as urbanization, unemployment, entrenched poverty, and poor public services, predisposed township communities to violence. Analysts also highlighted longstanding, pervasive violence against 'foreigners', noting that xenophobic and corrupt police forces leave such groups vulnerable. Numbers of foreign nationals, especially Zimbabweans, had grown rapidly, and sharply rising food and fuel prices added to the pain.

It remains unclear how much explanatory power analyses of the influence of poverty or relative deprivation really possess. Human societies across the ages have almost all been marked by extremes of oppression, suffering, and inequality. Men, women – and even slaves – have almost never rebelled in the face of inequality or injustice. One fear must be that the 'xenophobic attacks' may turn out to be something quite different: an expanding circle of victims that embraces Tsonga- or Venda-speaking citizens that may ultimately lead to widespread ethnic politicization and violence.

Another concern is that a decade and a half of radical change in political institutions has destroyed once-intelligible systems of community representation and mobilization, and replaced them with an incomprehensible patchwork of corrupt councillors, distant government departments, and opaque executive agencies. For ordinary citizens it is no longer clear where they can express grievances, or how change can be brought about. Discontented citizens cut loose from systems of political representation can only be brought together to rage sporadically about the injustices they believe they endure.

It is not merely immigration and related xenophobia that have been major concerns for South Africa's government and people. Emigration has also been substantial in recent years. More than 200,000 South Africans left permanently for English-speaking countries alone between 1989 and 1997, and many thousands – perhaps tens of thousands – more leave each year. Émigrés, usually beneficiaries of South Africa's highly unequal educational provision, sometimes bewail the limitations of the new South Africa in order to ease the guilt of exile.

Contrary to conventional wisdom, it is not South Africa's Whites alone who are leaving the country or considering doing so: it is professionals of all races and ethnicities, often blaming crime or limited job opportunities. The government has recently begun to recognize that emigrants can be a resource rather than merely a 'brain drain'. Returning migrants bring back with them skills and contacts. Those leaving permanently often retain a profound interest in South Africa, and have the potential to develop business relationships over the long term. It is always difficult, however, to transmute the bitterness of departure into a positive disposition towards a country of birth.

The government has not so far developed a satisfactory policy for managing population movements into and out of South Africa. In common with many other states, South Africa does not have an immigration or emigration strategy designed to minimize the economic harm caused by skills loss or to maximize the benefits that immigration and a benevolent Diaspora can bring. Xenophobia has limited legal in-migration to a few thousand per year with the potential economic benefits of the immigration of skilled workers from elsewhere in Africa disregarded. After

---

Box 2.5   The Truth and Reconciliation Commission

Meeting first in April 1996, and submitting its final report to President Thabo Mbeki only in March 2003, the Truth and Reconciliation Commission (TRC) had a threefold mandate. It was charged to investigate and report upon apartheid-era human rights violations; to grant amnesty to admitted perpetrators who had fully disclosed their actions; and to make recommendations concerning reparations. The TRC's principal achievement was to elicit and record the testimony of thousands of victims of human rights violations, and to establish on the historical record the extent and nature of such abuses committed during the era of political struggle. However, the ANC, IFP, and NP each selectively challenged the TRC's findings and so undermined its credibility. The institutional executors of apartheid – in business, the media, the judiciary, and the universities – avoided admission of (and so reflection upon) their own culpability. Individual perpetrators of abuse only rarely disclosed their actions and sought amnesty, and victims' testimony is likely only very exceptionally to support prosecutions. The government moved very slowly towards a reparations policy, announcing in 2003 that the victims of human rights abuses were to receive only modest consolatory payments.

---

more than a decade of policy confusion, there remains little likelihood of a coherent migration strategy developing.

Conclusions

Uprooting an entrenched sense of apartness remains one of South Africa's greatest challenges. The constitution enjoins the citizenry of the new democracy to recognize the injustices of the past and to heal the divisions of history. Yet even after a seven year 'truth and reconciliation' process (see Box 2.5), citizens remain divided by their history as well as over it. Some still view South Africa as 'two nations' – White and Black – divided by culture, wealth, and history. As we shall see in Chapter 4, however, a more complex reality contains a substantial non-White middle-class, growing levels of intra-Africa inequality, and a diversity of White living standards. Nonetheless, almost all of the poor in South Africa are African, and almost all of the rich are White. Changes in the labour market and employment patterns, moreover, have resulted in a growing gulf between the wealthiest in the society, who are predominantly White, and the poorest and the unemployed, who are overwhelmingly Black. Given the country's history of racialized political division, such a situation is not tenable in the longer term.

Middle class South Africans are building a degree of social harmony across racial divides. Everyday personal interaction is marked by the courtesy that often accompanies social division. At the same time, a society that never permitted interaction across racial boundaries on remotely equal terms is starting to do so. It is developing in its educational institutions, its public sector, and its private businesses the new forms of common understanding that can only come from personal experience and communication.

However, an asymmetry of power and wealth still almost always accompanies South Africans' relationships across races. They often seem to be guided by racial stereotypes and the potential for politicisation of racial difference is everywhere evident. In the past, the ANC's doctrine of non-racialism has been a bulwark against the political abuse of racial difference. Yet the failure of government and the privileged to change the structures of racial disadvantage may one day create fertile ground for a new generation of political entrepreneurs willing to exploit racial discord. The xenophobia and violence that has greeted so many of Gauteng's African economic migrants is no substitute for the sense of nationhood and social inclusion that South Africans are striving unevenly to attain.

3

The South African Economy

Introduction

At first glance the South Africa economy seems beset by paradoxes. It is the largest in the region, with higher output than the rest of Southern Africa combined. Yet, in global terms, it is a dwarf. It is the most advanced economy on the African continent. Nevertheless, it suffers from massive shortfalls in skills and infrastructure. Home to sophisticated financial services and information technology companies, it still contains a significant minerals sector that emerged in the late nineteenth century. The country's affluent suburbs and vulgar consumerism co-exist alongside an impoverished peri-urban poor. This uneven urban prosperity is divided by a chasm of inequality from South Africa's rural dispossessed who suffer levels of poverty similar to those endured by the world's very poorest peoples.

Many of these often remarked paradoxes are less puzzling than they first seem. Middle-income developing countries routinely display extreme contrasts in economic development, with high technology business and wealthy urban elites coexisting with extreme poverty and economic backwardness. South Africa is by no means the only state in the South to remain wedded to its economic past as a primary sector resource extractive economy. The country's seeming achievements, moreover, are exaggerated by their contrast with the desperate disappointment that has plagued most of the rest of the continent. As we shall see in Chapter 4, it is only in the country's terrible and multi-faceted inequality that its record is truly outstanding.

Output and Expenditure

The total value of goods and services produced in 2006 was US$239.5, the highest output of any country on the African continent (UNDP 2007).

With a little over 7 per cent of Africa's population, the country is responsible for more than one third of its output of goods and services. To place this achievement in context, however, the country's output amounts to less than 2 per cent that of the United States economy.

Gross Domestic Product (GDP) growth followed an unexceptional but unimpressive trajectory for most of the past five decades (Du Plessis and Smit 2007). An extended boom began before World War II, at the end of which manufacturing overtook the primary sector as the largest part of the economy. Growth continued throughout the 1950s and 1960s at levels of around 5 per cent per annum which were not dissimilar to other developing countries in this period of global boom (Moll 1990).

In common with most other developing countries, South Africa's economic fortunes declined sharply in the mid-1970s as the first major post-war recession was triggered by the increase in international oil prices. Thereafter, in the 1980s and early 1990s, GDP growth was heavily and negatively influenced by country-specific factors, such as changes in commodity (and especially gold) prices, political instability, and the international disinvestment that resulted from the struggle for non-racial democracy. In the 1980s, growth averaged less than 1.5 per cent, and the 1990s scarcely improved upon this disappointing rate. As a result of continued population growth, real per capita GDP actually declined after 1981 and per capita growth resumed once again only in 1995.

Since 1994, the country has enjoyed positive but quite low levels of economic growth (see Table 3.1). Average real growth of around 3.1 per cent per annum has translated after population growth into around 1.1 per cent growth in per capita GDP per year. South Africa's post-apartheid growth, moreover, has mostly been 'jobless growth', and the number of people employed in formal non-agricultural employment fell substantially between 1994 and 2000. As a result, the country has developed an especially severe and prolonged unemployment crisis.

The economy has become increasingly diversified. In the late nineteenth century, mining and agriculture dominated the economy. However, South Africa became progressively a manufacturing economy, with manufacturing surpassing other sectors by the mid-twentieth century. Services have achieved greater significance across the past four decades. The country entered the twenty-first century a reasonably diversified and robust economy, dominated by the tertiary (services) sector (66 per cent of output) with the secondary sector (including manufacturing) accounting for 20 per cent and the primary sector for only 10 per cent (Du Plessis and Smit 2007). Manufacturing, finance and government are the three biggest industrial categories (see Figure 3.1).

Table 3.1   Economic growth 1994–2007

Year	GDP*	% growth
1994	779,424	3.2
1995	803,710	3.1
1996	838,326	4.3
1997	860,515	2.6
1998	864,968	0.5
1999	885,365	2.4
2000	922,148	4.2
2001	947,374	2.7
2002	982,122	3.7
2003	1,012,763	3.1
2004	1,062,028	4.9
2005	1,115,136	5.0
2006	1,175,216	5.4
2007	1,235,627	5.1

*GDP at constant 2000 prices (Rand millions)
Adapted from Statistics South Africa 2008.

Figure 3.1   Contribution of various industries to GDP, 2007

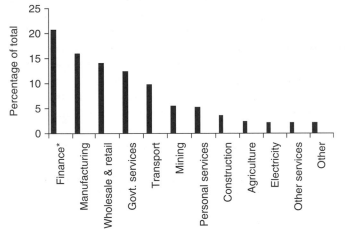

*Includes business services and real estate
Source: Adapted from Statistics South Africa 2008.

The fastest growth in recent years has been in transport, communications, financial intermediation, insurance, business services, and real estate. Despite this diversification, some scholars argue that resources remain at the heart of the economy. While mining itself accounts directly for a little over 5 per cent of GDP, there are strong relationships between mining and sectors such as electricity, non-metallic minerals products, iron and steel industries, fertilisers, pesticides, chemicals, and petroleum industries. For this reason, some analysts claim a 'minerals-energy complex' still accounts for a fifth or even a quarter of the output of the economy (Fine and Rustomjee 1996).

Economic Policy

The African National Congress (ANC) has adopted an orthodox or even conservative policy framework since 1994. The government's overall macro-economic framework emphasizes the pursuit of economic stability, market-friendly policy, and fiscal discipline as the prerequisites for sustained economic growth. A stable environment for private investment, the attraction of foreign investors, labour market flexibility, industrial policy, and partially privatized public assets are policies that according to Growth, Employment, and Redistribution (GEAR) can create the potential for a faster growing economy with higher levels of employment.

GEAR has been controversial within the ANC and especially among its tripartite alliance partners, the Congress of South African Trade Unions (COSATU) and the South African Communist Party (SACP). COSATU has complained that GEAR entrenches unemployment and has so far delivered few pay-offs in return for its conservative macro-economic position. While the government has recently reaffirmed in the strongest possible terms its commitment to GEAR, it has moved towards a more interventionist micro-economic strategy, an expanded industrial policy, and the creation of more elaborate systems of social welfare support to ameliorate the implications of economic restructuring for the poor. These interventionist strategies build on the tradition of a Reconstruction and Development Programme (RDP) which from 1994 embodied the developmental aspirations of the left of the ANC. Employment creation, an especially significant part of this new orientation of policy, is discussed in the next chapter.

Monetary and fiscal policy

From the mid-1970s, as the apartheid state came under increasing political and economic stress, fiscal policy became increasingly erratic as public expenditure and finance departments failed to maintain effective control over outlays and tax revenue. Since 1994, there has been a transformation on both revenue and expenditure sides of the budget. From 1987 to 1991, South Africa was running budget deficits of around 10 billion Rand per annum, around 5 per cent of GDP, and this rose to around 10 per cent of GDP in 1992 and 1993. Since 1994, strict control of government expenditure, combined with a revolution in tax collection by the South African Revenue Service, has steadily reduced budget deficits first to 4 per cent in 1997, then to 3.2 per cent in 2000. By 2007 South Africa was running a budget surplus.

The institutional power of the treasury within the government has also been entrenched, at times to the irritation of cabinet members and interest groups. The decade of the Mbeki presidency 1999–2009 has been the decade of Trevor Manuel's tenure in the most important cabinet office as finance minister. Under Manuel (see Box 3.1) the finance ministry has secured an exceptionally powerful position in national government and it has monopolized control of overall macro-economic policy. Treasury has become omnipresent across the cabinet subcommittee system. The South African Revenue Service, with its unprecedented access to personal and corporate financial information, reports to the finance minister. This minister is also responsible for the Financial Intelligence Centre, which has unparalleled capacity to track money-laundering and fraud.

Box 3.1　Trevor Manuel

As one of the world's longest serving finance ministers, Trevor Manuel has left a significant imprint on South Africa's post-apartheid governance. His political background in the 1980s Western Cape was in bus and school boycotts, in community mobilization around housing and civic issues and in the United Democratic Front (UDF). Manuel was the left's candidate for the headship of the ANC's economic planning department in 1991. As finance minister since 1996, he has overseen the conservative overall macro-economic policy known as GEAR, and he has been highly influential at the heart of the policy-making process. He persuasively defended GEAR's compatibility with the left-leaning RDP, and his view that the fiscal consolidation of GEAR provided the foundation for the sustainable delivery of the RDP gained many converts. Manuel instilled the lesson that it is the quality rather than the quantity of government spending that is decisive. Ideological antagonism towards Manuel has been amplified by his combative personality. He can be dismissive to the point of contemptuousness and the phenomenal application and attention to detail behind his critical positions have sometimes left his antagonists enraged.

The activist Finance Ministry under Trevor Manuel also moved to make the budgetary process more transparent and initiated a bold shift away from incremental budgeting in which year-on-year budget increases occur without systematic justification. Through the introduction of a rolling three-year medium-term expenditure framework in 1998, the government has also moved to reduce uncertainty and to increase the ability of economic actors to plan reliably for the future.

Monetary policy aims to secure a stable financial environment within which economic decisions are no longer influenced by variable and high inflation. Under the 1996 constitution, monetary policy is the joint responsibility of the Ministry of Finance and the South African Reserve Bank. In 2000, this joint authority agreed to adopt mechanisms of formal inflation rate targeting, with an initial target band of 3–6 per cent. The Reserve Bank's Monetary Policy Committee, consisting of Reserve Bank governors and officials, is charged with adjusting monetary policy to bring inflation into line with its target range, an approach that has become increasingly controversial in recent years, with leftists criticising the policy for reducing economic growth. The Reserve Bank also oversees the banking system as a whole, and acts as the central bank of South Africa.

One especially contentious responsibility of the Reserve Bank is its administration of the country's system of exchange controls. These instruments limit the amounts of capital South African businesses and citizens are permitted to move offshore. The government is committed to a gradual relaxation of these controls and ultimately to an open capital market, goals to which it has moved by means of increasingly generous allowances and technical mechanisms through which business and individuals are able to move capital. The government's gradualist approach has repeatedly received the full support of the International Monetary Fund (IMF).

Industrial policy and the idea of the developmental state

The government continues to proclaim the primary importance of fiscal and monetary stability, and to stress the priority it gives to market-friendly and competition-enhancing policies. Its competition policy, as expressed in the *Competition Act* (RSA 1998) aims to reduce opportunities for restrictive practices, the abuse of market dominance, and corruption. However, the South African government has also moved to establish a relatively ambitious industrial strategy. The Department of Trade and Industry aims to promote technology development in

---

Box 3.2   Key facts about South Africa's economy (2007)

GDP (US$ billions)	282.63
GDP (Rand)	1,993.89
GDP per capita (US$)	5,906
GDP per capita (Rand)	41,669
GDP per capita (PPP* US$)	9,761
GDP (PPP) as % of world total	0.716
Inflation (annual per cent change)	7.1
Population (millions)	47.9
Current account balance (US$ billions)	-20.56
Current account balance (per cent of GDP)	-7.27

*Purchasing power parity figures (PPP) adjust for price differentials between countries for purposes of comparison

Sources: UNDP 2007; IMF 2008; Statistics South Africa 2008a.

---

manufacturing industry, and manages spatial development initiatives that are designed to unlock economic potential in areas of socio-economic deprivation and to develop economic relations with neighbouring states. The most innovative (if unproven) elements of industrial policy concern micro-business promotion, through which the country's estimated three million micro-enterprises – businesses employing five or fewer workers – are to be provided progressively with technical support and advice.

Notwithstanding these initiatives, South Africa is a developing country without a clear framework for development. Responsibility for developmental issues is distributed within and between government departments and between institutions at different levels of government. Departments such as Trade and Industry, Social Development, Agriculture, Land Affairs, Health, Transport, Housing, Water Affairs and Forestry, and Public Works, and key parastatals such as Eskom and Telkom, have not yet found a way of working together. The different 'spheres' of government – national, provincial, and especially local government – will also have to work more effectively together if developmental strategies are to succeed.

Government has introduced integrated developmental strategies for both urban and rural areas, and it has attempted to build the capacity of municipalities to act as agents of economic development. More recently, the language of the 'developmental state' has entered ANC and government policy documents. Advocates of the developmental state sometimes claim that a country cannot 'make a speedy and successful transition from poverty' in the absence of 'a state that in some respects corresponds to [the] model of a developmental state' (Leftwich, 2000: 169), taking the high growth success stories of East Asia – Taiwan, South Korea, Singapore, Japan, and now China – as their models.

The institutional and contextual differences between South Africa today and these models are very great. Skills and social cohesion characteristics are quite distinct (Southall 2006: xvii). And nothing like the apparently requisite range of imitative institutional and political reforms – to regulatory frameworks, 'strategic' government departments, service delivery systems, and public sector human resources – could conceivably be made in South Africa today. The favourable external economic conditions enjoyed by the classical developmental states are also not reproducible. New obstacles include falling relative prices of manufactured goods and rising relative prices of commodities. Moreover, 'the rise of China and India has revived an old concern about export-led growth: the strategy may work for one country, but can it work for many?' (CGD 2008: 96). If developing countries simultaneously seek to emulate export-led growth strategies, an international glut of manufactures would depress prices, reduce returns to investment and provoke a protectionist counter-reaction (CGD 2008: 96–7).

Although there is limited interest in a 'shopping list' conception of how to grow fast, one influential set of growth studies (Rodrik 2003) shows that rapid economic growth can be stimulated by minor policy or institutional changes. There is no fixed menu of developmental prerequisites, and states can and have pursued their own idiosyncratic and unorthodox routes to faster growth. This has encouraged South African policy makers to look for creative policy innovations that might help the economy to grow.

Unfortunately political leaders in South Africa, as elsewhere, face pressing political and practical problems, and they normally adopt economic theories only when they seem to offer solutions to immediate challenges. The idea of the developmental state idea might easily be used to ratify poor or imprudent policy choices that are politically necessary or perhaps just convenient.

East Asian successes depended on an elite bureaucracy controlling industrial policy through powerful state institutions such as Japan's Ministry of Trade and Industry (Miti). In South Africa, sectoral interventions have been limited to the motor industry and textiles, and the bureaucracy is politicized and under skilled.

Even for policy makers, sceptical that South Africa might ever become a fully fledged developmental state, the ideology of the developmental state can be used to mobilize support behind relatively pragmatic policy interventions. First, developmental ideology provides a much-needed boost to informal and voluntary social dialogue. An aspirant developmental state can accumulate much of the sectoral information it needs to refine human resource planning, target infrastructure investment, and remove impediments to growth.

Second, a developmental state famously requires a bureaucracy closely linked to business but immune to capture by special interests – almost exactly the converse of emerging patterns in South Africa. By emphasizing that state capacity is crucial and sorely lacking, the idea of the developmental state justifies an aggressive attack on unproductive office-filling in the public service.

It also supports an intensified war on patronage and corruption. Those cheating the state or viewing public office as a platform from which to conduct personal business can be stigmatized if the technocratic state is presented as an essential part of a project of patriotic national development.

Finally, developmental states do not merely allocate resources, they also mobilize them to finance investment and growth. In order to assemble all the resources the public sector can contribute to national investment, government non-investment spending must remain tightly curtailed and a generally restrictive budgetary policy must therefore remain.

Certain elements of a developmental state are already in place. The Presidency boasts a policy unit committed to sector strategies, breaking down boundaries between departments, and prioritizing employment-creating growth. Housing and public infrastructure programmes are finally starting to yield developmental synergies. And a planning commission created in 2009 sets growth targets and then tries to orient infrastructure investment, sector strategies, and skills development towards these goals.

Although the developmental state ideal is unrealizable, it does not need to be fully realized to remain valuable. It is in the striving, and in the ideological cover that statist ideology provides for pragmatic reforms, that the real payoffs of the idea of the developmental state can be found.

Trade and Internationalization

South Africa's exports across the twentieth century were dominated to an unusual extent by a single commodity: gold. This over-dependence, which a variety of government policies failed to correct, left the currency subject to commodity-related swings in value, a property that itself served to further weaken export-oriented manufacturing. Despite a range of incentives and infrastructural provisions for export-oriented industry, gold (and then gold and platinum) continued to account for almost 40 per cent of external revenues. Imports have been dominated in the post-war period by industrial inputs (such as machinery), automobiles, chemicals, and oil.

Primary product demand has declined over recent decades, South Africa has re-entered a liberalizing global economy, and its currency has depreciated steadily. Together, these factors have brought about a substantial shift in the composition and volume of exports. Since 1994, both exports and imports in manufactured goods have demonstrated very strong upward trends, and the export base has diversified impressively.

European countries remain the major trading partners and investment sources and recipients for South Africa. Germany and the United Kingdom are South Africa's second and third largest trading partners, and are major sources of investment, while relations are also strong with France, Switzerland, Belgium, Sweden, Denmark, and Italy. The United States is another key trading partner for South Africa, and represents an especially important area for export growth in the aftermath of the *African Growth and Opportunity Act*, which allows duty-free export of specified products. South Africa has negotiated special trading relationships with the European Union and the United States, and it is also deepening trade and investment relations with Eastern European countries, Japan (which is South Africa's fourth-largest trading partner), Malaysia, and Latin America.

The focus of the Mbeki Presidency, however, has been on the development of economic relationships within the African continent. Around a third of South Africa's exports are destined for other African states, while the Republic is also a major source of foreign direct investment for many other African countries, especially members of the Southern African Development Community (SADC). Energy and transport parastatals, mining groups, agro-processors, retailers, and brewers have been among those businesses pursuing aggressive investment and acquisition strategies in Africa since 1994.

In part through the New Partnership for Africa's Development (NEPAD) championed by Mbeki, it is hoped that South African businesses will benefit from increasing external interest in the economies of the continent. However, NEPAD's currently diffuse mandate – addressing trade issues, debt relief, aid co-ordination, infrastructure investment, foreign direct investment, and conflict resolution – will require clarification if it is to endear itself with major western partners in the G8, the European Union, and the World Bank.

Investment Flows

While South Africa was the recipient of very considerable inward flows of capital to both mining and manufacturing sectors in the 1960s it became increasingly dependent on loan capital which itself dried up as the country's political situation worsened in the 1980s. Since 1994, there has been resurgence of portfolio or indirect investment, a welcome but in some respects concerning development. However, direct investment has involved far smaller sums, and perhaps two-thirds of this has been in mergers and acquisitions rather than into the greenfield investment that most directly expands capacity and creates employment and output (Muradzikwa 2002).

This is a problem for the African continent as a whole. While global foreign direct investment has soared in recent decades, only a little over 1 per cent of this amount has come to the African continent. Such disappointments have preoccupied South African policy makers. Some opinion formers complain bitterly about a shortfall of foreign direct investment which it had been widely hoped might compensate for low levels of domestic saving and provide access to technology, knowledge, managerial capacity, financial markets, and international distribution networks. Some critics complain that poorly informed institutional investors have been unduly swayed by negative press sentiment and exaggerated perceptions of African crisis, and have proven unable to differentiate South Africa from its northern neighbours.

A small group of extreme critics even accuse international business and finance of unfounded Afro-pessimism and implicit racism. Blaming western business people's intractable prejudices for weak inward investment, these critics in the ANC and its allies sometimes (and largely for domestic consumption) advocate protectionism, non-co-operation with international organizations, and special economic relationships with like-thinking partners elsewhere in the developing world.

Moderates complain that the country is unjustly associated with (purported) 'African' economic and social ailments – corruption, authoritarian leadership, and tribalism – and point to evidence that investors take an undifferentiated view of the performance of Africa's economies (Bhinda et al 1999; UNCTAD 1999). These moderates argue that South Africa should work – when appropriate with African partners – to confront negative perceptions, cement relationships with international businesses, and reshape foreigners' and expatriates' perceptions of South Africa. They argue for both a 'business-friendly' policy framework comparable to that in developing countries elsewhere, and sometimes for additional orthodox initiatives, such as spatial development plans, business promotion agencies, investment drives, and tax incentives.

Liberal sceptics – a tiny minority within the ANC but representing business orthodoxy – tend to disparage activist prescriptions with regard to perceptions or sentiment. They argue that South Africa is in fact fortunate to enjoy today's levels of investor interest. Such sceptics stress that South Africa is a medium-sized economy in a small region, locked into a slow growth path, and that these features represent the decisive impediments to investment. Foreign direct investors, like the domestic actors from whom they often take their cues, are not very susceptible to misinformation or misperception. They take business decisions on narrow business grounds, and will continue to adopt defensive strategies – such as telescoped business plans, local borrowing, and the immediate repatriation of profits – so long as South African conditions demand them. Such sceptics argue that the government should focus its attention, not on 'perceptions' or 'uncertainty', but on objective and remediable obstacles to doing business: inherited structural weaknesses, uneven infrastructure, unskilled, expensive and unionized labour, crime, corruption, and a host of others.

Since 1994, it is an incontrovertible fact that South Africa has been the beneficiary of substantial inflows of capital. Although direct investment has indeed been disappointing, portfolio investment has poured into the country and made a positive contribution to financing domestic investment. Sustained high-growth economies appear to have maintained investment rates at 25 per cent of GDP or higher, often together with additional (non-accounted) investments in education and health (CGD 2008: 24–5). In South Africa, although planned increases in domestic investment will have to come from domestic sources, external finance is already extremely high. For this reason, the moderate position is likely to continue to dominate in the ANC. Senior policy makers are reconciled to prevailing international orthodoxy about prudent government as a result of recognition of dependency. At the same time, like their counterparts elsewhere on the continent, South African intellectuals have been unremitting critics of the injustice and political domination that is integral to the international economic order.

Public and Private Sectors

South Africa's qualified but determined accommodation of international intellectual orthodoxy is also found in the government's approach to the role of the state in a modern economy. From 1948, parastatals were used as the engines of the Afrikaner nationalist project, driving up the living standards of Afrikaners both through public service provision and employment creation. Key state-owned enterprises today include Eskom, Transnet, and Telkom, which together employ around 200,000 people.

The next three largest state-owned enterprises are the Industrial Development Corporation, The Development Bank of Southern Africa, and the Land Bank of South Africa, which have a substantial role in urban and rural development. In addition there are a number of smaller parastatals, including Denel (formerly Armscor), Rand Water, the Post Office, the Airports Company, and the South African Broadcasting Corporation. There has been extensive restructuring in the parastatal sector, with managed liberalization and rationalization in transport, energy, and telecommunications.

In contrast to this general if qualified retreat of the state, public works programmes are likely to undergo expansion in the face of alarming levels of unemployment and associated poverty. The Community-Based Public Works Programme targets areas of exceptional poverty in rural areas, and maximizes employment creation and capacity building, particularly among women. Among other effective employment creation and poverty alleviation measures is the Working for Water programme, led by the Department of Water Affairs and Forestry, a labour intensive scheme for the clearance of 'alien vegetation' which can potentially affect water security, ecological systems, and the prevalence of fire and flood. The programme employs almost 20,000 people annually.

Most notable among the government's initiatives has been an increase in partnerships between private, public, and voluntary sectors. Recent initiatives have recognized the importance of voluntary work in supporting the poorest of the country's communities and in enhancing the personal security and well-being of the aged and ill. The HIV/AIDS pandemic will make such voluntarism still more important across the next decade in the absence of an appropriate health and welfare infrastructure. In a number of areas – water and sanitation, waste removal, electricity generation and reticulation, prison construction and management, education, and toll road construction – the government has also embraced the concept of public-private partnerships. There is much scope for further partnerships in rail and harbour redevelopment, government property upgrading and development, and energy generation.

Private finance initiatives, however, have been the object of unremitting scorn from the trade union movement, and this has exacerbated tensions within the ANC–SACP–COSATU alliance. Such projects often bring considerable problems, most notably in the exclusion of the very poor from effective participation as market actors. However, while market imperfections and failures will be an inevitable consequence of public-private partnerships, especially in a context of extreme inequality, they will often represent the least worst option.

Selected Sectors of the Economy

Resources, extractive industries, and energy

The modern South African state was created by the late nineteenth century minerals revolutions. While extraction remains technically difficult, South Africa has around half of all known gold reserves and continues to account for thirty or forty per cent of world gold output. The fortunes of the South African economy have been closely related to the price of gold, and this has brought an unhappy degree of instability to the country's economic environment. Gold has also been blamed by some historians for the political trajectory of apartheid. Always dependent on extremely low cost labour, some analysts claim that the migrant labour system – in which workers would be employed on short contracts in the prime of their working lives, while their families, children, and old people languished in the reserves – was a direct product of the gold economy.

Over the twentieth century, the country experienced a diversification of mining activity. By the middle of the century, South Africa was one of the world's largest producers of a whole range of materials: gold, platinum, diamonds, chromium, manganese, titanium, vermiculite, zirconium, vanadium, uranium, copper, silver, and asbestos. In addition, South Africa has immense reserves of coal – which have supported its energy generation industries and a host of related energy-intensive industries – as well as considerable reserves of iron ore. Platinum-group metals now equal or even surpass the contribution of gold to the economy. In 2000, total sales of gold amounted to some R25 billion (Euro/$2.5), while sales of platinum group metals totalled R27 billion. Coal sales totalled some

R20 billion, and base and ferrous minerals around R5 billion each. Other minerals amounted to some R15 billion in sales. Official figures indicate that the mining industry contributed 5–7 per cent to GDP in 2000, but perhaps 15 per cent through associated multiplier effects. Mining also employs some 400,000 people on 750 mines. The industry indirectly supports many tens of thousands of other employees. A little under R25 billion in wages was paid out in this sector in 2000. Stakeholders, including the Chamber of Mines, the National Union of Mineworkers and the government's Department of Minerals Affairs and Energy, have striven together to maintain the viability of marginal mines and to safeguard employment in this sector.

South Africa suffers strategic energy dilemmas. It has very significant coal reserves, perhaps 55 or 60 million tons, equal to 10 per cent of the global total, or the fifth largest known amount. In addition, it has substantial uranium resources. However, it has almost no petroleum and is therefore vulnerable to oil price fluctuations.

Electricity generation is primarily based on coal reserves in the north of the country. Due to substantial over investment in the 1970s and 1980s, and slow economic growth in the 1990s, there was for a long time substantial oversupply of generating capacity. Energy prices for industry were consequently very low, encouraging waste and the development of energy intensive industries.

The parastatal Eskom has dominated generation, accounting for some 95 per cent of electricity production and transmission. Coal accounts for 90 per cent of production, gas less than 5 per cent, and nuclear and hydroelectric power for most of the residual. Electricity distribution is often chaotic. Eskom is the biggest single distributor, but there are also 300 municipal electricity departments involved, overseen by councils. Some 100 of these municipal suppliers have fewer than 1,000 customers. This fragmentation results in high costs, low efficiency, limited scale economies, discrepancies in tariffs, and cross-subsidisation of other municipal functions. Numerous disconnections for non-payment, illegal reconnections, debt traps into which consumers have fallen, and politicized payment boycotts indicate widespread citizen discontent.

In January 2008, South Africans were hit with a wave of power cuts that demonstrated that this era of cheap power was at an end. The power cuts have had a substantial economic impact and severely damaged the credibility of government policy makers.

The government's policy of 'managed liberalisation' began promisingly at the turn of the millennium with the institutional separation of the three activities of generation, transmission, and distribution that were almost monopolized by the giant parastatal. In the generating field, private independent power producers (IPPs) were invited to break Eskom's near monopoly of generation. It was hoped they would reduce the parastatal's thirst for capital, bring in new international technologies and technical expertise, and create the possibility of price competition between generators.

Eskom's transmission system – or 'grid' – was supposedly turned into a standalone servant of public and private generators alike. Meanwhile, the inefficient patchwork of Eskom and municipal distribution systems was to be rationalized into a small number of regional electricity distributors (REDs). The intention was to construct a wholesale electricity market. Eskom and independent producers would vie for the business of REDs and big industrial users, and this competition would supposedly keep a lid on prices.

The first challenges arose on the generation side. Modelling of demand trends meant Eskom and the government were well aware of rapidly falling reserve margins. Having made their bed, however, ministers refused to lie in it, dithering over IPPs because of ideological confusion, opposition from COSATU to 'privatisation', and growing international scepticism about managed liberalization.

Since the entire sector restructuring would make no sense without IPPs, the government had no real choice but to introduce a moratorium on Eskom generator investment after 2000. Low prices already made South Africa unattractive to foreign investors, however, and Eskom made matters worse by obstructing the tendering process, boasting about its continuing control of the grid, and deepening its longstanding relationships with major industrial users.

Eskom also achieved a high degree of political invulnerability by dressing itself up as the key regional instrument of President Thabo Mbeki's New Partnership for African Development, and by allowing Mbeki to claim credit for the numerical achievement of 3-million household electricity connections.

During this period of indecision, reserve capacity fell from 1994's 30% to about 10% in 2005, at which time the Eskom investment moratorium was lifted. In a second key development, the transmission system was neglected while senior executives and skilled technologists vied for positions in more glamorous international and generating divisions.

In the third key area, the cabinet finally decided only as late as October 2006 how many REDs there would be and which areas they would service. Wealthy municipalities unwilling to cede assets or to pool revenues still cannot be compelled to participate, and any review of their constitutional reticulation rights will take years the government does not have. In the meantime, uncertainty around distribution has inhibited local infrastructure investment and precipitated a spate of local supply disruptions in major metropolitan areas.

Eskom brazenly denies any culpability for power cuts. Its managers insist wet coal was the proximate cause of the load shedding debacle, and that R20bn or R30bn spent restoring inexplicably depleted coal stockpiles constitute an appropriate precaution against a recurrence.

It likewise treats the government's previous moratorium on investment as its longer-term scapegoat for load shedding. The parastatal now wants to bounce the government into picking up the tab for a capital requirement estimated at R300bn over the next five years and upwards of R1,3-trillion over the next two decades.

Eskom and the government alike are hesitant to confront the all embracing character of the problems confronting the sector. Potential transmission and distribution system crises, maintenance overruns such as those that caused cumulative generation shortfalls in mid-January, and the negative effect of 'black economic empowerment' (BEE) programmes (see below) on the coal supply chain present urgent challenges that remain outside the scope of current recovery plans.

The parastatal's celebrated status as a low-cost supplier of electricity was always based in part on apartheid-era overinvestment, abundant surface coal, state debt write-offs, a high tolerance for pollution, and exemptions from taxes and dividend payments.

Nevertheless, Eskom has been rightly proud of its post-1994 tradition of competent management. It is an open question whether this tradition has been compromised by a new trend of political appointments to vital managerial and technical positions.

Manufacturing and finance

South Africa's reasonably diverse manufacturing base has weathered the difficult decade of the 1990s surprisingly well. As a consequence of apartheid policies, industry had been encouraged to adopt capital intensive strategies to minimize the demand for Black labour in urban areas. Manufacturing was especially hard hit by the economic downturn of the 1980s and the dismantling of protectionist instruments since 1994. Yet it has responded well to the opportunities offered by the increasing international integration of the economy and the trend decline in the value of the Rand. The sector has a broad technological base, skilled managers, and abundant but poorly skilled labour.

South Africa has sophisticated, liquid, and deep financial markets, including active primary and secondary capital markets, money markets, the Johannesburg Stock Exchange, a South African Futures Exchange, and the Bond Exchange of South Africa. Financial sector regulation is a responsibility of the Reserve Bank (for the banking sector) and of a Financial Services Board (for non-bank institutions). The banking sector is dominated by four major banks associated with major mining groups: ABSA Group, Standard Bank, First National Bank, and Nedcor. In addition, over a dozen foreign banks were active in the country in the 1990s (although many have since withdrawn). The insurance sector, like banking, has deregulated and demutualized. The South African Reserve Bank reports that the total assets of long-term insurers in 1999 amounted to some R665 billion. Other financial institutions include the Development Bank of Southern Africa, charged with promoting economic development and growth across the regions, and the Land Bank, whose role is to provide retail and wholesale banking services to the commercial farming sector.

There are two key issues facing the financial sector today, the first of which is to ensure that the ramifications of further integration in the international economy, especially the removal of exchange controls, are well-managed. The second is responding to the financial services needs not just of the small minority of wealthy South Africans but those of the wider and poorer members of the society. Bank accounts and formal sector credit are expensive and difficult to obtain. Black South Africans often depend on informal networks or on co-operative rotating savings schemes (stokvels) to raise capital, and have often been at the mercy of unscrupulous elements in the micro-lending industry.

Tourism, small business, and the informal sector

After decades of limited development in this sector, a consequence of apartheid, tourism has become the fastest growing sector of the South African economy, contributing almost 5 per cent of GDP and employing perhaps 7 per cent of the workforce. Because of the vast untapped potential that remains, it is hoped that tourism will continue to grow rapidly and may become South Africa's major employer within the next two decades. Of the many millions of foreign travellers to South Africa each year, the majority come from elsewhere in Africa. The tourism industry, however, has hitherto focused its marketing efforts on bigger spending tourists from the OECD zone.

Promotion of tourism has been most successful in the Western Cape, with the first eight of the country's top twenty tourist attractions lying in or around Cape Town. Other major attractions include the national game parks and private game reserves, and increasingly 'township tours' which aim to give visitors some experience of typical peri-urban living conditions and lifestyles. A major challenge lies in the need to harness the energies of the industry to the wider projects of job creation, poverty alleviation, sustainable rural livelihoods, and BEE. It is hoped that the 2010 soccer World Cup will make a substantial difference to South Africa's tourism industry by providing a massive injection of investment, raising the country's international profile and introducing tens of thousands of new arrivals to a country to which they might well return.

Small, medium sized, and micro-enterprises (SMMEs) are essential to both the economic development and the political stability of South Africa. Small business (with less than 50 employees) account for more than half of those employed in the formal sector of the economy. Micro-enterprises, employing five or fewer people and often comprising single person operations, provide means of support for poorer families and communities. A variety of institutions play a role in aiding small and micro-enterprise, in particular the Department of Trade and Industry, but there have been concerns about the efficacy of the department's interventions. One key challenge in creating an enabling environment for small business has been the burden of regulation, including labour and taxation issues, that favours larger businesses over small, and makes movement from the informal to the formal sectors difficult.

Labour Relations

Public and private sector labour relations and collective bargaining processes have each improved markedly since 1994. A new legislative framework for labour relations was put in place in the mid-1990s through the *Labour Relations Act*, the *Basic Conditions of Employment Act*, and the *Employment Equity Act* (RSA 1995, 1997, 1998a). The labour relations and basic conditions legislation, both recently amended, have served to mitigate industrial relations conflict by creating new and effective institutional forums for dispute resolution. The employment equity legislation has sought to impose reporting and transformation requirements upon employers, to eliminate unfair discrimination and to provide redress for the effects of past discrimination in the workplace.

Three key institutions created to advance this ambitious policy agenda are the National Economic Development and Labour Council (NEDLAC), the Labour Court, and the Council for Conciliation, Mediation, and Arbitration (CCMA). Nedlac provides a quasi-corporatist forum within which policy change impacting on producer interests can be debated and negotiated by representatives of organized business and labour (with a residual civil society representation). Business representation, however, continues to be institutionally fragmented in South Africa, with well over 200 registered employers' associations. The major conglomerates act severally to lobby government where particular interests are threatened, and chambers of business continues to be riven with divisions along regional and racial lines. A long-touted merger between the South African Chamber of Business (SACOB) and the National African Chamber of Commerce (NAFCOC) was put on ice yet again in 2002 after further divisions within and between the federations.

Labour is also fundamentally divided. Different trade unions have historically aligned themselves with opposing political parties. Industrial relations disputes have characteristically been shop floor driven and therefore not easily subject to binding union-business mediation. There are still around 400 trade unions, although rationalization and consolidation is underway. Perhaps three quarters of those in formal non-agricultural employment are unionized, with about a quarter of the economically active population members of trade unions.

The CCMA was empowered by the Labour Relations Act to mediate and resolve conflict between organized labour and business. Unlike its highly adversarial predecessors, it has achieved a settlement rate of around 70 per cent, thus reducing both industrial action and the burden on the courts of labour disputes. It seems that the relatively high degree of credibility the CCMA has established among both business people and representatives of organized labour has permitted it to play an important facilitatory role in reducing the impact of industrial relations conflict on the South African economy. The country lost around 1.4 million days to strike action and stay-aways in 2000 which contrasts quite sharply with the high-point of apartheid era conflict in 1987 when almost 6 million working days were lost to stoppages. While these achievements have been considerable, critics complain that the labour relations framework is partially responsible for the country's intractable unemployment problems, an issue we discuss under employment policy in Chapter 4.

There are also concerns that South Africa remains a 'low trust society'. In such a society, it is hard for employers and employees to engage in constructive dialogue, and for agreements of mutual benefit to be struck between labour, capital, and the state. According to influential econo-mists, it is 'high trust' societies that have been most successful at achiev-ing long-term growth. South Africa's limited social dialogue explains why government departments are locked into permanent crisis. Workers are poorly paid, but they are also unproductive even when they work hard. The absence of trust makes it impossible to introduce productivity-enhancing labour relations and managerial reforms. This low-trust stale-mate has recently been extended into what is almost a class war within the state by the government's refusal to prevent senior public servants developing links to external businesses.

An increasingly dysfunctional state will eventually destroy the con-ditions for sustainable private sector growth. Political stability in years to come will also depend on averting any dramatic deterioration in the capacity of the state. At the delivery end of departments, where civil servants interact directly with citizens, a hostile and embattled work-force will deliver ever-worse public services. This will result in wide-spread dissatisfaction and ultimately in violent protest.

Black Economic Empowerment (BEE)

The fuller participation of Black South Africans in the formal economy has been a key aspiration of policy makers since 1994. Government's current 'broad-based black economic empowerment' (BBBEE) strategy aims to increase the ownership, management, and control of businesses by Black citizens, and especially by women. It also seeks to support the emergence of new skills and small businesses, to make finance more readily accessible to Black entrepreneurs, and to use 'preferential pro-curement' by the state and its agencies to spread empowerment across the private economy.

Broad-based BEE (BBBEE) is only one part of government's wider strategy to deracialize public institutions, provide employment, and social benefits to the poor, accelerate land reform, and improve public service delivery. The spatial dimension of apartheid policy, prohibitions against asset accumulation, and the systematic undermining of human capital through 'Bantu Education' created deep-seated racial disadvantage. As politician and businessman Ramaphosa (2004: 74) has emphasized, empowerment initiatives must be broad given the pervasiveness of the centuries of economic disempowerment they are intended to redress.

Afrikaner economic empowerment has influenced many ANC intel-lectuals. Afrikaners' long march towards equality with English-speakers began in the 1920s when organized farmers pressed successfully for tariff protection, state research support, and direct subsidies. After the National Party's (NP's) 1948 election win, Afrikaner nationalists exploited affirmative procurement, targeted state contracts, and employment-creation in the parastatals. They built up ethnic insurance companies and banks, and transformed their language and educational institutions into instruments of collective progress.

While it seems strange to talk about empowerment in the context of the post-1948 NP governments, Black empowerment also originated directly in efforts to bolster the viability of the systems of segregation and Bantu self-government. Africans were provided with specific new opportunities that were designed to deepen racial segregation, by building a Black professional and business class to service Black populations, and by bolstering the homelands.

Moribund Black business policy was unexpectedly energized by the political upheavals of 1976. In the aftermath of Soweto, both the NP and its liberation movement enemies saw a Black middle class as a necessary bulwark against Black radicalism and political unrest.

When Mandela came to power, he endorsed a tacit bargain about ownership between ANC and business. The liberation movement would protect private property and business freedom. In return, big business would not obstruct transition and would later help redress the racial injustice that characterized the economy.

Post-1994 government began as a 'government of national unity' in which emphasis was given to confidence-building in economic policy. To the degree that BEE policy was articulated at all, it took the form of employment equity policy, the first stages of de-racialization of the state, efforts to take control of parastatal and regulatory institutions, and the nurturing of small and medium sized business. BEE across the wider private sector was left to voluntary initiatives and networks, and the private economy remained for many ANC members a hostile realm responsible for an 'investment strike' and 'malicious acts of capital flight'.

The voluntary process of Black empowerment was cruelly undermined. Deals had been financed using 'special purpose vehicles' (SPVs) established to allow purchase of equity in an established target company. SPVs used shares as collateral against loans, and the 1998 emerging market crisis saw the banks wind most of them up. The unsustainable financial structuring of BEE deals resulted in Black ownership on the JSE falling in 1998 from 7 per cent of market capitalization to perhaps 2.2 per cent.

By the time he became state president, Thabo Mbeki was associated with the argument that the ANC needed to create a Black capitalist class. The case for creating a Black bourgeoisie turns on the need to build effective communications between business and politics. A Black elite can create relationships between politicians and businesspeople and nurture the confidence upon which long-term investment is based in what has been a society of mutual distrust.

Empowerment was re-invigorated by the 2001 report of the Black Economic Empowerment Commission (BEECom) compiled under the chairmanship of ANC-leftist-turned-businessman Cyril Ramaphosa. At BEECom's intellectual heart, however, was a compelling rationale for 'broad-based' empowerment, rooted in the report's understanding of the broad-based character of historical Black dis-empowerment.

BEECom inspired the Broad-based BEE Act of 2003 that has combined a range of empowerment measures. Its key instrument is a 'balanced scorecard' that measures every enterprise against wide-ranging criteria. The key fields of assessment, each accounting for a fifth of points, are ownership; management control and employment equity; skills development; preferential procurement; and enterprise development and corporate social investment. Every element of the scorecard is clarified by 'codes of good practice' dealing with employment equity, skills, procurement, enterprise development, the status of transformation charters, and a framework for BEE rating agencies. The codes are binding on all state and public entities, and will be applied in all decisions involving procurement, licensing, concessions, public-private partnerships, and the sale of state owned assets. Moreover, no private company can escape the codes because the requirements of the procurement component will cascade down public sector supply chains.

Concerns about this policy relate to its overall feasibility, its direct economic costs, the character of the 'empowerment state' it might produce, its implications for ANC unity, and the shadow of uncertainty that it casts over the country's future. For observers who believe there is no such thing as a free lunch, BEE is largely a mirage. The overall ownership targets for BEE suggest that a quarter of the private economy should be owned by Black South Africans within a decade. Despite increasingly frenetic activity, we have so far seen something of the order of R200 billion committed to empowerment deals. Yet private sector assets total around R5 trillion (R five thousand billion). It remains quite unclear how this massive scaling up can occur, especially given the continuing shortage of Black capital.

Black partners continue to buy high-risk equity while the financial structuring of their debt leaves them vulnerable to economic downturn. The current generation of transactions, in short, may prove as unsustainable as its predecessors. Even if favourable economic conditions endure, only a fraction of the hoped-for ownership revolution will be realized. Even an unencumbered 25 per cent shareholding may not in fact confer real power over the activities of a company because minority shareholders have few formal legal rights and cannot compel action from an executive board.

The ownership scorecard may create a swathe of dysfunctional empowerment partnerships. Many deals will be 'broad-based' partnerships such as development trusts or employee share schemes, which lack an economic rationale and are administratively costly. There will also be growing prevalence of 'influence-based' partnerships, usually operating through diversified investment holding companies whose key asset is political influence. BEE will also discourage some of the foreign investment that might otherwise compensate for the savings shortfall.

Numerous lesser controversies surround broad-based empowerment: the legal status of the scorecard has been problematic because it conflicts with earlier preferential procurement legislation; enterprise development is poorly understood by business; the concerns of foreign and small businesses, although catered to, remain serious; corporate social investment is expensive and its beneficiaries often see no returns; 'trusts' are being abused to circumvent the law and exploit Black partners; and verification agencies seem unable to solve the problem of false empowerment self-assessments by business. In general, established White business generally complains that BBBEE is altogether too intrusive and places a heavy regulatory burden on business; emerging Black business argues that limited ambition, exploitation and fronting have been their main experience of empowerment to date.

There has been concern about the character of the emerging empowerment state. Such a state might become the slave of narrow interests, rather than the 'developmental state' that government has recently championed. BEE requirements can disguise the growth of patronage relationships between officials and entrepreneurs. They could ultimately lead every business to believe they need a state patron to land government contracts or to secure licenses.

Industrial policy could become a life support system for politically well-connected companies. Given a drastic shortage of empowerment finance, public sector and parastatal pension funds might be drained in support of risky investments. Government departments might increasingly act at the behest of individuals rather than in the national interest.

Intelligence systems and diplomatic capital might be put at the disposal of companies with high-risk foreign investments simply because of their close relationships with ministers or officials. Major infrastructure investments – in power generation and transmission, nuclear energy, or new-generation rail systems – might be still more often secured by golf-course hand-shakes rather than by social and economic cost-benefit calculations. The key financial beneficiaries will continue to be established businesses, but with politically connected Black empowerment receiving a cut for their political influence.

Along the way, regulatory institutions, individual regulators, and peripheral institutions such as the public broadcaster may become casualties in battles between well-connected empowerment groups. In sectors such as oil and armaments, where scale, technical complexity, and secrecy make media and parliamentary oversight difficult, BEE vehicles have allegedly been instruments for personal enrichment. Media houses and the public broadcaster have been used to attack business rivals and to destroy the careers of scrupulous officials and regulators. 'Revolving doors' problems have also arisen, with no effective confidentiality requirements or cooling off periods constraining departing government officials. There are also widespread conflicts of interest between officials' roles as public servants and their external directorships.

A fourth set of critics worry about the implications of empowerment for the integrity and stability of the ANC. Capitalism evidently structurally limits the ability of Black owners and managers to act in the interests of the oppressed. However, there is little to prevent influence moving in the opposite direction. Highlighting deals involving Manne Dipico, Popo Molefe, and Valli Moosa, one journalist recently asked if the ANC might not already be 'mortgaged to private capital'. Procurement scandals have meanwhile raised the spectre of alleged 'retro-kickbacks' to party funds. And one broad-based empowerment scheme, Batho Bonke, run by politician-entrepreneur and presidential aspirant Tokyo Sexwale, enriched thousands of prominent South Africans, sometimes to the tune of millions of Rand.

Empowerment vehicles have been implicated in the alleged abuse of preferential procurement to bring kickbacks to party funds, and in the purported interference of business in the presidential succession process. BEE mechanisms can also cloak spreading patronage and corruption. SACP intellectuals worry that South Africa is following the road of some other post-colonial states in which liberation movement elites have thrown off colonial oppression only to become parasitic looters of state resources themselves.

Challenges

Of all the responsibilities of any government, achieving economic success is the burden for which it is most readily and unreasonably held to account by its citizens. The South African people are no exception. While citizens have remained sympathetic towards the government's difficulties in extending public services, the lack of employment opportunities has been a matter of profound and growing dissatisfaction for South Africans of all classes. The definition and measurement of levels of unemployment is highly controversial in South Africa, not least in the degree to which 'discouraged workers' should be excluded from the labour force (those able and willing to work). According to official definitions, the unemployment rate is more than 25 per cent. As we shall see in Chapter 4, a more appropriate 'expanded' definition places unemployment at closer to 40 per cent. According to official statistics, the number of economically active people in 1999 stood at around 13.5 million whereas the number of people employed (in both formal and informal sectors) was around 10.4 million. While the number of people employed is growing, so too is the number of those unemployed.

While 'jobless growth' would present a great long-term threat to social and political stability in South Africa, so too would low growth or no growth at all. Currently many business people perceive the economy to be locked into a relatively low trend growth rate of around 3 per cent, whereas most would view something in excess of 5 per cent as a prerequisite for a sustained reduction in unemployment. The slow growth is both caused by, and perpetuates, other problems such as low skills levels, poor education, and long term unemployment. Contributory factors include HIV/AIDS, crime, corruption, and the emigration of skilled labour.

Unfortunately the challenge of raising the productive potential of the economy is a complex one. It demands energetic and sustained responses to a series of deep and intractable problems. Many of the barriers to faster growth – in the labour market, business and effective public investment – lie largely beyond government control. The country remains vulnerable to international financial and economic crises. Key problems – such as poor education and low skills levels – are profoundly difficult to correct within a generation, let alone within the decade or two across which the ANC can hope to extend its honeymoon with the voters. South Africa must make progress, moreover, in the face of

HIV/AIDS, which will worsen skills shortages and place institutions under exceptional stress.

Uncertainty continues to surround the likely economic impacts of HIV/AIDS. One recent review points to agreement on factors likely to reduce growth: a higher death rate among the economically active, an overall decrease in the capital and human resources available for production and investment, a fall in the rate of saving, declining disposable incomes, and reduced domestic consumption (Ford *et al* 2002). The magnitude of these GDP effects, however, remains in dispute because of a lack of consensus over appropriate methodologies, the absence of robust data, and the likelihood that both policy and behaviour changes may radically alter the trajectory of the epidemic.

Models variously predict declines in the rate of GDP growth of anything between 0.3 per cent and 1.6 per cent per year, a 17 per cent smaller overall GDP by 2010, or a 25 per cent smaller GDP by 2020 (ING Barings 2000; Stover and Bollinger 1999; Arndt and Lewis 2000; Haaker 2002; Ford *et al* 2002:10–11). One influential study (Bureau for Economic Research 2001), applying heroic assumptions about labour surplus and investment planning, predicts a mere 5.7 per cent overall 'GDP shortfall' by 2015 – notwithstanding its expectation of a 21 per cent shortfall in the labour force by that date. As Nattrass (2002) emphasizes, moreover, HIV/AIDS may well reduce population more rapidly than it reduces GDP growth, so increasing per capita income.

Scholars increasingly focus not on bald GDP data but rather on the effects of HIV/AIDS on the structure of the economy. De Waal (2003:8–9) suggests that a decline in returns to training will reduce incentives to invest in human resource development, and so transform the skills base and structure of the economy. One study under the auspices of the World Bank dramatically suggested that HIV/AIDS will erode not just existing human capital but also the mechanisms through which human capital is transmitted across generations. As a result, and in the absence of a changed policy response to the epidemic, South Africa will face 'complete economic collapse' within three generations (Bell *et al* 2003).

There are also wider social and inequality effects. Human development impacts are greater than income effects, with South Africa's human development ranking more than 50 places below its per capita GDP rank (UNDP 2007). HIV/AIDS will exacerbate South Africa's income inequality, initially through increased demand for skills, and the disproportionate access of the wealthy to anti-retrovirals (Mattes 2003).

HIV/AIDS will also impact upon the survival strategies of the very poor. One lost income will have repercussions for many dependent family and community members. Relatives will be forced increasingly to abandon casual work to care for relatives, and children to drop out of school. Household income will be redirected towards symptomatic treatments, while the wives and children of deceased men may face the injustice of eviction from their homes.

HIV/AIDS may also precipitate a fiscal crisis in some states. On the revenue side, some economists believe sharp HIV/AIDS-related falls in GDP growth will result is a much smaller than anticipated tax take (ING Barings 2000). Eroding administrative capacity in the South African Revenue Service might encourage tax evasion or avoidance, and self-employed HIV-positive workers may become less tax law compliant. On the expenditure side, we can anticipate rapidly escalating demands on the health and social welfare budgets, and then progressively on other budgets as government personnel fall ill and planners try to mobilize resources to minimize the spread and impact of the virus. Yet, even here, the calculations are contestable, with some departments potentially landing 'windfall gains', for example through a decline in the number of children requiring schooling, or a reduction in the number of old people claiming pensions (Ford *et al* 2002).

Governance problems also threaten to undermine economic growth. At national and provincial levels, where legislation supposedly bars dual employment, the auditor-general has reported a high prevalence of external directorships among public servants. Senior public servants often combine broad ideological hostility to established business with personal and particular interests in outside commercial activity – almost the exact converse of the state of affairs developmental state theorists usually recommend. Revolving doors have sometimes taken senior public servants directly into commercial relationships or employment with firms advantaged by state procurement of licensing decisions (Butler 2006). South Africa's public-sector bureaucracy is arguably beginning to form itself into self-serving class that is forging dangerously unregulated alliances with business and political elites.

BEE raises many problems. It remains an open question whether a liberation movement already changed by its interaction with economic power will be able to steer empowerment in a benign direction.

A widely shared aspiration for BEE over the next decade is that it will progress so rapidly that the need for intervention will fade away. There is little reason to believe that such hopes will be realized in the near future. It may be, however, that some costs and dangers of BEE will decline.

Once all established businesses are 'black-influenced', the ground rules for open competition for government business and for a more pluralist politics of policy influence may be easier to establish. A successful BEE policy that encourages more intense interaction between Black business, established capital, and the state, might also establish clearer rules to manage such relationships. By so doing it will create a more transparent and plural politics of competing interests.

4

Social Structure and Social Policy

This chapter explores South Africa's social structure and investigates government's efforts to address the poverty and inequality that scar the everyday life of so many citizens. First, we place the society into comparative context, using international human development indicators to identify its relative developmental strengths and weaknesses. We go on to explore the country's key dimensions of relative and absolute disadvantage. Here we address the vexed conceptual and empirical issues that surround the analysis of inequality and social division. Just who is disadvantaged and why? Is South Africa essentially divided by race? Or is its inequality better explained in terms of class structure, rural deprivation, or gender oppression? In the second half of the chapter we appraise some key government strategies to improve the situation of the less advantaged through employment creation, social welfare, public service delivery, social infrastructure, and education policy.

Human Development in South Africa

In November of 2007, the pages of South African newspapers were the scene of an unlikely conflict between a Non-governmental organization (NGO), South African Institute of Race Relations (SAIRR), and state president Thabo Mbeki. SAIRR released a report, using the World Bank's definition of extreme poverty as living on less than US$1 per day, claiming that 1.9 million people were living in extreme poverty in 1996 whereas 4.2 million were doing so in 2005.

In a furious response in party newsletter *ANC Today*, Thabo Mbeki used a different definition of poverty – a R3,000 poverty line – to argue that 53 per cent of the population lived in poverty in 1996 and that this had fallen to 43 per cent by 2006. Government's response did not end there. Presidency policy chief Joel Netshitenzhe wrote an extended reply to SAIRR, pointing to alternative definitions and sources of evidence and a series of complex issues in data interpretation.

The debate demonstrated how hugely complex and contested the definition and measurement of inequality and poverty can be in any society. Poverty is notoriously hard to define, and there are advocates for a variety of 'relative' and 'absolute' understandings of what it is to be poor. For purposes of policy making, most societies agree upon a 'poverty line', but South African policy makers have so far been unwilling to take this step.

Inequality is an equally complex and contested concept, embracing not just material outcomes but also wider socio-political goals such as political equality and equality before the law. Measures such as the 'Gini coefficient' are often used for purposes of comparison but these have also become a subject of controversy in recent debates.

South Africa is a middle-income developing country. Its Gross Domestic Product (GDP) per capita (adjusted for purchasing power parity [PPP] for purposes of cross-country comparison) was $11,110 in 2005. This places its income per head on a par with Poland ($13,847), Chile ($12,027), Uruguay ($9,962), Costa Rica ($10,180), or Mexico ($10,751). In a ranking of countries by per capita income, South Africa would emerge in fifty-sixth place out of 177 countries (UNDP 2007).

Yet income per head tells us only a little about the quality of human experience in a society. To explore the ability of households and individuals to command the resources necessary for a 'reasonable' standard of living, it is necessary to use more complex multi-factor measures of poverty that include non-monetary elements in fields such as health and education. Perhaps the best known indicator, and that used most widely by policy makers to compare human wellbeing in different countries, is the United Nations Development Programme's (UNDP's) 'Human Development Index' (HDI). The HDI measures a population's ability to develop its three 'most basic capabilities': to be able to lead a long and healthy life; to be knowledgeable; and to have access to the resources needed for a decent standard of living. Life expectancy is used as a proxy for the first capability, literacy and school and college enrolment for the second, and GDP per head for the third. The UNDP assesses a score for each proxy and the HDI is a simple average of the three dimension scores.

Such indices can only be broadly indicative. However, UNDP argues that the HDI helps to draw the attention of policy makers away from blunt economic statistics to focus instead on human outcomes, emphasizing that the overall lives of ordinary people should be the ultimate criteria for assessing the development of a country. To discover that two countries with the same level of income per person have very different human development outcomes, for example, can help to stimulate debate over which governments and policies are succeeding and why.

South Africa fares exceptionally poorly through the lens of HDI, especially in the light of its relatively high GDP. It is currently HDI ranked 120th out of 177 countries. Countries with a similar GDP per head fare far better: Poland is ranked 37th, Chile 40th, Uruguay 46th, Costa Rica 48th, and Mexico 52nd.

Brazil, with a per capita income of just $8,402, comes in at 70, a full 50 places ahead of South Africa. In HDI terms, let us emphasize, South Africa is ranked alongside countries that are far poorer in terms of income: Mongolia ($2,107 per capita), Kyrgyzstan ($1,927), Bolivia ($2,819), Gabon (6,954), or Morocco ($4,586). All told, South Africa lies some 65 places below the ranking one would expect for it judging purely on the basis of its income (UNDP 2007).

Why does a relatively affluent 'middle income' developing country like South Africa perform so badly in terms of HDI? One answer is that the country's overall GDP data do not take account of the extreme inequality of income in the society, one of the greatest in the world. South Africa's score on the most widely used measure of inequality, the Gini coefficient,

---

Box 4.1   South Africa's Human Development Index, 2005

Life expectancy at birth, annual estimates (years), 2005	50.8
Adult literacy rate (% aged 15 and older), 1995–2005	82.4
Combined gross enrolment ratio for primary, secondary and tertiary education (%), 2005	77.0
GDP per capita (PPP US$), 2005	11,110
Life expectancy index	0.430
Education index	0.806
GDP index	0.786
Human development index value, 2005	0.674
GDP per capita (PPP US$) rank minus HDI rank	–65

Source: UNDP 2007.

was 0.59 in 2000, making it one of the most income unequal societies in the world (RSA 2006).

While income may be quite substantial overall, much of it is concentrated in a small and privileged segment of the population. In 2000, the richest 20 per cent of households were responsible for 65 per cent of expenditure. By contrast, the poorest 20 per cent accounted for just 2.8 per cent. Almost half of the country's people live in poverty with little access to money or credit.

Levels of unemployment – the key determinant of poverty in South Africa – are exceptionally high, as a result of the opening of the economy after 1989, tariff reductions and conservative fiscal policy after 1997, productivity gains, and the growth of capital intensive export industries. There were also huge job losses in sectors such as agriculture and domestic work.

Because unemployment grew over the first decade of democracy, on conservative official measures from 17 per cent in 1995 to around 28 per cent in 2003, inequality correspondingly deepened with it (Kingdon and Knight 2007). Incomes from work have also declined for many poorer households, with profit growth vastly outstripping wage growth.

A second explanation for South Africa's poor performance lies in unequal access to public services. Access to such provision continues to be difficult for the very poor. Services such as public education, health, water, sanitation, and transport should contribute to a healthy and knowledgeable population and compensate for inequality in the labour market. While availability of such services has been considerably extended since 1994, poor households often cannot pay the charges required to access them. One result is appalling deficiencies in health care, educational opportunities, and other public services in rural areas.

If income inequality and uneven public service provision explain much of South Africa's poor HDI performance, the country does badly even when compared to other highly unequal societies. Moreover, it is one of a small number of countries whose HDI has slipped since 1995. For example, it has fallen behind Brazil, its historical twin in terms of entrenched inequality (see Table 4.1). A comparison between the UNDP appraisals of Brazil and South Africa is indeed instructive because it brings out the significance – perhaps the distorting influence – of life expectancy in South Africa's falling HDI.

The relatively impoverished Brazil has relatively poor educational and income per capita outcomes. Life expectancy in Brazil, however, in common with many other developing countries, has advanced impressively, from 59.5 in 1970–75 to 67.2 between 1995 and 2000, and more than 70 today. Brazil's infant mortality has been steadily reduced, and under-five mortality has come down quite dramatically in recent years. In South Africa, by contrast, both infant mortality and under-five mortality have declined very slowly.

Most importantly, South Africa, unlike Brazil, faces the implications of a devastating HIV/AIDS epidemic that will claim the lives of many millions over the next decade. South Africa's life expectancy index has been declining fast, a reflection of the current life expectancy at birth in the country of little more than 50. It is expected to fall significantly as AIDS-related deaths continue to accelerate.

Indices such as the HDI are intended to help policy makers and citizens remember that the overall lives of ordinary people, and not bald economic growth statistics, should be the ultimate criteria for assessing the 'development' of a country. HDI has been much criticized in South Africa. It is true that the weight that UNDP places on the proxy of 'life expectancy' does have a distorting effect on the overall index, particularly for countries that are in the middle of a major health crisis. It is also true that African National Congress (ANC) successes in disbursing poverty-reducing social grants, building houses, and providing water and household energy are not directly reflected in the UNDP indicator.

Governments, however, should use indicators such as HDI in the spirit in which they are intended, as a spur and aid to reflection. It cannot be right simply to rule out of consideration any measure of the human condition that does not reflect well on the performance of the national government. If mortality patterns remain unchanged, a child born today in South Africa has the same chance of surviving to the age of 40 as a child born today in Guinea-Bissau or Cameroon.

Table 4.1   South African and Brazilian Human Development Index 1975–2005

Human Development Year	HDI value RSA	HDI value Brazil
1975	0.649	0.644
1980	0.663	0.679
1985	0.683	0.692
1990	0.714	0.713
1995	0.724	0.737
2000	0.695	0.757
2005	0.674	0.800

Source: Adapted from UNDP 2007.

Explaining Inequality

Once we set aside these exceptional affects of HIV/AIDS, there can be no single correct way to set out or explain the society's problems of inequality and human development. Segregation and apartheid created distinct racialised sets of economic opportunity and public service entitlement and their effects persist today. These 'legacy effects' are exceptionally important in political as well as human terms because they have bequeathed a divided country in which White South Africans' HDI, if one were to calculate it, is similar to that of Italy, whereas Black citizens' HDI is equivalent to that of Swaziland (May et al 2000).

Inequality, however, is not simply a black and white issue. All societies exhibit inequality, regardless of racial politics, and South Africa's distinctive patterns of relative disadvantage should not be attributed solely to a racialised policy history. Professional social scientists also seek to explain inequality in terms of rural-urban divides in a developing society, through the lenses of gender or intergenerational inequality, or even through the prism of disability. There is a gulf between those living in rural South Africa and urban South Africans, Black and White, who have potential access to the resources of the formal economy. Likewise, gender plays a significant role in disadvantage, with women disproportionately bearing the burden of poverty, disease, physical labour, and unemployment. Taking these factors together, for example, perhaps six in ten rural African women are unemployed whereas only three or four in ten urban African men are similarly disadvantaged.

Social scientists, however, explain inequality primarily in terms of 'class'. Class here is not simply a way of referring to gradations of inequality between the wealthy, the middle class, the skilled workers, and the variously very disadvantaged. Rather, it refers to the ways in which the fundamental social relationships within a capitalist society – between capital and labour – generate differences in income and opportunity. Class analysts argue that what appear to be divisions based on race are in fact founded at a more fundamental level upon class relations between the owners of the means of production and workers. The disadvantaged must sell their labour power to survive, and many are unable to secure anything other than pitiful remuneration or even to participate in the employment market at all. There is only a tiny small commercial farmer sector, and informal employment and small-scale entrepreneurial activity account for a very small part of the economy. South Africa is therefore a society in which people are overwhelmingly dependent on employment and wages.

Today the very poor are still overwhelmingly Black while Whites dominate the ownership of resources. However, White and Black no longer correspond to rich and poor. The poor, on a class interpretation, are poor not because they are Black, but rather because they live in a household with a very low income, either because none of its members has a job, or because the jobs they do have pay extremely low wages (Seekings and Nattrass 2005).

In the 1950s, the income hierarchy was essentially racial, in the sense that Whites monopolized well paid employment and almost all Whites were reasonably remunerated. Indians and Coloureds occupied middling class locations, while Africans were at the bottom of a colour-coded employment hierarchy. Such an overlap between class and race was already eroding in the mid-1970s. While overall levels of inequality remained very high, rapid economic growth had already resulted in the development of a large African working class and a substantial middle class. While race was still overwhelmingly closely related to income, its effects were now mediated by other factors, such as education and access to new white-collar jobs.

Racial division today has been further eroded by the deracialization of public policy, and by the removal of colour bars and other forms of employment discrimination. Greater equality of access to education, the removal of controls on the free movement of labour, and the ability of Black South Africans to enter into business and the professions, have contributed to the emergence of a Black middle class. There are new 'income gaps' in the society, between a multi-racial middle class and the rest of society, and between an African urban industrial working class and the African unemployed and very poor (Seekings and Nattrass 2005).

Yet the impact of the country's history on the racial composition of classes persists. In 1998 Thabo Mbeki famously described South Africa as a country divided into two nations, one Black and the other White. The White nation, he argued, 'is relatively prosperous, regardless of gender or geographic dispersal. It has ready access to a developed economic, physical, educational, communication and other infrastructure'. The second and larger nation is 'black and poor' and 'lives under conditions of grossly underdeveloped economic, physical, educational, communication and other infrastructure' (Hansard 29 May 1998, col. 3378; cited Seekings and Nattrass 2005).

He was speaking in the context of a country that seemed to be becoming more unequal when viewed through a racial prism. The household income of the 'average African household' fell by about a fifth since in the first few years of non-racial democracy. The average White household, by contrast, saw a 15 per cent increase in income. At the end of the first ANC government, the average White household was earning six times as much as the average Black one (Statistics South Africa 2002b). Even by 2007, only 2 per cent of Africans were professionals or managers whereas 22 per cent of whites occupied such positions. Half of all households had to survive on less than R2,000 (US$300) per month. In a society in which work determines life chances, White unemployment remained at around 5 per cent while the African unemployment rate (on the most favourable definition) was 30 per cent (Statistics South Africa 2006).

Although the assessment of changes in poverty and inequality are made difficult by limitations in the available data, there is a broad specialist consensus that both worsened in the late 1990s but that the situation probably improved somewhat after 2000 as a result of faster growth, job creation and especially an increase in social transfer payments (Van der Berg 2006, Seekings 2007, Simkins 2004).

Addressing Poverty and Inequality

Understanding the causes of poverty and inequality is a prerequisite for effectively reducing them. Evidence suggests that government policy directly targeted at racial redress, housing and land programmes, rural uplift, or gender equality can have some impact on inequality and poverty. However, the labour market is the crucial site in which the battle against poverty and inequality will be won or lost, and the education and health systems are an additional key to addressing the bitter legacies of apartheid.

Here we will consider four dimensions of government's response to its developmental crisis. Since unemployment and poorly remunerated work are key determinants of poverty, employment growth and the labour market will be our first area of concern. Second, we explore the social welfare system and government's use of social grants to alleviate income poverty.

Third, we examine government's record in providing public services such as water, sanitation, healthcare, and public transport essential for reducing human capital poverty. Fourth, we trace the history of post-apartheid education and healthy policy, sectors especially important for addressing the perpetuation of inequality across generations. Finally, we address one key area of failure: gender has a special significance in South African patterns of disadvantage, but it has not figured prominently or successfully in government strategy.

Employment policy

South Africa's unemployment crisis is relatively recent in origin. In the two decades after 1948, the state advantaged Whites and particularly White Afrikaners by manipulating the labour market. Full employment, in combination with labour controls, limitations on the free movement and employment of non-Whites, and the use of colour bars at company level, contributed to high levels of disposable income for the White population. Meanwhile Africans were steadily deprived of their right to work, own property, and even to subsist in rural survivalist production.

While the last decade has seen a move towards 'normality' in the labour market, with the removal of residual formal restrictions on employment opportunity for Black South Africans, the beneficial effects of this change have been mitigated by a radical change in overall levels of unemployment. In the 1950s, South Africa suffered from labour shortages because of the constraints on entry into the labour market constituted by 'influx control' at a time of rapid economic growth. By the 1970s, as the post-war economic boom came to an end, unemployment started to rise among the non-White population, reaching devastating levels, especially in rural South Africa, by the 1990s.

While official statistics paint a grim enough picture of post-1994 unemployment almost doubling from 16 per cent in 1995 to 30 per cent in 2002, this official measure in fact understates a harsher reality, based as it is on a 'strict' definition of unemployment, which includes only those actively seeking work. A more appropriate 'expanded' definition would include 'discouraged' workseekers, who have no hope of finding employment where they live and cannot fund the transport and other costs associated with workseeking. Unemployment on such a definition may be as high as 35 per cent and not far short of 45 per cent for Africans (see Table 4.2).

Unemployment is an extremely serious problem that continues to run at levels unknown elsewhere in the world (with the exception of states in conflict). It has an enormous immediate impact in terms of poverty and inequality and it remains government's greatest failure in the eyes of the electorate. Yet the ANC has adopted a conservative approach to employment in its Growth, Employment, and Redistribution (GEAR) macroeconomic framework. This strategy is orthodox in that it views raised productivity as the primary route to higher employment, even if such productivity growth implies the loss of jobs in the short term. Whether

Table 4.2   Unemployment in South Africa, 1993–2007

	1993	1998	2007
Unemployment (strict definition)			
African	15.7	33.4	26.8
Coloured	15.1	15.8	20.7
Indian	7.1	14.8	9.7
White	3.2	4.5	4.5
Total	12.7	26.1	23.0
Unemployment (expanded definition)			
African	37.7	47.6	n/a
Coloured	20.9	23.9	n/a
Indian	11.0	12.8	n/a
White	4.6	6.6	n/a
Total	29.4	38.6	35.0

Source: Adapted from Seekings and Nattrass 2005; Statistics South Africa 2008b.

the government is correct to take this view has been the subject of strenuous debate, particularly between the ANC and its alliance partners in the trade union movement. While public sector labour has been largely cushioned from the impacts of GEAR, the labour shedding process in the private sector (and to a degree in parastatals) has had considerable knock-on effects in an economy where one formal sector worker often supports very many family and community members.

After advances made by the left at the ANC's national conference in 2007, there has been a renewed insistence that employment must be at the centre of a new economic strategy, but the precise policy implications of this change remain unclear. The unemployment problem has deep roots in apartheid era maldistribution of access to assets and skills. According to the government's critics in the Congress of South African Trade Unions (COSATU) and the South African Communist Party (SACP), however, the current crisis was precipitated in the past decade by the opening of the economy to international trade, by the reduction in tariff protection for domestic producers, and by ANC fiscal austerity that simultaneously reduced government demand for goods and services.

Such critics prescribe short-term job preservation and an expansionary fiscal policy to boost medium-term demand for labour. Job creation can only work, such leftists claim, if the economy moves away from its dependence on capital intensive activities such as mining and mineral processing. The poor, moreover, require access to infrastructure, new skills, and finance so that their nascent businesses can grow and absorb labour. Labour intensive activities, such as small-scale farming, and labour absorbing activity, such as construction and public works, need to be promoted, and private investment on services, agriculture, and construction incentivized.

A second set of critics, primarily in business, have a quite different diagnosis, focusing on unintended consequences of labour market regulation. The wage bargaining system (through 'bargaining councils') is inflexible and encourages industry level wage agreements that disadvantage new businesses and reduce overall employment levels. While the industrial relations framework mitigates conflict between employer and employee, the overall level of regulation is a strong disincentive to employment creation, especially for small- and medium-sized businesses. Regulation imposes heavy administrative and cost burdens and discourages job creation through excessive protection against dismissal. Shedding labour can be a protracted and difficult exercise, and it is almost uniquely expensive for a developing country. One consequence has been a proliferation of subcontracting arrangements through which businesses try to avoid compliance with employers' regulatory obligations.

While labour and its academic allies insist that current labour market regulation does not discourage employment growth, it is difficult otherwise to explain why such growth has been so slow. New industries need to be able to create and fill jobs quickly, reforms 'easier to recommend than to enact' (CGD 2008: 46).

Defenders of extensive regulation argue that because each formal sector worker supports many family and community dependants, the devastation caused by retrenchment is far greater than in an environment with high levels of employment and labour mobility. Regulation, it is true, advantages the currently employed over the currently unemployed. But employment relations in agriculture and domestic work have been extremely exploitative. Such trade-offs are inescapable, and there is no technical formula for balancing enhanced worker security and dignity against unemployment.

In 2002, government reaffirmed its commitment to the current labour relations framework through a serious of consolidatory amendments to post-1994 legislation. The right to strike was extended to striking over retrenchments, and companies are now obliged 'meaningfully' to consult before laying off workers. The loophole of subcontracting work to 'independent contractors' has been partially closed to prevent employers' evasion of worker benefits and tax contributions. At the same time, government has pursued an ambitious minimum wage strategy, setting lowest legal wages first for agricultural labour and then for domestic (household) work despite potentially substantial impacts on employment. Such commitments undoubtedly make more difficult the achievement of the conflicting goal of employment creation and so poverty and inequality alleviation.

One compromise solution might be to offer a once-and-for-all wage subsidy to citizens who turn 18 in order to address the youth unemployment crisis or to allow crucial export-oriented industries to recruit labour on less stringent terms (Hausmann 2008, CGD 2008: 47). However, the currently ascendant trade union constituency of the ANC is unlikely to embrace such initiatives in the near future.

Social welfare policy

For a middle income developing country, South Africa has an ambitious social welfare system that is now equivalent to 3.5 per cent of GDP, up from 2 per cent in 1994 (Seekings 2007: 19). The Department of Social Development (DSD) accounts for a tenth of government spending, much of it directed through a national social security agency but administered largely at provincial level. The centre-piece of the social welfare system, and for many years the key instrument of redistribution though the budget, is the national old age pension or 'aged person's grant'. This is distributed to almost 2 million South Africans and provides a bulwark against poverty in the poorest rural communities. The pension was deracialised in 1993, primarily through increases in the level of the formerly African pension. It has since been undergoing a managed erosion of about 1.5 per cent in real terms per annum but still accounts for half of social welfare transfers.

In addition to these social assistance transfers, the DSD runs a Poverty Relief Programme, which adopts a community-based approach to poverty alleviation. This programme has a primarily rural bias, and is aimed to provide short-term employment for women. The current focus of departmental activity is on mitigating the impact of HIV/AIDS upon those living with it and their dependants and communities.

From around 2000 there has been an explosion of government welfare activity, with the most important innovation being the child support grant. This grant reduces the intergenerational perpetuation of poverty, and has assumed an extra significance given the growth in orphans as a result of the HIV/AIDS epidemic. The age of entitlement for the grant has been raised from 7 to 14, and the bureaucratic impediments to claiming the benefit – for example the inability of the very poor and orphaned to secure citizenship papers in rural areas – are gradually addressed. A remarkable 7 million monthly payments are now made under this scheme (Seekings 2007: 20).

The DSD also manages disability grants and foster care grants reaching hundreds of thousands more South Africans. In all, more than 11 million citizens are now beneficiaries of transfers. These payments are well targeted towards poor households, which has resulted in them having a very substantial positive impact on levels of poverty (RSA 2006, Van der Berg 2006).

Over the past few years, a variety of campaigners in the trade union movement, churches, NGOs, universities, and the official opposition Democratic Alliance (DA) have together clamoured for the government to go further and institute a 'Basic Income Grant' (BIG). As an instrument to reduce poverty and allow the poorest to live with dignity, the BIG is not such a bad idea. A proposed monthly state payment of about R100 could help the 12-million poor South Africans who live in households in which no members are eligible for a pension, disability, or child support grant. A basic income could help rescue the two out of three children who grow up in poverty. It might allow desperate AIDS-affected households to stay afloat.

The BIG, proponents claim, would also stimulate consumer spending and economic growth. It would create healthier and more productive workers, better able to invest in their own education and to create new businesses. By reducing the extremes of poverty, it might entrench political stability and so encourage the longer investment horizons needed to grow the economy.

Many impressive non-governmental networks with experience in addressing complex social welfare issues have promoted BIG: the Black Sash, Alliance for Children's Entitlement to Social Security and the Children's Institute, to name but a few. They are supported by committed analysts. Together, the serious proponents of BIG have wrestled with obstacles to its feasibility.

BIG would be expensive. Estimated costs range between R50 billion and more than R150 billion a year, though much of this would be clawed back through the tax system. A basic income would be difficult to deliver. Administration costs would probably eat up 20 per cent of expenditure – though it could be far more – and opportunities for corruption would be legion. The very poor who most need the grant would find it hardest to access.

The case for BIG would be stronger if technologies on which it would depend – such as the planned home affairs national identification system – were at a more advanced stage of readiness.

The treasury argues that South Africa's aged persons, disability, and child support grants are already unprecedented – and possibly imprudent – for a middle-income developing country. In this context, BIG might become an 'untouchable' item in the budget, with opposition parties and government 'bidding up' the value of the grant in electoral campaigning. Influential government spokesman Joel Netshitenzhe even contrasted BIG 'handouts' to the dignity of public works remuneration – perhaps cruelly so, given that many older citizens will not secure employment in their lifetimes.

In general, BIG should not discourage people from seeking work. However, it might prove a disincentive for poorly paid agricultural labourers and, most importantly, for the young. Netshitenzhe is right that a poverty alleviation instrument like BIG should not be used to tackle labour market problems: the young unemployed need training and work experience rather than 'handouts'.

For all these reasons, treasury, cabinet, and the ANC have made it clear that BIG is not on the cards, and even growing COSATU and SACP power since December 2007 seem unlikely to improve its prospects. Why then has there been so urgent a campaign for something that is not going to happen in the foreseeable future?

Three groups have arguably exploited BIG's emotional appeal and used it as a badge of moral virtue behind which they can advance their interests. The DA has adopted the BIG in seeming disregard for the party's deep-seated anti-statist philosophy. The DA's broad agreement with the ANC's unpopular economic policies, and its hard-earned reputation for favouring the interests of the privileged, together severely damage its electoral prospects. It has latched onto a policy that differentiates it from government and reaches out beyond its wealthy constituency.

A second key advocate has been the COSATU, which sees BIG as the centre-piece of its jobs and poverty campaign. COSATU's key demands around poverty, unemployment, and the delivery of basic public services pose troubling questions for organized labour itself. Government has delivered the financial resources needed for better schools, clinics, and municipal services, only to see them swallowed up in the wages of members of COSATU affiliates.

Unions are sometimes seen as major impediments to the management innovations required for better public service delivery. COSATU's resistance to wider labour market reform, meanwhile, impedes employment growth, which is the primary remedy for poverty. BIG also poses internal political problems for COSATU because the net effects of BIG on union members depend on how it is financed and its introduction might well make most of them much worse off. COSATU's recent focus has been on securing 'comprehensive social protection' centred upon a contributory social security system. It is seeking health, unemployment, and disability insurance programmes that will most strongly benefit organized workers.

The third set of actors championing BIG comprise a disparate range of churches and NGO's from outside the social welfare sector. Some – such as the Alternative Information Development Coalition and South African New Economics Foundation – view the grant as a palliative for the worst effects of what they see as 'unbridled neo-liberalism'. Others find some consolation in the simple morality of BIG.

Critics complain that religious institutions such as the South African Council of Churches and the Southern African Catholic Bishops Conference champion BIG – but not the condom – as a key weapon in the battle against poverty in an AIDS society.

On one account, the BIG coalition represents an important episode in the politics of a new democracy in that it shows that civil society can struggle heroically – in the face of immense ANC hostility – to overturn government policy. On a more cynical reading, the ANC has signalled that campaigning for BIG is acceptable to the movement, but that such campaigning will simply be ignored.

Although the adoption of BIG remains unlikely, there is likely to be an intensification of efforts to increase take-up of existing grants, an extension of child support grants, and a progressive reduction in the entitlement age for the aged person's grant.

Public Services and Social Infrastructure

Apartheid era public service provision heavily advantaged Whites, who received near-universal access to housing, electricity, water and sanitation, together with public transport, social welfare support, and post-employment pensions. Non-Whites were deprived of basic public services, with non-urban Africans especially disadvantaged. The extension of public services to the population as a whole is a tremendous opportunity as well as a challenge (see Table 4.3). By providing services to those who do not have them, the government can counteract the patterns of unemployment-driven inequality.

While the government set out attractive sectoral policy frameworks, however, and came close to hitting tough delivery targets in house building, electrification, water supply, and health, critics have complained with increasing urgency that ordinary citizens are experiencing insufficient

Table 4.3   Social infrastructure and services, 1993–2004

Households having....	% 1993	% 1999	% 2004
Formal dwelling	68.3	74.2	73.6
Piped water	59.3	65.7	67.8
Electric lighting	51.9	69.5	80.2
Electricity for cooking	45.2	52.7	59.4
Phone/cellphone	28.2*	42.4**	n/a
flush/chemical toilet	52.6	55.5	57.2

*1996 **2001
Source: Bhorat et al 2006, GCIS 2002.

improvement in their living standards. Wider availability of services has been accompanied by rapidly escalating user fees and a backlog in payments as a result of the economic insecurity of households. Perhaps one in seven households have had their electricity disconnected at one time, and eight in ten of Telkom's new telephone lines have been disconnected.

Household energy

Household energy provides a fascinating window onto the problems facing the government. Energy policy in South Africa has been dominated historically by commercial electricity use, with industry, mining, and business still accounting for some 60 per cent of consumption. Households account for 25 per cent of electricity consumption. Around eight in ten households had access to electricity in 2004, up from around half in 1995, with around 4 million households electrified in the past decade and a half. Yet while 80 per cent of households use electricity for lighting, far lower numbers are able to use it for cooking and heating.

Electricity is therefore bringing the educational and leisure benefits of reading after dark and television, which was hitherto car-battery dependent. However, the other anticipated benefits of electrification have not materialized. Citizens' health is still undermined by indoor coal burning. Death and disease from paraffin fires continue. Air quality still suffers from coal and wood fire emissions. Women still bear the burden of wood collection. Electrification has also not brought promised economic development, because low amperages and high prices preclude its use for refrigeration and power tools. Expensive electricity also brings extra user costs for schools and public institutions wishing to use it to support delivery and administrative improvements.

As we have seen (Chapter 3) government's attempts to restructure the electricity industry have run aground. Severe power cuts beginning in 2008 have been followed by a rapid escalation of tariffs. Meanwhile the proposed reorganization of electricity distribution has stalled leading to further disincentives to essential investment in municipal infrastructure.

Water and sanitation

Household water provides another window onto the problems of delivering mass public services for the first time. South Africa's water affairs policy was until 1994 driven by supply side and water resource management issues. Government's interest was primarily in river basin, dam, and reservoir management, and to oversee bulk routing of water over longer distances. Commercial agriculture and forestry accounted for about half of water use, with mining, manufacturing, and power responsible for around a fifth. Domestic water supply to mainly White consumers had been provided by 16 water boards, and the Black population was severely underserviced. In 1994, 12 million South Africans had no access to clean water and 21 million had inadequate access.

The Department of Water Affairs and Forestry (DWAF) has achieved some notable successes in improving access to convenient and drinkable water, with around 90 per cent of citizens now having access, of one kind or another, to clean water. However, around 10 per cent of the population continue to access water from unsafe sources, such as streams, dams, or wells, a figure that has remained quite constant across the post-1994 period. As with household energy, moreover, many poor women continue to expend time and energy carrying water substantial distances from communal taps to dwellings.

DWAF has wrestled with a series of constitutional and institutional obstacles to improving water services. The 1996 Constitution allocated responsibility for water to local government, and the national department's role has properly been to build but not maintain or operate infrastructure. DWAF currently provides funds for infrastructure and it implements the provision of new services through water boards, municipalities, NGOs, or occasionally private partners. It has set out frameworks to ensure that maintenance arrangements are robust, and uses Build Operate, Train and Transfer protocols with private and NGO partners to ensure that the capacity of municipalities to act as water service providers is gradually enhanced. Statutory Water Boards, established under the Water Services Act of 1997, are enjoined to assist local government, manage resources, facilitate cost effective delivery, monitor standards, provide bulk supplies, and transport and treat sewerage.

Key shortfalls in DWAF's mission have included the slow pace of change in water boards, and very limited municipal capacity. In rural areas, in particular, there has been a high level of project failure. Many such problems can be traced back to very low consumption. New water infrastructure is expensive to build and costly to maintain and poor consumers often pay very high per unit charges for their water. DWAF is having to subsidize projects heavily to make them viable, and infrastructure such as pumps and pipes has often fallen into disrepair through a combination of poor community engagement and a shortage of local technical skills. Cost recovery has been low and the anticipated health benefits of wider access to clean water have not fully materialized.

In recent years, government has introduced a 'lifeline tariff' through which free basic water is to be made available to all households. Supporters of this programme claim it is the only way to reach the very poor, who cannot afford the most minimal tariff, and to ensure that the use of unsafe sources is minimized. Such a scheme is costly, however, and poor municipalities usually lack wealthy users to cross-subsidize the numerous poor. Critics have claimed that the poor continue to shoulder unsustainable costs and that the free basic allowance is too small to meet basic criteria concerning health and human dignity.

Housing

Housing has been another avowed government priority. ANC housing policy first focused on a subsidy scheme that empowered individuals and communities to build property for the first time. Since 1994, the government has created more than two million 'housing opportunities' in this way. Housing subsidy programmes are now quite differentiated, and include rental subsidies, project-linked and individual subsidies, hostel subsidies, subsidies for people with disabilities or with HIV/AIDS, and a variety of others.

The achievement pales, however, in the face of the current housing backlog of more than two million units. Critics, moreover, claim that housing policy has created a very large number of poor quality homes in areas distant from potential work or economic opportunities. It has therefore entrenched apartheid's spatial patterns rather than challenging them, and substituted poor quality formal housing for often high quality informal housing. In addition, many new homeowners have proven unable to meet the heavy and sustained costs associated with home ownership, and they have been obliged (or incentivized) to sell to more wealthy purchasers, so undermining the intentions behind the housing subsidy.

Housing policy has also been criticized for its failure to empower individuals to build their own homes, and by so doing to develop their skills, capacities, and communities.

The government has responded energetically to these perceived failings. In particular, there has been a new emphasis on quality in place of crude numerical targeting. Participation has also moved centre stage, with a 'people-centred' approach enabling communities to access the resources that will enable them to construct their own housing. An insistence on building houses has been replaced by a more flexible approach to the delivery of services such as water, sanitation, roads, and drainage, while leaving households and communities to build their own structures. Equally importantly, the former fixation with ownership as the central goal of housing policy has been replaced by an approach recognizing that renting is often the most appropriate strategy for low-income families and individuals.

Another major shift of emphasis has been a recognition of the significance of the spatial dimension to housing policy. Apartheid resulted in the creation of immense urban settlements at great distances from work opportunities, and there has been growing attention to land availability in or near to urban employment opportunities. Like similar states, South Africa is struggling to manage an urbanization process that brings ever-increasing demands for public services and land in urban areas.

Behind the disappointing statistics and burgeoning backlogs for housing and household services lie three major processes of social change. First, the urbanization of South Africa's population is continuing at a rapid pace as a result of ever-declining opportunities in rural and former Bantustan areas and the natural growth of younger urban populations. Second, the size of households is falling quite rapidly. In 1995, the average household contained 4.5 people. By 2000 this had fallen to less than 4 (RSA 2006: 12). This decline in household size, which is continuing, has affected poor as well as non-poor households. And third, there has been quite substantial immigration into the country from neighbouring states. Taken together, these changes mean that government has to run merely to stand still, providing for housing and public services to be available to ever more numerous peri-urban households.

One important response to the multiple challenges of public service delivery, poverty alleviation and urban development has been a new emphasis on the local sphere of government as the key developmental agent of the state. The country now has 'wall-to-wall' municipalities covering the entire land area, including six major metropolitan 'unicities' which are solely responsible for the administration of municipal

---

Box 4.2   Land reform

Given the high profile of land transfers and seizures in Zimbabwe's current political and economic crises, government's low key approach to land reform has surprised many commentators. The South African programme has three prongs: restitution of land lost through racially discriminatory apartheid era laws; tenure reform to create legal coherence out of the diversity of inherited tenure forms; and land redistribution. While tens of thousands of outstanding restitution claims are being slowly processed, and tenure reform has advanced slowly but steadily since 1994, the redistribution strategy lacks urgency. Government aims to transfer 30 per cent of agricultural land to previously disadvantaged individuals and communities by 2015, an immensely ambitious target that becomes more unrealistic with each passing year. Projected resources for agricultural support and development seem to be insufficient, current policies create farms too small to be highly profitable and low confidence is hindering the investment the sector needs to thrive. South Africa differs from its less developed neighbours, moreover, in that contestation over land is primarily an urban or peri-urban phenomenon, with people in an urbanizing society looking not to farm but rather to make a home within striking distance of urban employment.

---

government within their areas. Government has determined that municipalities will be at the centre of integrated development, and will be responsible for bringing together the whole range of public services and for stimulating economic development. Unfortunately, this sphere of government has proven unable to shoulder the many burdens that government has placed upon it.

Education policy

While initiatives in municipal infrastructure and public service delivery have been a major focus for innovation, public spending is still dominated by health, education, and social development (see Table 4.4). These sectors, in addition, have a major direct impact alleviating inequality as well as involving both benefits in kind and direct government expenditure.

Education spending is the largest single item in the budget, accounting for one in every five Rand the government spends. Poor quality or inappropriate education is an obstacle to economic development and to the alleviation of poverty within a society. More equal access to an effective education system would ameliorate many of South Africa's various

Table 4.4   Consolidated national and provincial spending on social services 2008/9

Function	2008/9 in R millions	% of total spending
Education	120,494	20.6
Health	72,852	12.4
Social security and welfare	105,078	18.0
Housing	13,440	2.3
Community development	37,254	6.4
Social Services (total)	349,118	59.6

Source: Adapted from National Treasury 2008.

developmental challenges. It would help reduce fertility rates, increase citizens' ability to avoid HIV infection, and increase knowledge about nutrition and family planning. Understood as enhancement to 'human capital', education also contributes to productivity and economic growth.

The right to education is a special human right because it has the capacity to 'unlock' other rights by creating capable and knowledgeable citizens. The education system, moreover, has special significance as a mechanism through which cross-generational inequality can be perpetuated or eroded and as the key instrument through which the apartheid-era legacies of exploitation and dispossession can be ended.

South Africa spends a lot on education for a middle income developing country (a pattern not atypical in Anglophone Africa). Yet its education outcomes are in many respects unsatisfactory. The school system has been racially polarized and highly fragmented. Under apartheid, 'own affairs' departments managed Coloured and Indian education, while each of the Bantustans had its own department of education. Only in 1996 were 19 departments rationalized into single education system.

A small minority of Africans received a relatively good education in mission schools, but most received little or no formal education. A 'Bantu education' policy enacted after 1953 allowed increased spending on mass education but deliberately aimed to constrain the skill levels of Africans so as to fit them better for their designated roles within the apartheid economy. Africans in any event were rarely able to complete schooling because of economic pressures.

Whites enjoyed a massively subsidized and effective public education system. They were also heavily resourced at tertiary level, with English and Afrikaans medium universities striving to secure 'European' educational content and standards for this minority group. Non-White, and especially African, schools and colleges were starved of resources.

Today there are around 12 million students (or 'learners') in schools – around 3 million in KwaZulu-Natal (KZN), 2 million in Eastern Cape and not far short of 2 million in Limpopo and Gauteng – and some 395,000 teachers ('educators'). Not far short of 97 per cent of learners are in public schools, demonstrating the success of government's strategy of keeping middle class pupils in the state system.

Fifteen years of ANC government have seen the nominal racial integration of schools at all levels, pupil feeding schemes, major construction of buildings and facilities, the introduction of 10 years of compulsory school, outcomes based education' and a deracialisation of the school curriculum.

Two factors appear to be most critical to a high-quality education: teacher quality and staff to student ratios, but these factors have proved hard to change for the better. Government's first wave of reform in the mid-1990s saw voluntary severance packages for schools with 'too many teachers' – primarily white suburban schools – and many highly qualified teachers were lost to the profession. Efforts to improve learner to educator ratios have had some success with most classes in urban and peri-urban areas remaining below 40 pupils.

Inequality remains great. Formerly white ('ex-Model C') public schools have used rapidly escalating school fees to recruit 'governing body teachers' to supplement government funded staff. Although these schools have become partly racially integrated, in the sense that they often accommodate twenty or twenty-five per cent black students and smaller but growing numbers of black teachers, they remain the vehicles for the perpetuation of white suburban privilege.

Most schools remain mono-racial. African learners in township and rural schools, moreover, are rarely receiving an adequate education. This is in part a matter of resources but it is primarily a matter of teacher quality, experience, and management. There is still no effective training programme for what are often under qualified teachers. Much teacher behaviour seems to be a perpetuation of the dysfunctional practices of the past, and there is widespread absenteeism, pupil sexual abuse, and alcoholism among staff.

Overall, schools continue to perpetuate class disadvantage, and to provide unequal access to the skills that will determine success in the labour market. Yet it has proven very hard to change them. South Africa's educators are highly unionized, with around 100,000 being members of the National Professional Teachers' Organization of South Africa (NAPTOSA) and more than twice that number members of the South African Democratic Teachers Union (SADTU). The unions have been an obstructive force in attempts to introduce higher teacher standards of discipline, training, and attendance.

The racist curriculum of the apartheid era has been largely replaced. Moreover, the National Education Policy Act of 1995 introduced a controversial system of 'outcomes based education' (OBE), intended to replace authoritarianism and rote-learning with a learner-centred focus on creating independent-minded, creative, and critical citizens. Because OBE involves teaching according to interest, adjusting the learning pace to individual learners, group study and 'formative' continuous assessment it has proved impossible to implement effectively in many, perhaps most, of the country's schools.

Formal education today nevertheless reaches the vast majority of children between the ages of seven and fifteen, with school attendance estimated at around 95 per cent in this age group. Girls are not, as in so many other countries, excluded from education in substantial numbers out of economic necessity.

School leaving certificate pass rates vary wildly, with many schools having a very small number of passes (or even none at all). Relatively few scholars complete secondary education and continue to tertiary institutions. Less than 20 per cent of matriculants secure the 'exemptions' necessary for higher education admission and of these only a small minority have the passes in mathematics that allow then to take scientific or mathematical subjects.

Meanwhile the tertiary sector is undergoing an upheaval. Newly reorganized further education institutions are finding it hard to produce graduates with the skills demanded by employers. The universities have been through a period of merger and racial integration. Historically African universities, such as Fort Hare and the Bantustan universities, have been undermined by the decisions of African students who have opted to enter the now integrated formerly white universities. Apartheid's racial inheritance lives on in class terms in the privileges accorded to universities that historically serviced Whites, such as the country's two premier universities, Witwatersrand and University of Cape Town. It is the formerly White Afrikaner universities, such as Stellenbosch and University of Johannesburg (formerly Rand Afrikaans University) that have responded most energetically to the opportunities and threats of the new era. Like the English universities, however, they have yet to wrestle with the reality of fundamental change and they are failing to reproduce the research output successes of the ageing generation of scholars and scientists. Like universities everywhere, of course, these institutions are having to face the implications of bewildering technological and scientific advance, a rapidly changing labour market and a new internationalization of employment options for some groups of academics and scholars.

The underperformance of South Africa's education system is well known. There remain failings in literacy, numeracy, and cognitive skills. For an aspiring developmental state, however, there is also a need to focus on the requirements of a knowledge economy. 'For countries in the vanguard of the world economy' the World Bank (1998) observes, 'the balance between knowledge and resources has shifted so far towards the former that knowledge has become perhaps the most important factor determining the standard of living ... Today's most technologically advanced economies are truly knowledge-based'.

A society like South Africa, with an increasingly knowledge-driven economy, needs constantly to upgrade its educational and high-level technological skills at the same time as addressing other educational deficiencies. Knowledge will continue to become more important as a result of further advances in information and communications technologies, an increasing rate of technological advance and lower communications costs. Economic theorists now see knowledge as central to economic growth (Crafts 1996).

Women and Disadvantage

Among the cross-sectoral challenges that policy makers confront, it is the disadvantage of women in South African society that is the most prominent. Gender equality is important not merely because human rights are premised on equal worth of all human beings but for the more pragmatic reasons that greater gender equality is essential to the reduction of poverty and the increasing of economic growth. In South Africa, as in other countries, there are numerous impediments to women's exercise of their human rights and poverty impacts disproportionately on women. Their access to health services is poor. They are subject to sexual harassment and violence, have poor access to justice, and lack productive opportunities. They have primary responsibility for household maintenance and rural physical labour. A variety of traditions, cultures, and religions systematize and legitimize their exploitation.

There have been some gains in South Africa in recent decades, primarily through the efforts of women themselves. Whereas 25 years ago, brothers, uncles, or husbands mediated and controlled all aspects of women's entitlement to property and land, such unequivocal control is becoming far less common – although the ANC has been equivocal in its support for women's emancipation.

Women today have greater access to credit than in the past. Lacking education and facing discrimination in educational provision in most of the developing world, women in South Africa are also more likely than men to finish secondary school. Numerous women participate in government at the highest level, including in parliament and the Cabinet. The ANC recently adopted a policy of 50 per cent of senior offices being reserved for women. Employment equity and black empowerment policies make special provision for increasing the opportunities available to women.

Yet the broader picture of disadvantage remains clear. Perhaps three quarters of African women live below the poverty line and female unemployment in rural areas is at staggering levels. Apartheid's migrant labour system encouraged women-headed households. Women have been primarily responsible for household energy and water supplies, forcing them to engage in the extended and backbreaking labour of water and firewood collection. Land ownership and allocation, dominated by men, has systematically discriminated against them.

South African women (and their children) also experience exceptional levels of sexual and physical violence. Around 50,000 rapes are reported per annum, or more than one reported rape per hundred persons in any given year, the highest incidence in the world. Such figures, moreover, should be interpreted in the light of the extreme under-reporting of this crime. Violence and rape are often characteristic of established relationships or marriages, and the rape of young children has become an increasingly widely recognized scourge in South African society.

Over the past decade, many governments, donors, and NGOs have adopted a 'gender mainstreaming' approach, with the aim of delivering rights to women and equality of opportunity. Such an approach seeks to place a gender perspective at the heart of any policy or programme so that, before a policy decision is taken, an analysis is made of its effects on women and men. This process initially requires gender analysis, data disaggregation by sex, and new project design, monitoring and impact assessment approaches. The roles, resources, and priorities of women need to be identified and explored, and basic equitable practices introduced. Clear equity commitments need to be made in each sector. Organizational capacity must be built and skilled staff trained to catalyse policy formation and commission relevant research.

South Africa has progressed only a very short way along the road towards gender mainstreaming. The Constitution guarantees formal equality before the law, and the ANC is committed to the development of a non-sexist South Africa. Employment equity and economic empowerment initiatives have been targeted at women and Black people, and many government projects – in departments such as Housing and Social Development – have been designed to reduce gender inequality. Mainstreaming, however, is as far away as ever. There remains a paucity of relevant data and research. Participatory methods are often poorly designed, and there is little gender analysis of the budgetary processes.

There are few institutional levers through which policy can be influenced, by and for women. The Office of the Status of Women (based in the Presidency) is largely inactive. The Commission for Gender Equality, a statutory body, has placed land reform at top of its agenda, seeking strategies for access and security of tenure for rural women. The Commission, however, has been lambasted for its poor organization, limited capacity, and funding (as well as suffering financial scandals). The Parliamentary Committee on Women has come under heavy political pressure from the Executive. The political leadership necessary to give substance to the vision of equality embodied in the constitution has not been manifested by the ANC.

Towards a More Equal Future?

There is no single correct way of mapping social structure or isolating the forms of inequality and disadvantage prevalent in a society. South Africa, as we have seen, is a society divided by race, class, employment status, location, and gender. While striving unevenly towards a more equal future, and building public services open to all, its government faces immense obstacles to success in reducing inequality. Indeed, like most other societies South Africa faces the prospect of a deepening of some dimensions of its inequality. It is relatively easy to end comprehensive discrimination by race or by gender and to create opportunities for many women and Black people to advance within the society. It is far harder to transform the structure of opportunities itself and to reduce overall inequality of outcomes. Unemployment is currently the major force behind widening inequality in South Africa and there is no panacea for this problem. Wider economic forces reward those possessing scarce skills and assets while penalizing those who cannot add value in an increasingly knowledge-based economy, and governments everywhere have struggled to create instruments with which to respond.

5

Government

⌊The contemporary South African state emerged out of a tumultuous history. It was in its first manifestation a product of forced unification by the British imperial power that was completed in 1910. Unification required the suppression of Afrikaner and especially African societies, and the progressive harnessing of their energies to a dynamic minerals economy. Across almost all of its short history, this state failed to command popular legitimacy. The 1910 *Act of Union* embodied a racial politics, cemented an alliance of interests between Boer and English-speaker, and excluded almost all Blacks from political participation.

After 1948, a state that had been an agent of imperial power was transformed into an instrument of Afrikaner nationalist advance. It was used to impose an increasingly brutal social engineering while launching Bantustans into quasi-independence and servicing Coloured and Indian South Africans through a labyrinthine bureaucracy of 'own affairs' departments. As domestic resistance to apartheid intensified, and as neighbouring countries secured liberation from colonial rule after 1974, the state increasingly became a dual instrument of internal oppression and external destabilization. By the mid-1980s, a powerful security establishment occupied the centre of the state surrounded by a fragmented machinery of mass service delivery. At every level the legitimacy of the state was under attack, from the vast majority of South Africa's people and from the wider international community that united against apartheid as against no other modern political regime.

The Making of a Constitutional Settlement

Political scientist Jon Elster observes that there is a paradox at the heart of the making of a constitution. On the one hand, any constitution is

110

designed to endure in an unforeseeable future, and so it must embody the highest possible degree of foresight and detachment. Its creators must detach themselves from the concerns of the present, and design binding rules for a future they can never know. On the other hand, constitutional settlements are forged in times of political upheaval, in which negotiators are buffeted by intense and immediate political and emotional pressure. In Elster's (1993) evocative phrase, their task is to rebuild a boat while it is sailing on the open seas. To surmount such a challenge requires constitution builders who are able to combine powerful intellectual detachment with cunning and the application of brute political force.

The 1993 interim constitution decisively shaped the 1996 final constitution. The latter was intended to guide the society across future decades. Yet it was negotiated in a context of mass political upheaval and violence and by necessity reflected the balance of political forces of the day. Its greatest significance was probably the fact of its being, rather than its particular content: it represented the triumph of constitutional government itself. South Africa now subscribes to the doctrine of 'constitutionalism', which specifies that citizens and officers of the state alike should be subject to the rules outlined in the constitution impartially applied. The South African constitution characterizes itself as 'the supreme law of the Republic' (RSA 1996: Section 2). All actions, individuals, and bodies are formally subject to its authority.

While an immediate context shaped the constitution's form, the inheritance of the 1910–94 period was also significant. Even through the period of security state dominance, the law was often a check on executive action, although the principle of 'parliamentary sovereignty' severely limited judicial authority. Cabinet government survived until an 'imperial presidency' emerged in the 1980s. In addition, parliament had a tradition of adversarial multi-party politics, albeit one stifled by National Party (NP) dominance after 1948.

The road to talks had been long and winding. Throughout the 1980s, powerful forces pushed the leaders of the African National Congress (ANC) and the NP towards negotiation (Asmal 1995). By the time FW De Klerk seized the state presidency in late 1989, there had been a wide variety of contacts between liberation movement leaders and representatives of the regime's civilian intelligence services. Equally importantly, South African business had created channels of communication that would allow the second 'hidden transition' – in the economy – to take place without ideological conflict.

Nevertheless, the negotiation period was marked by severe violence, especially in the area of what is today KwaZulu Natal (KZN) where a

low intensity civil war was conducted between the ANC and the traditionalist Inkatha Freedom Party (IFP) for the support of Zulu-speakers.
In addition, the White right, primarily Afrikaans-speakers, threatened
military and civil insurrection. The military affiliates of anti-apartheid
actors were meanwhile conducting high profile bombings and shoot-
ings. There was much debate about the kind of constitution best suited
to such a 'deeply divided society' in which, for some, racial and ethnic division were entrenched and had to be accommodated within the
constitution.

There were external pressures for liberal constitutionalism, from
international powers and from domestic and international business.
Many different models were mined for ideas. The Germany Federal
system, in which the provinces enjoy considerable autonomy and co-
operate with the federal government according to consensual principles,
influenced some negotiators. The United States, from whom a bastard-
ized Separation of Powers was borrowed, had a pervasive influence. The
United Kingdom, whose unitary state was most closely related to the
pre-existing South African state form, ultimately proved an exceptionally important model.

The ANC and the NP dominated interim constitution negotiations,
while the IFP took brinkmanship to new extremes in its efforts to influence their outcome. The NP favoured a 'consociational' settlement, in
which veto powers and proportional representation in the public service
would be guaranteed to all designated ethnic groups. The IFP sought
a high degree of autonomy for the province of KZN given the weak-
ness of its support base elsewhere. The ANC, however, insisted upon an
essentially unitary state, albeit one with certain guaranteed powers for
the provinces and municipalities. A parliamentary system was chosen in
preference to a presidential model, although elements of presidentialism
and a partial separation of powers were included. The ambitious and
carefully designed constitution, moreover, incorporated not just conventional liberal protections, but also certain socio-economic rights – to
adequate housing, health care, water, and so on – which the government
was charged with responsibility for progressively realizing.

The ANC's immensely impressive negotiating team, led by master
strategist Cyril Ramaphosa, and backed by the liberation movement's
power on the streets and in the factories, achieved most of its goals. South
Africa emerged after 1994 with a complex constitutional settlement that
might have made possible cabinet government, a high degree of federalism, and an active policy-making parliament. However, the constitution
also made possible an executive-centred and unitary state of the kind
ANC largely favoured.

Box 5.1   Cyril Ramaphosa

Born in Soweto on 17 November 1952, Ramaphosa is the most gifted of an exceptional generation of ANC political leaders. As a law student and black consciousness activist at University of the North in the early 1970s, he was twice detained and held in solitary confinement for 11 months. After completing his legal studies in 1981, he joined the Council of Unions of South Africa (CUSA) which charged him with launching a National Union of Mineworkers (NUM). At the time of its inaugural congress in December 1982, it had just 14,000 members in nine branches. By the middle of 1986 an astonishing 344,000 mineworkers had signed up to the union. In 1987 a massive and extended NUM strike launched a major challenge to the minerals sector at the heart of the apartheid economy. Helping to found the ANC-aligned Congress of South African Trade Unions (COSATU), Ramaphosa and his NUM became a backbone of mass protest actions against the Botha and de Klerk regimes. Ramaphosa headed the reception committee that greeted Nelson Mandela on his release from prison, and in 1991 he became head of the ANC's constitutional negotiating team and secretary general of the ANC. He oversaw the drafting of the country's interim and final constitutions in 1993 and 1996. Losing out to rival Thabo Mbeki for the Deputy Presidency in 1994, Ramaphosa moved to the business sector in 1997, where he has been a prominent proponent and practitioner of Black Economic Empowerment (BEE). He has remained a member of the ANC's National Executive Committee and has recently returned to a more active role in political life.

Few powers are unambiguously devolved to provinces or to local authorities, and the policy process has been left essentially to the national executive branch. There is a strong centre in which executive power is vested in the president, who is head of state and of government. The president is supposed to exercise power 'together with' cabinet members, but at the same time he is responsible for their appointment. Parliament's position, as we shall see, has been essentially reactive, a position determined by political rather than constitutional factors.

The three 'powers of government' – legislation, execution, and adjudication – are each assigned to one branch of government at national level: to parliament, president and cabinet, and the courts. In theory, such a 'separation of powers' avoids the concentration of too much power in any single institution. While the President has some legislative powers in assenting to laws and promulgating regulations, and some judicial authority in pardons, there are mechanisms that leave his office open to the influence of the other branches of government. The President is elected by National Assembly (NA) rather than directly by the people. He is vulnerable to impeachment (by two thirds of the NA) or to a vote of no confidence by the majority of the assembly, which triggers a general election. (As we shall see in the next chapter, such constitutional provisions do not guarantee that the power of the executive will be contained, especially where the ANC can effectively fuse executive and legislative power through its parliamentary caucus.) The parliament has two chambers with legislation passing through the NA and a National Council of Provinces (NCOP). This second chamber of the bicameral parliament has ninety members, ten from each of the provinces. The legislature approves the budget, and its portfolio committees (NA) and select committees (NCOP) oversee the activities of government departments.

Ministers are collectively responsible to the legislature, in that the Cabinet collectively determines policy and ministers are obliged to defend government positions rather than personal ones. If ministers wish to protest or oppose cabinet positions, they are obliged to resign. Ministers are also individually responsible to parliament, and they are obliged to account for the actions of the executive behaviour to parliamentary committees. Neither form of cabinet accountability works well in practice. Collective responsibility has limited public debate, and ministers have almost invariably shirked responsibility for mismanagement and maladministration in the departments for which they are responsible.

The constitution also mandates a number of 'independent' offices which are designed to protect against illegal actions or abuses of power. These include an auditor-general's office, a public protector or ombudsman, a human rights commission, a commission for gender equality, a national language board, and an electoral commission. These bodies have performed unevenly as a result of constricted funding by the government, administrative incompetence, and because most appointees are senior members of the ANC and so cannot maintain distance or objectivity when government's failure are under scrutiny.

The system of provincial government contains certain additional checks on the centre. The notion of 'concurrent powers' is much employed in the constitution. In conjunction with the treatment of national, provincial, and municipal government as 'spheres' rather than 'tiers' of government, concurrency is intended to suggest a notional parity. In practice, the centre has been able to limit the autonomy of the provinces in South Africa, primarily by the imposition of national ANC discipline upon provincial liberation movement structures. The municipalities, and especially the new 'unicities' of the major metropolitan areas, enjoy the greatest degree of autonomy from the centre, and have become to some degree fiefdoms that the executive and the ANC alike have found it difficult to control.

Political Authority under the New Constitution

Some commentators have claimed the constitution is 'federal' in character while others see South Africa's new political system as essentially 'unitary'. There are no uncontested definitions of these terms. The major African colonial powers, France and Britain, have historically been strongly unitary states with a marked centralization of power at national level (although European integration has significantly changed this distribution of power). At the other extreme, the United States and Germany have been influential models of highly decentralized political systems in which most significant policy and political decisions are taken, or at least shared, by sub-national units. Such decentralization, if it implies constitutional entrenchment of regional government with significant powers protected by the constitution, is usually treated as indicative of a 'federal' system.

South Africa's constitutional negotiators explored a variety of federal and unitary systems, including the inescapable United States model. In most respects a unique case, the original American states' constitutions predated the federal constitution of 1789, and contemporary citizen identity is primarily defined and shaped at state and city level. States have their own separation of powers between legislature, judiciary, and executive, and a dualistic legal system, with parallel federal and state jurisdictions, leaves the latter dominant in criminal and civil law. Legislative activism is embedded at state level, and both states and cities can raise revenues and so act with a considerable degree of autonomy. Almost all public policy is determined at state level or lower, with federal government setting structures of incentives or intervening to regulate interstate activity. Policing, transport, and social security are dominated by states, and even economic development and energy policy – national functions in almost all other societies – are primarily state level activities in the United States.

The US model illustrates many of the strengths and weaknesses of federalism. It protects against central tyranny, increases citizen participation, encourages innovation and learning, strengthens community identity and values, and can partially defuse deep conflicts of belief. At the same time, it leaves government slow to respond to challenges, and the plethora of levels makes decision-making processes cumbersome. These were perceived by many constitutional negotiators as fatal flaws for a fragmented old South Africa looking for coherent government in the new era.

Non-ANC constitution builders were also impressed by the moderated federalism of the Federal Republic of Germany whose 1949 'Basic Law' or Constitution was designed by the western allies to prevent the re-emergence of a powerful centralized state (such as Hitler's Third Reich). The Basic Law decentralizes power, encourages coalition government, and entrenches the autonomy of provinces. The constitution lists provincial prerogatives – education, mass media, and any other matter not explicitly preserved to federal government – and 'concurrent' competencies, including economic development, environmental policy, federal issues, defence, foreign trade, and macroeconomic policy – a feature partially borrowed by South Africa's constitution. Provinces are represented in the upper house of the federal parliament (the Bundesrat), a 'conclave of states' with the authority to block decisions by the lower house (or Bundestag). Bills changing the tax balance can be vetoed, and German provinces have significant sources of tax revenue from indirect taxes and from a guaranteed share of the national government budget.

Most ANC negotiators were never very much taken with the strengths of the federal model. Within the ANC and its alliances, there were (and remain) social democrats and socialists attracted by the potential of central state intervention. Such intervention is especially attractive in developing countries or states going through periods of upheaval. A powerful centre was presumed to be an aid to the creation of a nation, and it was expected to counteract potential centripetal tendencies – among them the ethnic tension that has been a problem in so many post-colonial African polities. The likely desire of richer regions and provinces to increase their autonomy from the centre, and to retain their advantages in terms of standards of living and income, also made a unitary form attractive. The exile leadership of the ANC, furthermore, had a preference for centralization because of its fears that the ANC itself lacked cohesion domestically, and worried that provincial ANC structures – and the domestic activists who had brought apartheid to its knees – might be difficult for the exile-nurtured liberation movement leadership to control.

Perhaps the most important influence on the new constitution was the historical legacy of the highly unitary 'Westminster model' derived from the former colonial power, Britain. The United Kingdom has historically possessed a dominant national executive, in which a cabinet system, and in recent years a powerful prime minister, together create policy. A weak parliament plays a reactive and limited policy-influencing role. Revenue raising and expenditure is monopolized by a strong and intrusive Treasury, and there have been (until recently) no regional elections or institutions and no real revenue raising powers at regional or local level.

The conventional wisdom is that the Westminster system enjoys efficacy at the cost of representativeness, its strong and unchecked executive able to formulate policy, generate legislation, have it rubber stamped by parliament and implemented by national, regional, and local government agents. In a federal system like Germany, by contrast, consultation between national and provincial levels leaves all groups represented and all interests consulted. Policy makers – in part admittedly because of accompanying corporatism and coalition government – must advance by consensus. While highly representative, critics claim, the system is slow and muddled.

Such an analysis of the relative merits of the two systems misunderstands the relationship between consultation and efficacy and exaggerates the advantages of a unitary state. While the UK's unitary structure makes the formulation and passage of legislation fast, the country also has a history of major policy failures. A lack of consultation makes for rapid change but policy implementation can be less effective because citizens resist policies in which they have had no say and in which they believe themselves to have no stake. (The United Kingdom and Germany, of course, are now part of the European Union's multi-level system of governance in which authority is distributed across provincial, national, and pan-European institutions in accordance with a complex and fast-evolving set of conventions and intergovernmental agreements.)

South Africa appears federal at first glance, because of the prominence of sub-national institutions and the presence of nine provincial legislatures. The constitution, however, promotes or at least sanctions a highly integrated system of government in which the national level can prevail over the provincial in both shared 'concurrent' responsibilities and supposedly 'exclusive' provincial competencies. The South African constitution speaks the language of German consociationalism but it embodies the reality of executive dominance in a unitary state.

The National Executive

The executive is the dominant branch of government everywhere in the modern world, with the partial exception of the United States. It is responsible for executing the laws of Parliament but it also contains the government, or the political executive, which is constituted in South Africa by the President, the Cabinet and the senior public service. So complex and interrelated are the activities of a modern administration that certain actors will be involved in the majority of significant policy initiatives in the country as a whole. The 'core executive', as it is some-times called, in South Africa includes the Cabinet, the Presidency (which contains a policy co-ordination unit and a secretariat for the manage-ment of cabinet business), the Directors General (DG) who are the senior public servants in each department, the Treasury, and the intelligence and security services.

The executive has grown in power across the world since the modern South African state was created in 1910. The complexity and technical nature of policy has grown, the volume of legislation has increased, and expert and interest group lobbies circle ever more frenetically around policy makers. In addition, the state has become ever more ambitious in policy co-ordination, trying to get public and private actors to work har-moniously together. Executive leadership in South Africa as elsewhere has been bolstered by the tumultuous history of the twentieth century. Economic interventionism has also played a role, as frameworks for budgeting, changing ownership structures, and creating regulatory sys-tems each require specialist knowledge and the authority of the state. Increasingly, private lobbying and the demands of executive-related international institutions have enhanced the leverage of the executive and undermined the legislature.

Corporatist relations between the executive, business, and labour, and the emergence of welfare states have contributed to this trend. Foreign and defence policy have also played a major role in expanding the influ-ence of the executive. Modern industrial war is driven by the executive branch and its relations with capital. It calls for concerted action and justifies central control and intervention. In addition it allows the raising of new taxes – which are never fully withdrawn after the cessation of conflict – and predisposes populations to listen and respond to national political leaders. In addition, the executive branch has responsibility for international agreements and institutions – in South Africa's case, dealing with environmental treaties, World Trade Organization (WTO) regulations, the Southern African Development Community (SADC), the African Union, and the New Partnership for Africa's Development, among myriad others.

The South African constitution places the Cabinet towards the apex of this system of executive authority. Cabinet ministers, who give political direction to a million public servants, are appointed by the President. There are 29 departments. A cabinet system is designed to manage government business by ensuring that all relevant parties are informed of, and contribute to, policy that impacts on their area of responsibility. This is given effect in Pretoria by a committee system based on 'clusters' of related departments. The key principle behind this system is that the departments in a cluster need to plan their activities together mindful of the impacts one department may have on others. Thus the justice cluster brings together the justice department with the safety and security department that manages the South African Police Service and the correctional services department responsible for prisons. A change in sentencing policy, for example, will impact on all three departments and they all need to be made aware of policy changes that have implications for how each of the others acts.

A social sector cluster in the same way co-ordinates the interactions of departments responsible for education, health, household infrastructure, and social welfare. An international relations cluster brings together foreign affairs, defence, and intelligence. And an economy cluster, dominated by the national treasury, accommodates trade and industry, labour, transport, and others. A final cluster – something of an oddity in an otherwise function-based system – is a governance cluster that includes department responsible for public administration and the relationships between the spheres of government.

In a cabinet system, decisions are taken where possible by inter-departmental agreement, if possible among officials and without the need of ministers to become actively involved. Hard problems or turf wars are taken to cabinet 'cluster' committees, to ministers and ultimately to cabinet. Only intractable disputes between departments need to be mediated by full cabinet. The committee system therefore relieves pressure on cabinet itself by defining points of disagreement and excluding irrelevant actors. Only if disputes are intractable, or a policy is highly significant politically or in terms of resource implications, is a dispute likely to make its way to Cabinet. This procedure gives recognition to the fact the Cabinet is not a good decision-making body, being overloaded, large, and unwieldy, and comprised of non-specialists in any particular policy area.

'The Executive power of the Republic vests in the President', according to Section 85 of the Constitution, but he or she is supposed to exercise this power jointly with cabinet. Yet, the 'clustering' system itself is managed by a cabinet office within the Presidency, one of the most controversial institutional innovations of the Mbeki Presidency. The

Presidency has also since 1999 included a policy co-ordination and advisory services (PCAS) unit vetting policy proposals and monitoring the implementation of policy within clusters.

At the apex of the presidency is the President himself. At first sight he possesses a formidable array of powers. He is head of state and head of government, as well as usually being the head of the largest party. He appoints ministers and oversees the appointment of DGs; he chairs the cabinet and determines its overall operation; he chairs some cabinet committees and appoints the chairs of others; he shapes international policy; and he can adopt other policy areas more or less at will and dominate them. A president also appoints a vast range of members of public bodies, giving him a huge realm of patronage running into thousands. In close liaison with the Government Communications and Information Service, he is well placed to manipulate the media. In addition, he can undermine full cabinet, cow his ministers with the threat of dismissal, and use outside advisers to double guess them while denying them any real opportunity to speak beyond their brief. He can also use alternative co-ordinating or dispute resolution procedures in the Treasury or within the ANC to override opposition.

Despite this appearance of overwhelming power, however, presidents are tightly constrained by a variety of factors. Any president will lack the time, knowledge, and resources required to dominate to the extent permitted by the office. He relies on the knowledge resources of departments and ministers. In addition, he is politically vulnerable and must balance cabinet by faction, region, ethnicity, race, and gender, while respecting powerful colleagues with party constituencies. He must rely on a relatively small pool of genuine administrative talent, and accommodate members of alliance parties.

Ministers, meanwhile, are scarcely political innocents. They are sometimes charismatic and almost always devious, they are media-savvy and opportunistic, and over time they will accumulate and nurture grievances against a president and his confidants. Above all, however, it is events themselves – the unending stream of exhausting challenges that confront a president day in day out – and the loneliness of the office that will deplete the resources of any incumbent who tries to dominate the system of government.

The relationship between president and cabinet – and the third key institution of the Treasury – has been highly controversial in recent years. The Constitution envisages a balance between cabinet government, an executive Presidency and a treasury with wide powers. Cabinet government is generally benign because it creates opportunities for the analytical deliberation of policy, and it allows government departments to bring sectoral policy communities and interest groups into play.

Since 1999, however, the relationship between these three centres of power has become unbalanced. The Treasury controls broad economic policy but it also micromanages public expenditure. Its bilateral relationships with individual departments have arguably proven to be incompatible with the overarching strategic thinking and co-operative behaviour required for effective government in a 'developmental state'.

President Thabo Mbeki's 'new integrated Presidency', designed to introduce strategic, proactive, and 'joined-up' policy making, has largely failed to do so. While ministers and DGs have sometimes used the 'cluster system' to take on the Treasury, they have done so not as a result of high-level strategic analysis but to scratch one another's backs.

According to his critics, Mbeki has further undermined the capacity of the cabinet to take well-considered collective decisions by introducing a swathe of loyalist deputy ministers, playing divide-and-rule games with ministers and DGs, and usurping the cabinet's role as ultimate adjudicator in interdepartmental conflicts.

How could the post-Mbeki cabinet system be strengthened? First, merit criteria could play a bigger role in the appointment of DGs and cabinet ministers. Second, the 'management of ministers' by senior officials might be curtailed by empowering ministers to appoint a wider range of external advisers. Third, institutions in the Presidency that duplicate departmental functions might be dismantled. Fourth, the Cabinet could take control of elite public sector recruitment, training, and discipline. Finally, to give effect to these changes, the cabinet office needs to be moved out of the Presidency altogether, and it needs to take with it elements from the President's current support system.

Cabinet ministers, even working together, lack the capacity to act as a counterweight to the treasury. The Treasury is not too powerful, however; the Cabinet is too weak. Some of the powers the Cabinet needs can be found in the Presidency's PCAS, which is currently being pulled in two directions – political and co-ordinating – and might sensibly be split to reflect this implicit divide.

Any president needs a policy office to create and communicate a sense of coherence in government, to elaborate an overall framework of priorities, and to relate the government's broader vision to the political ideology of the ruling political party. But it is cabinet ministers who need co-ordination support. The cabinet office could take on permanent cross-cutting issues, such as the condition of women and the youth, as well as contingent cross-sectoral emergencies such as HIV/AIDS.

The Cabinet requires procedural and policy co-ordination capabilities: systems for arbitration between conflicting ministers, monitoring policy implementation, providing legal and specialist analysis to officials, and more broadly for managing the machinery of government.

The Cabinet itself, through an empowered cabinet office, could undertake long-term strategic reviews, and create new partnerships with the private and voluntary sectors. It could even conceivably manage dedicated central funds to promote co-operation between departments and to support cross-sectoral and high priority apex initiatives.

Reforms of this kind might rebalance relationships at the centre of government, allow a renewed cabinet to become accountable to a rejuvenated Parliament, and avert what might otherwise become a dangerous concentration of power in the Presidency and the Treasury.

The National Legislature

In the early history of the doctrine of 'separation of powers' it was legislatures (and the 'tyranny of the majority' they threatened) that were viewed as the key opponent of 'balanced government'. But, over the course of the twentieth century, the power of legislatures was eroded, primarily by the expansion of executive power. In developing countries, this executive dominance has often been accompanied by a more systematic subjugation of the judiciary and legislature to the executive and its leaders.

South Africa's NA, like its UK equivalent the House of Commons, is sometimes described as a 'rubber stamp' ripe for reform. Parliamentary reformers, however, tend to underestimate the constraints on the autonomy of any modern legislature. The past 100 years have seen a mostly irreversible growth in the power of the executive branch around the world. Wars developed new executive capacities that were not relinquished in peace. 'Corporatism' shut legislatures out of long-term deals between state, business, and labour. Social welfare programmes grew beyond the capacity of parliamentarians to understand them.

Changes in the character of the mass political party simultaneously stripped backbenchers of residual powers. Parties are primarily instruments for securing state power, and they survive in competitive systems only through relatively rigorous organization to ensure effective recruitment, candidate choice, and campaigning. Power and information in electorally successful parties are concentrated in the hands of party elites, and the expulsion of dissidents is used against independent members to maintain a facade of unity.

Given these general constraints, some observers believe ordinary parliamentarians in South Africa have been performing quite well. Political scientist Joel Barkan (2005) has noted that the NA amends as much as 80 per cent of all legislation, and often quite substantially. Portfolio committees are reasonably well resourced, several are ably chaired, and they often enjoy the respect of interest groups and civil society organizations. To the degree that the executive and legislature are inevitably partly fused in Westminster-type systems such as South Africa's, moreover, this has brought benefits during the period of relentless law-making that began in 1994. Unnecessary inter-branch conflict has been minimized and decisive legislative action by the majority party facilitated.

The features that have made Parliament an effective legislator, however, equip it poorly for the challenges of tomorrow. The overhaul of apartheid legislation is more or less complete, and today's Parliament needs to adapt so as to exercise its second, but not secondary, executive oversight function more effectively.

The natural tendency of executives to subordinate legislatures can be averted only through a deliberate counterstrategy to build oversight capacities. In an ideal world, it might be desirable to establish an electoral link between Members of Parliament (MPs) and constituencies, and to elect a smaller number of more professional MPs, who would enjoy a far greater level of resources and support. More practical and immediate reforms would include a committee career structure that increases the status and remuneration of committee chairs. The research and analytical resources available to individual committees should be enhanced, and Parliament as a whole could be provided with at least a minimal capacity to formulate, cost, and analyse complex packages of integrated policy alternatives. Such support systems could make possible the oversight of cabinet clusters rather than merely of individual departments.

Given the disadvantages of legislatures, it is important for a national president to demonstrate through his actions that Parliament is deserving of respect. Such a president would be willing to expose himself to parliamentary interrogation both more frequently and more freely, abandoning the current practice of screening out challenging questions in advance. A president should celebrate robust executive oversight, and haul his ministers and DG over the coals if they fail to demonstrate the respect that Parliament deserves.

For any programme of renewal to succeed, however, a change of strategy will be required from an ANC that has tended to mistrust Parliament as a bourgeois liberal institution. It is surely unnecessary that ANC leaders, rather than committee members themselves, select portfolio committee chairs, and that Parliament does not deliberate as a body over the choice of a rules committee chair, the speaker, or the deputy speaker.

In interventions that might be rethought, the ANC's national working committee exercises too direct a sway over the party's parliamentary caucus, ANC 'study groups' are encouraged to pre-empt the decisions of committees, and the caucus code of conduct prohibits ANC MPs from using parliamentary structures to undermine party policy.

After a decade of perceived centralization, a consensus may be emerging in the ANC that power needs to be distributed more widely, both in the movement and in the country, and that parliament might be one useful vehicle for such a change of direction.

The Judiciary

The third branch of government, the judiciary, is concerned with the application of the law. Laws are binding decisions that are made into rules and enforced by the state. In South Africa there is formal equality before the law: any law, in theory at least, is enforced equally on all regardless of position. Yet, the sources of law are not as clear cut as one might expect. Law originates primarily in the legislatures, including 'delegated' legislation in different spheres of government. The Constitution sets out a clear hierarchy, in which the Constitution is supreme, and below it lie national, then provincial, then municipal spheres. Law can also originate in statutes promulgated by the executive. In addition, the courts themselves make new law in their interpretation and application of existing laws. 'Common law', 'customary law', law established through the practice of 'traditional' courts, and Muslim family law, are also recognized in South Africa but are at the same time subject to the constitution (implying that ultimately they will move into line with it).

The application of law is always open to dispute. For example, the courts must adjudge whether a right has been infringed, a legal offence committed, what the nature of the infringement might be, what exactly the law says, and how precisely the law ought to be applied. The system through which such judgements are made in South Africa involves a number of different types of courts. Magistrates, appointed by the Minister of Justice, may serve in either district or (higher) regional courts, and deal with the overwhelming majority of cases. High Courts, whose judges are appointed by the President concurrently with the Judicial Services Commission (JSC), deal with appeals from lower courts but also with many constitutional issues. The Supreme Court of Appeal has been highest court of appeal in all but constitutional matters.

The Constitutional Court is at the apex of the judiciary. South Africa enjoys constitutional supremacy. All laws and state actions are supposed to be consistent with the constitution (including its Bill of Rights). The Constitutional Court is a special and specialized court which interprets, protects, and enforces the Constitution. It is 'independent' in that it is appointed by the President and Cabinet in consultation with party leaders in the NA, and the JSC submits a list from which these judges must be chosen. The JSC itself is a representative body comprising, in roughly equal measure, senior judges, parliamentarians, and acting lawyers. The key areas of jurisdiction of the Court include the consistency of legislation with the Constitution – if such legislation is referred to it by the President or a Premier – and disputes between spheres of government. The Court also rules on the constitutionality of constitutional amendments (in which cases there are complex rules for different kinds of amendments) and on the consistency of government actions with the constitution (including the Bill of Rights).

One key issue that has arisen in South Africa with regard to the role of the Constitutional Court is whether the courts are genuinely 'independent', given that the executive – in fact the state President – dominates appointments. In addition, it is often asked whether they should be independent, given that the courts may obstruct the 'will of the people' as expressed in democratic elections. Some criticize the courts as unrepresentative and suggest that they should play no role whatsoever in making policy. Yet such a role is an inevitable consequence of the Constitutional Court's function of interpreting whether the executive is progressively realizing people's social and economic entitlements under the Bill of Rights to decent housing, health care, and education.

Controversy will continue to surround the authority of the courts. Constitutional government is essential to sustain national consensus and prevent the accumulation of power in the hands of fallible political leaders, but judges cannot be 'above politics'. The law, as Chief Justice Pius Langa has observed, is never 'neutral and objective', but rather 'expresses a particular politics and enforces a singular conception of society'. A constitutional court is a site of special political struggle because the matters before it are ones that have not been settled in lower courts by means of legal reasoning.

There can be merit in explicitly recognizing the political character of a constitutional court. In the United States, the judgments of aspirant Supreme Court justices are scrutinized and an open Senate confirmation process allows judges' legal and political philosophies to be interrogated. In South Africa, citizens are shut out of the opaque proceedings of the JSC and the state president possesses a *de facto* power to select our most important judges.

The legitimacy of the courts has long been fragile in post-apartheid South Africa and a substantial constituency within the ANC has never accommodated itself to constitutional democracy. Lawyers have sometimes been among the Constitution's worst enemies as a result of explosive conflicts among themselves concerning racial and cultural transformation. Yet the law's limited legitimacy has deeper roots. In this intensely conservative society, Constitutional Court judgements concerning abortion, sexuality, and tradition have rendered justices as defenders of minority values and freedoms. A prickly executive has made it hard for the transformational character of the Constitution's socioeconomic rights to be fully expressed and popularly recognized.

Whites have sometimes claimed the Constitution as their own and so denied it to others. Rather than defending constitutionalism, they have tried to freeze in law the historical balance of power that existed during the constitutional negotiations.

Constitutional law does not belong only to minorities and it is too important to be left to the lawyers. If the Constitution's authority is to be entrenched, the wider citizenry needs to be drawn into debates about the character of the law and the jurisprudential inclinations of the judges who are entrusted with its interpretation.

The National Sphere

We have so far looked at the state in terms of the division of labour and authority between its three branches at national level. In the following sections, we look at the three 'spheres' of government, national, provincial, and local, through which the resources of the state are allocated (see Table 5.1). These spheres have been designed to create an integrated state after decades of apartheid-inspired division.

South Africa's segregated society was administered by a fragmented state. A multiplicity of institutions was required to support segregated public services. After 1948 this fragmentation worsened under the impact of petty apartheid legislation and growing imperatives of racial classification and residential segregation. 'High apartheid' took state fragmentation to new extremes, creating supposedly 'independent' sovereign states for each ethnic group. Those classified as Coloured or Indian under this system were accorded specific rights of residence, employment, and access to public services, so necessitating an elaborate bureaucratic nightmare of 'own affairs' departments in every sector.

Table 5.1 Government functions by sphere

Sphere	Key functions	Executive authority	Key challenges and controversies
National	Governance; Policy making; Budgeting; Economic policy; International affairs; Intelligence; Security	President and cabinet; National government departments	Intergovernmental relations; Implementation failures; Monitoring and evaluation; Policy development
Provincial	Health systems; Education Systems; Social welfare (administration); Delegated competencies	Premiers; Provincial executive committees; Provincial government departments	Efficiency and effectiveness; Corruption and patronage; Lack of capacity; Viability of weak provinces
Local	Water and sanitation services; Waste removal; Electricity distribution; Housing and planning; Local economic development; Primary health; Integrated development; Municipal police	Executive Committees OR Executive Mayors	Capacity to implement; Debt; Skills crisis; Lack of basic financial systems; Corruption and patronage; Role of cities

National departments cover the range of activities we expect in any modern state. There are spending departments in health, housing, defence, and education; external affairs departments, in foreign affairs, defence, and intelligence; and security and justice departments, including intelligence, safety, and security, correctional services, justice, and constitutional development, and home affairs. In addition, there are economic

Box 5.2   Kgalema Motlanthe

Kgalema Motlanthe was raised in the Johannesburg township of Alexandra, the son of a clerk and a textile factory machinist. He was profoundly influenced in his youth by a communalist Anglican sect and seriously contemplated a life in the church. Turning instead to anti-apartheid politics, he was sentenced in 1976 under the Terrorism Act to 15 years on Robben Island. There he benefitted from an extensive political education and became a prominent disciple of communist intellectual Govan Mbeki. On his release in 1987 he was employed by the National Union of Mineworkers. He rose to the office of general secretary of the union, and in 1997 he became secretary general of the ANC. While he did not prove to be an especially effective leader or administrator in these positions, he secured for himself a reputation as an unflappable centrist and a principled defender of the unity of the liberation movement. In the turmoil that wracked the ANC in the leadership contest between Thabo Mbeki and Jacob Zuma, Motlanthe emerged as a potential unifier and voice of reason. He was elected deputy president of the ANC in 2007 and he became state president in 2008 upon the ouster of Thabo Mbeki by the new ANC leadership.

departments, such as departments of trade and industry, labour, and minerals, and energy, and others concerned with intergovernmental relations and public sector reform.

The key department is the Treasury which incorporates the roles of finance ministry and public expenditure control department. Under the decisive leadership of Trevor Manuel from 1996 (see Box 3.1), the Treasury launched an ambitious financial management infrastructure for the public service.

Alongside the Treasury, the Presidency is charged with reversing the historical legacy of apartheid fragmentation through policy co-ordination and cabinet committee innovations. As we have seen, it became an especially prominent centre of power during the presidency of Thabo Mbeki (1999–2008) and his immediate successor Kgalema Motlanthe (see Box 5.2).

Provincial Government

The second sphere or tier of government is made up of nine provinces. These provinces are designed to be effective developmental but also political units, roles which sometimes come into conflict with each other. Provinces are responsible for many of the key spending and social transfer functions of government, in education, health, and social welfare (although much of this last function has been transferred to a national agency). For this reason, more monies are allocated to provincial government expenditure than to national – although it is important to recognize that provinces spend this money under tight nationally imposed constraints.

The functions of provinces are set out in some detail but with considerable ambiguity in the constitution. There are areas in which provinces are delegated exclusive responsibility, but primarily their function is in maintaining essential national standards, establishing minimal service standards, and securing essentially national goals of economic development and national security. Where there are conflicts between national and provincial spheres, the national almost always prevails.

Provinces have legislative power over matters in schedules 4 or 5 of the constitution. The schedule 5 'exclusive competencies' of provinces are limited to such areas as ambulance services, liquor licenses, and abattoirs. 80 per cent of provincial budgets are spent on the schedule 4 'concurrent' powers which are exercised together with the national sphere. These include the social sector broadly – especially education (excluding universities), health, and welfare services – but also agriculture, cultural affairs, housing, police services, and public transport. Policy is primarily defined by national government and it is implemented by provinces subject to national norms and standards.

Oversight rather than legislating has been the primary role of provincial parliaments, where they have been active at all, and provinces have a limited capacity to draft legislation. Hence it is national political imperatives and standards for delivery that have held sway, and a national budgetary framework and regulations on financial reporting and accountability that have defined the responsibilities of provincial officers.

Provinces have a Premier and an executive council of 10 members (Members of Executive Council [MECs]). The main portfolios to be found in every province are finance; education; health; social development; agriculture; the environment; housing; local government; safety and security; transport; roads; public works; and sports, arts and culture. Since there are more than ten key provincial portfolios, some MECs in every province are responsible for more than one portfolio.

While their role is primarily to implement national rather than provincial legislation, provinces have scope for developing some provincial policy and for co-ordinating departments to best possible effect. Premiers are elected by the provincial legislatures, but since 1997 the ANC's

National Executive Committee, and then the ANC president, took over responsibility for choosing the premiers in ANC controlled provinces. This power was largely restored to ANC provincial structures in 2007.

MEC's portfolios are broad and the Premier and MECs are collectively and individually accountable to the legislature. Provinces have limited financial powers, with almost all of their revenue coming from central government either through project funding or more normally according to an 'equitable share' formula that is designed to advance equity. The Financial and Fiscal Commission (FFC) (a constitutionally established instrument) details the 'division of revenue' by sphere and then by province taking account of basic service provision and need, the capacity and efficiency of provinces and municipalities, provinces' developmental needs, economic disparities, national legislative obligations, and issues of predictability and stability. A Budget Council made up of Treasury and Finance MECs ultimately dominates the allocation process but it is obliged to take account of the FFC framework and advice in its decisions. There is very limited fiscal federalism with around 97 per cent of provincial budgets made up of transfers from the national fiscus.

The constitution advances an ideal of 'co-operative governance' in which spheres must assist, support, and inform one another, should co-ordinate activities, adhere to agreements, and avoid using the law to settle disputes. The NCOP acts on basis of delegated votes from the provinces. In addition, there is an Intergovernmental Forum (IGF) comprising provincial premiers and national intergovernmental relations ministers, and a Technical Intergovernmental Committee (TIC) made up of Provincial DGs, the DG in the Presidency, the FFC Chair, and the DGs of intergovernmental relations departments. There have been moves towards tighter control by Presidency with the IGF severely downgraded recently. Within the ANC leadership, in addition, there has been much debate about the future of provinces, with many believing that it is the municipalities – and their relationship to national government – that must lie at the centre of effective developmental governance. There has been speculation that some of the provinces may be merged or that the key education and health functions they control will be removed to national agencies.

Local Government

The third 'sphere' of government – the municipalities – has the most troubled history and faces the starkest challenges. Local government under apartheid enjoyed very little popular legitimacy. The quasi-states of the Bantustans were effectively an imposed third tier of government, unelected and unable to deliver public services. Widespread corruption and cronyism plagued them. Over much of South Africa there were simply no local government structures at all, the commercial farmers and White rural populations securing services directly from government agencies while the Black poor went unserviced. This troubled history has guaranteed the municipalities cannot easily fulfil the mass public service delivery role the government envisages for them. Problems with effectiveness and capacity of local institutions are likely to persist for a long time to come.

There are now 282 municipalities which are divided into three categories. There are nine 'Category A' municipalities – known as the metropolitan municipalities or sometimes the 'unicities': Johannesburg, Cape Town, eThekwini (Durban), Nelson Mandela Metropole (Port Elizabeth), Tshwane (Pretoria), Ekurhuleni (East Rand), Buffalo City (East London), Mangaung (Bloemfontein) and Msunduzi (Pietermaritzburg). The 'metros' are all characterized by high population density, extensive economic development, multiple business or industrial districts, and a complex and diverse economic base. They enjoy considerable legislative and executive authority over their area, manage a single municipal budget, and operate a unified tariff system for household services.

Category C municipalities, or 'district councils' are often rudimentary capacity building bodies in areas that often did not possess local government under apartheid. The 46 category C authorities are sometimes based on old 'Regional Services Councils', which were late apartheid creations designed to deliver mass public services in poor rural areas. Brand new districts suffer from a wide variety of capacity and skills deficits. The rural areas they cover often suffer vast backlogs for even the most basic services. Such councils always include within them smaller Category B municipalities.

Category B or 'stand alone' councils share authority with a Category C municipality. Although there are more than 230 of them, they still often cover a vast area. Some are centred on towns or small cities serving historically advantaged communities but they are all the creations of a merger process that was designed to break down apartheid-era demarcations. These have latterly started to provide services to their poorer hinterlands, but usually not very much beyond. Critics of such councils argue they are perpetuating the advantages of historically White towns while doing too little to develop the historically disadvantaged communities that surround them.

The responsibilities of municipalities are diverse and constantly growing. They deal with key infrastructural services such as the reticulation (final point delivery and user-charging) of water and electricity, and waste disposal services. It is in just such areas that the backlog of delivery is most pronounced and the problems of user charge collection are most severe. In addition, municipalities deal with social services and primary health care, and they are responsible for the application of a variety of laws passed by central government. In recent years, their planning, housing, and integrated development roles have received emphasis. Although some Category B councils are performing well, the general picture is of institutions burdened with too many tasks by national government and lacking the skills and capacities to discharge their responsibilities effectively.

While the role of unicities is relatively clear – they enjoy unparalleled authority within their boundaries to develop and deliver services and to discharge their responsibilities – the division of labour between district and local councils is less clear cut. Many responsibilities have been moved to district level and there may over time be a gradual shift of staff, infrastructure, assets, liabilities, records, powers, and functions to districts, in order to permit them to perform a 'developmental' role. A strong lobby within the ANC believes wealthy category B municipalities have been dragging their feet over development and redistribution, and argues not merely for the further empowerment of districts but also for the transfer of further provincial functions and resources to them.

The Treasury and some departments are strongly opposed to this development, arguing that the existing capacity of functioning municipalities cannot be sacrificed and redistributed to unproven and often scarcely operational district councils. Category B authorities that are well-established and organized should instead be obliged to devote more of their energies and resources to improving public services in historically disadvantaged environs. This highly politicized dispute about the roles of different municipalities and the provinces is unlikely to be resolved rapidly.

Decision-making within municipalities follows a complex system. There is mandatory election of councillors every five years, through proportional or mixed systems. The councillors elect a Speaker and either an Executive Mayor or an Executive Committee. Mayors are largely elected by party groups, in most parts of the country by the ANC. Some office holders will be 'full-time' and so are paid – a matter that has become increasingly controversial as salaries have begun to grow without any clear relationship to skills or market-related considerations.

The notion of the Executive Mayor is sometimes proclaimed as an innovation, in the sense that there was no provision for this office in the constitution, although it seems to be derivative of a similar (and mostly unsuccessful) initiative in the United Kingdom. Executive mayors have very generally defined powers, primarily involving the monitoring of council management, which is overseen by the municipal manager, who is also the accounting officer of the municipality. An Executive Committee (which is not a compulsory feature) co-ordinates council structures, makes recommendations, and deals with delegated material from the national and provincial levels. Ad hoc committees on specific issues may include non-councillors.

The functions of municipal executives vary quite widely depending on the nature of the authority in question. Primarily, they are responsible for delivering services, promoting local economic development, and creating a 'safe and healthy environment'. As an elected tier, they are expected to respond to community feedback and to add value to provincially determined policy by tailoring it to local conditions. Most challenging for many municipalities, they are formally charged with achieving financial viability, and this leaves them preoccupied on a day-to-day basis with trying to increasing cost-recovery through service payments, enforcing stringent new legislation on financial management, and attempting to keep control over staff budgets which make up the bulk of their expenditures.

The key issues facing municipalities over the next decade are resources and capacity. All suffer problems of arrears and some are close to technical insolvency. Many district councils are unable to meet statutory requirements for financial management, let alone to conform to the vast range of other guidelines imposed upon them by central government. Financial and service delivery crises have marked many municipalities in recent years. Despite a series of initiatives led by the department of provincial and local government to boost the human resources and administrative systems of failing local authorities, the unhealthy state of local service delivery seem set to continue for years to come and may even substantially worsen. The near collapse of financial management and technical skills in the worst rural municipalities poses a major human development challenge but also a political threat to national government.

At the same time, there remains fundamental conflict about the role of municipalities, the degree to which they can aspire to be the motors of local economic development, and the relationship between local government and the provinces in which they are located. The impending creation of a 'single public service' may result in greater national and provincial intervention in the operations of municipalities.

The unicities confront a different kind of challenge as the engines of national economic growth in the age of globalization. Taken together, the six metropolitan centres together with a handful of other towns are already responsible for half of South Africa's population and two-thirds of economic output. Some of the 'metros' have bigger budgets and more powerful policy and management systems than the smaller provinces, and in the economic heartland of the country, Gauteng, the three metros combined have a budget equivalent to the province in which they are located. Most big cities also boast more complete and skilled administrations – in particular legal, planning, and economic staffs – than almost all government departments. Trends in urbanization and economic growth suggest that big municipalities will increasingly dominate their national and regional economies.

In consequence of these apparently promising trends, there has been much debate about the potential for the country's major urban centres to join the class of 'world cities'. Johannesburg, Tshwane (Pretoria), and Ekurhuleni (East Rand) together, it is sometimes anticipated, will soon emerge as one of the world's great 'city regions'.

Issues of co-ordinated governance between provinces and cities have already emerged, however, and are not always being resolved pragmatically. Provinces have often blocked the devolution of the housing function to cities, for example, in a series of local-provincial power plays. The institutions that co-ordinate governance at national level incorporate the interests and voices of the provinces but not of the cities. This problem is amplified by the fact that the ANC is essentially a province-based organization and provinces are therefore able to dominate cities – to the detriment of the interests of the society as a whole – through ANC structures rather than formal governmental ones.

Challenges and Controversies

The three spheres of government have been settling down after a period of tumultuous change in both structures and functions and it is unfortunate that further upheaval may be inevitable. National government is developing according to a model of co-ordinated and coherent policy making dominated by the Treasury and Presidency. Problems in intergovernmental relations have been addressed with some success by complex institutions operating within provinces and between provinces and national government. The municipalities are moving slowly towards their designated role as developmental arms of the state.

The constitution provides a uniquely South African solution to the problems of accountability and coherent policy making that have bedevilled all modern states. A powerful executive with mechanisms for intergovernmental co-ordination provides the possibility of coherent and integrated policy making, and a sustained drive towards development and growth. At the same time, legislature oversight and the entrenched constitutional authority of the judiciary provide mechanisms through which the abuse of such concentrated power can be averted. The bill of fundamental rights allows for redress where the executive is adjudged to have failed in its duty progressively to deliver on citizens' socio-economic rights. The robustness of this system of accountability, however, and the degree to which other institutions and actors in society are willing or able to support it, remain open questions whose answers will be decided politically. Many authoritarian regimes have enjoyed enlightened constitutions, claimed to guarantee rights, maintained 'independent' judiciaries, and proclaimed adherence to the rule of law. Ultimately any executive is held to account not by careful institutional design but by the efforts of a country's citizens using the full range of its political institutions and associations.

The challenges facing the system of government are bewildering in their variety and depth. Viewed along one dimension, there are massive failures of 'service delivery'. As we saw in Chapter 4, health and educational outcomes are exceptionally poor and backlogs continue to bedevil housing, local infrastructure, and service delivery. Viewed somewhat differently, many of the state's institutions are mired in financial mismanagement, the collapse of basic administrative systems, and the emergence of new forms of corruption and patronage.

These problems are linked to one another by conflicts over the proper distribution of power across the state. At the ANC's 2007 national conference at Polokwane, the movement mandated its leadership to make far-reaching changes to education, health, and social development policy, a proposal underpinned by a renewed conception of popular participation.

Delegates endorsed free basic education and a mass literacy campaign advertised as featuring 80,000 tutors and 5-million adult learners. Health policy was to be revitalised by bringing citizens onto hospital oversight boards. The government and ANC, the conference insisted, must 'take the lead in mobilising communities and all sectors of society to promote responsible sexual behaviour, encourage regular voluntary testing and counselling, improve the access of all to appropriate care and treatment, and to support healthy lifestyles'.

Housing policy innovations such as the promotion of renting and faster state land acquisition were also accompanied by a new embrace of participation. One resolution committed the government to consider 'assisting people with building materials' to encourage 'self-involvement in the provision of housing needs'. Equally, on crime, the ANC identified a need 'to mobilise our communities more effectively', commenting on the positive role street committees could play.

The leftist forces ascendant in the ANC leadership are gambling that participation is a big idea whose time has come and they have also argued that South Africa must become a 'developmental state' (see Chapter 3). The new focus on participation makes sense after a decade of Mbeki's top-down 'delivery state'. It suggests the people can lead the struggle against poverty. Widespread service delivery protests that have become almost a daily phenomenon point to the movement's failure to remain engaged with communities. Channelled, organized participation could bring practical benefits. Community members might ease the burden of the creaking bureaucracy by tracking down corrupt councillors, monitoring school and clinic standards, fighting crime, and acquiring skills to build their own houses. In this way South Africans might feel themselves for the first time full citizens, participating in the remaking of their own country.

Problems overshadow this impressive vision. Many of South Africa's most important challenges, partly overlooked in the rush to mass mobilization, are not very amenable to participatory solutions: ensuring energy security, protecting state technical capacity, developing a sophisticated skills base. Moreover, popular mobilization is a complex and sometimes counterproductive cousin to vigilantism and rule by emotion. It will require a radical change in the culture of public sector intervention and in relations between state and civil society.

A successful developmental state does not merely make good policies that help an economy to grow. It also has the capacity to implement and administer them, to maintain an effective machinery of government, and to protect and grow a culture of honesty and high performance in the public sector.

Many of the fast-growing so-called developmental states of East Asia – such as Japan and South Korea – were famous for the effectiveness of government administrative systems, the high levels of talent attracted to the public service, and the cadres of highly trained and motivated public servants.

A dispassionate analysis of the South African state along these dimensions is not encouraging. On one account, it shows signs of emerging dysfunctionality (Southall 2006). The weaknesses of the South Africa state are no surprise. The ANC created a new system of government out of a late apartheid shambles. The scale of its achievement in incorporating former Bantustans, creating new municipalities and provinces, reconfiguring the centre of the state, developing an integrated national planning framework, and moving to medium-term financial planning, has gone mostly unrecognized (Picard 2005). The transition from authoritarian rule created further vulnerability to corruption and criminality. Moreover, the local state, the legal system, and the police were compromised by the history of apartheid. Bantustan bureaucrats brought with them traditions of bribery, money laundering, and nepotism.

The public health system is close to crisis. The criminal justice system is short of management skills, criminal investigators, and forensic scientists. The local (developmental) state suffers deficiencies in engineering, project management, financial management, and technical skills. The public school system is failing when it comes to basic scientific and mathematical competencies.

The recent and largely unplanned turnover of public officials has not been backed by appropriate training and educational programmes. Institutions have been forced to undergo rapid change that has destroyed institutional memory and the capacity to reproduce skills (Picard 2005). As Sangweni and Mxakato-Diseko (2008) observe, 'It does not matter what slant or take you have on the developmental state: at the end of the day, a strong, coherent and astute public service is critical'. Sangweni picks up Chalmers Johnson's vision of an 'apparatus of plan rationality' (Johnson, 1995: 21–37) in 'a small, inexpensive, but elite bureaucracy, staffed by the best in managerial talent available in the system.' The quality of this bureaucracy, he observes, 'should be measured not so much by the salaries it can command as by its excellence, as demonstrated academically and competitively, preferably in the best schools.' Participation may be one part of the solution to the country's emerging crisis of state institutions. The building of the capacity of the state to match the ambitions of the government and the needs of the people will be another, quite different, task.

Controversy has also surrounded the institution of 'traditional leadership'. Despite the historical association of the chiefs with the Bantustans and with the divide-and-rule strategies of the apartheid era, the Constitution provides for the recognition of the institution and status of traditional leadership. Government has legislated to clarify and formalize the role of traditional councils in development and the scope of application of customary law. A new department of traditional affairs is being created to regulate what appear to be the resurgent powers of these institutions. Critics claim that such moves are a retrograde step and encourage anti-democratic and patriarchal practices at odds with the new constitutional order. Defenders counter that tribalism and sexism were merely apartheid era perversions of traditional authority and that there must be a place for these supposedly indigenous systems in the governance of rural South Africa.

As we will see in the next chapter, there are wider issues surrounding the legitimacy of parliamentary democracy and constitutional government. The supreme law, as we shall see, is by no means yet supreme.

6

Political Life

South African politics in the last century was dominated by the exploitation and oppression of the majority of the country's people by its White minority and by the struggle to establish fundamental social and political equality. After 1948, a key secondary issue was concealed behind this overarching conflict: the implications for the quality of political life of increasingly authoritarian single party domination by the National Party (NP). The shadow of apartheid continues to hang over the country's political life. While a democratic system has transformed the political class and aspects of political participation, South African politics still turns around historically familiar issues. How can the vast racial imbalances of wealth and opportunity in the society be reduced? What will be the implications of one-party electoral dominance – today of the African National Congress (ANC) – for the quality of the country's new democracy?

The Electoral System

South Africa is a representative democracy with elections at national, provincial, and local levels. The 1996 constitution prescribes that two legislative bodies are to be elected at national level, the National Assembly (NA) and the National Council of Provinces (NCOP). In addition, it stipulates that the electoral system must be based on a common national voters' roll and that it must result 'in general' in proportional representation. The system chosen to fulfil this mandate for the national parliament was a highly proportional party list system, in which each party draws up closed and rank-ordered national and provincial lists of candidates for parliament. Elections are held every five years. The NA has 400 members, 200 of whom are elected on national lists and

200 on the basis of provincial lists (with each province getting provincial list members in proportion to its population). The NA elects the President who is the head of the executive branch of government, and who is responsible for governing in conjunction with the cabinet, which he appoints.

The nine provincial legislatures are elected on a separate but simultaneous ballot. Provincial legislatures in less populous provinces (such as Northern Cape and Mpumalanga) have a relatively small number of members. Because the thresholds for winning a single seat are extremely low, the system encourages a very wide range of parties to compete both nationally and provincially. Local authorities are elected on a different cycle to national and provincial spheres. Elections in major unicities, especially in eThekwini (Durban) and Cape Town, have been strongly contested and have the potential to produce surprises in future elections.

Members of national and provincial assemblies and municipalities lose their seats if they are ejected, or resign, from the party on whose list they were elected. (Government enacted controversial and opportunistic 2002 legislation to enable windows of 'floor crossing' during which changes in party affiliation were possible. This allowed the ANC to secure a mid-term two-thirds majority in early 2003, and threatened the viability of many smaller parties. It has since been repealed.) Critics complain that the electoral system is bedevilled by excessive centralization of party control, and provides for too little interaction between representatives and citizens. Some have argued for the introduction of a partially constituency-based system to reconcile participation with proportionality. Notwithstanding the commissioning of a major review of the electoral system by the Minister of Home Affairs, however, further changes to a system that well suits ANC party managers are highly unlikely.

The Electorate

The South African electorate is sophisticated in both regional and global terms. As a result of the country's long history of rural-urban migrancy and political organization, the politics of the peasantry that characterizes many developing countries has been little in evidence. Anti-apartheid campaigning created national cross-class and anti-ethnic political networks. South Africa entered the democratic era with strong levels of partisan identification, with nine out of every ten voters strongly committed to the support of a particular party. Strong racial and ethnic echoes could be seen in White and Coloured support for the NP, rural Zulu support for the Inkatha Freedom Party (IFP), and overwhelming support among Africans more generally for the ANC (although this party secured votes from all racial and ethnic groups).

The analysis of voter behaviour was until recently highly unsatisfactory because researchers' assumptions about race and ethnicity undermined attitude, opinion, and voter surveys as well as other kinds of social science research (Taylor and Orkin 1995). Whites were treated as 'normal' objects of political enquiry, whereas 'Blacks politics' was viewed through the lenses of anthropology or as a 'mass' social phenomenon. Priority was accorded to ethnic and racial categories and assumptions were made about ethnic identity and social structure that were often highly inappropriate to the social fluidity and geographical mobility of the country's individuals and households. Ethnicity – as opposed to income, age, gender or any other factor – was on occasion the only analytic category employed in major surveys (for example in Johnson and Schlemmer 1996).

In recent years, however, scientifically reliable data on public opinion has been made available in South Africa (and elsewhere on the continent) by Afrobarometer, and the development of new data sets has encouraged a wealth of new empirical research and analysis (see for example Mattes 2007). Two trends in the character of the electorate that such research has identified are especially significant. First, levels of identification with particular political parties have declined quite steeply among South African electors. A growing number of citizens can now be described as 'floating voters' who are not strongly bound to a particular party and may increasingly use evaluations of party performance to inform their electoral choices (Schulz-Herzenberg 2007).

Second, and a matter for some concern, floating voters are not yet at least 'realigning' themselves with parties they have chosen on the basis of interest or an evaluation of performance. Instead they are becoming alienated more generally from the party political system. While the percentage of actual votes cast for the ANC increased to almost 70 per cent by 2004, the percentage of potential voters – of the eligible electorate as a whole – that did so fell to less than 40 per cent. This fall in participation in national elections has been hidden because it has impacted equally on both the ANC and on opposition parties (see Table 6.1). It raises the concern that the ANC may be elected in future years by a growing proportion of a declining electorate.

The improved quality of social science research for the first time allows study of the country's political and social attitudes in comparative context and over time. Such studies can provide insights into how

Table 6.1   Trends in voter turnout, 1994–2004

	1994	1999	2004
Potential voters (PVs)* millions	22.71	22.59	27.87
% Turnout of PVs	86.0	71.8	57.8
Actual votes (AVs) cast millions	19.53	15.98	15.61
% of AVs cast for the ANC	63.1	66.35	69.7
% of AVs cast for the opposition	36.9	33.65	30.3
% of PVs voting ANC	53.8	46.9	39.0
% PVs voting for opposition	32.1	23.7	16.9
% of PVs abstaining	14.0	29.4	43.9

*Voting age population (over 18) eligible to vote by RSA citizenship

Source: Adapted from Schulz-Herzenberg 2007.

citizens understand democracy, what they view as significant issues, and the degree to which they respect and trust state institutions and political leaders.

South Africans are quite positive about their system of government but they tend to view democracy instrumentally. Two-thirds of them see democracy as primarily a matter of delivering jobs, basic necessities, and education rather than as a set of processes such as free elections, multi-party competition, and freedom of speech (Mattes 2002). Public confidence in state institutions showed a steady improvement in first decade of democracy, but it has since demonstrated a marked decline, perhaps as a result of political scandal and the prolonged inability of government to deliver on electoral and other implicit political promises.

Party Support and Political Parties

The key fact of political life in South Africa is the degree to which the ANC dominates the county's electoral and political life. Conceiving itself as a 'liberation movement' rather than merely a political party, the ANC currently commands the allegiance of around two-thirds of those who vote in national and local elections. Through a series of alliances with the Congress of South African Trade Unions (COSATU) and the South African Communist Party (SACP) – but also with key 'opposition' parties such as IFP and the former New NP – the ANC has dominated the political terrain and seems set to do so for many years to come (see Table 6.2). Its own intellectual frameworks and political

Table 6.2   National election results 1994, 1999, 2004 and 2009 (per cent)

Party name	1994	1999	2004	2009
African National Congress	62.6	66.4	70	65.9
Democratic Alliance*	1.7	9.6	12.4	16.7
Inkatha Freedom Party	10.5	8.6	7	4.6
Congress of the People	–	–	–	7.4
United Democratic Movement	–	3.4	2.3	0.9
Independent Democrats	–	–	1.7	0.9
(New) National Party	20.4	6.9	1.7	–
African Christian Democratic Party	0.5	1.4	1.6	0.8
Freedom Front Plus	2.2	0.8	0.9	0.8
Pan Africanist Congress	1.2	0.7	0.7	0.3
Other	0.9	2.2	3.4	2.0

*Formerly Democratic Party

Source: Sadie 2001; Electoral Commission 2004, 2009.

processes – rather than the institutions of constitutional democracy – will forge the society's sense of collective purpose and make its key political and policy choices.

The African National Congress

The ANC emerged relatively recently as the pre-eminent force in South African politics, and as the almost unchallenged voice for its people's liberation. Founded in 1912 as the South African National Native Congress, the Congress has an extended history of internal factionalism, detachment from mass political organization, and political conservatism. In the 1920s and 1930s, these weaknesses lead to the marginalization of the Congress. In the period of economic growth and influx to the urban areas of the 1940s, however, the Youth League was established by a militant generation of leaders, including Anton Lembede, Oliver Tambo, Nelson Mandela and Walter Sisulu, propagating a mild variant of pan-Africanist Black nationalism. Faced with NP government from 1948, the ANC launched a series of defiance campaigns that for the first time brought it a position of national leadership, and provided a foundation for mass membership. The ANC joined with other anti-segregation forces in the 1950s to propagate the 'Freedom Charter', a quasi-socialist and non-racialist agenda which retained influence in later decades. Papering over divisions between Africanists and non-racialists, the charter did not, however, prevent the breakaway in 1959 of the Pan Africanist Congress (PAC) with its more activist Black nationalist agenda.

The political turmoil of the 1940s and 1950s culminated in the suppression of opposition activity from 1960. The ANC was declared illegal and commenced an underground armed struggle operating increasingly from neighbouring countries. The military wing of the ANC, 'spear of the nation' (Umkhonto we Sizwe or just MK), embarked on a long and ultimately fruitless campaign of espionage against a state with overwhelming military and intelligence superiority. Key ANC leaders, including Mandela, were jailed for treason in the 1963 Rivonia trial, and other ANC leaders moved into extended 'exile', in neighbouring countries, the United Kingdom, Scandinavia, the Soviet Union, and East Germany among others.

The behaviour of the ANC as a political movement in government has been greatly influenced by three broad traditions: imprisonment, exile, and domestic civic and labour struggle. Beyond the famous older Robben Island generation, including Mandela, the experience of prison was diverse, with generational, gender, and racial divides. The exile experience, if anything, was still more varied, with exiles engaging in all manner of activities – military, intelligence, or diplomatic – in a host of sometimes authoritarian settings. Domestic struggle, likewise, took many forms, with certain key individuals formed by trade union activity while others were politically forged through community activism. The foot-soldiers of the final decade of domestic struggle achieved a form of collective self-determination that was ultimately to collide with the hierarchical and authoritarian organizational traditions of exile and imprisonment.

Ideological diversity has also been marked, with many deeply religious activists co-operating with equally numerous communists and traditionalists. Communism was especially influential in the development of the ANC. The institutional embodiment of communism, the SACP, was formed in 1921, and went through periods of failed multi-racialism and Stalinisation before adopting an unexceptional if slavish pro-Moscow profile after the Second World War. After its banning in 1950, it engaged actively in entryism of the ANC and became influential in the Congress movement's adoption of a non-racial position. Members of the SACP continued to consider themselves as a vanguard within the ANC, or as the most 'progressive' element within it, a self-conception that sometimes persists notwithstanding a repudiation of Leninist categories of cadre organization.

The 'tripartite' alliance between the ANC, COSATU, and the SACP has on occasion been convulsed with conflict but it has in the past allowed the ANC to represent an exceptionally wide constituency. The SACP was very much affected by the demise of communism in the USSR, and this epochal event led to mass resignations as well as to many doctrinal and political changes. The legitimacy of a party that does not stand for election under its own banner cannot be sustained forever. Economic policy, in addition, led to inevitable and growing tensions between the ANC and COSATU. The three movements' memberships, however, overlap very substantially. Almost all SACP cadres are also ANC members, and the leadership of COSATU has strong links with both parties. Until recently it was difficult to conceive of circumstances within which a conclusive rupture might occur.

With its leadership mostly imprisoned or in exile between the early 1960s and the early 1990s, the ANC played a marginal role in the decisive labour movement and popular domestic struggles of the 1980s. Nevertheless, the ANC embraced labour and civil society allies in the transition period and it was widely acknowledged as the natural party of government. As it became a mass political movement it demonstrated a capacity to reconcile disparate interests and to develop a coherent overall programme of government. Over its first decade of rule, it also became an impressive electoral machine. Yet the ANC's current leadership as a whole seems to possess no special attachment to representative democracy. The liberation movement's democratic tendencies co-exist with democratic centralist and hierarchical conceptions of legitimate authority. The struggle between these elements is unlikely to be decisively resolved in the foreseeable future.

The ANC has used its dominant position to pursue a number of important goals. Political violence has been drastically curtailed, and the territorial conflict that characterized the 1994 elections has been reduced. It has elaborated an integrated programme of government that has helped to contain social conflict and stabilized the democratic settlement. Its carefully constructed programmes have helped to structure citizens' electoral choices, filtered, prioritized and reconciled demands, and neutralized potentially divisive ideological conflict. Electoral invulnerability, moreover has allowed the ANC to enforce an unpopular but necessary programme of economic stabilization.

Finally, it has discouraged the racial and ethnic conflict that many thought inevitable in post-apartheid society. The liberation movement has emphasized that tribalism was 'invented' by missionaries and colonial administrators to 'divide and rule', control native populations, and exploit their labour. Ethnic tensions have been subtle, and occur as much within as between language groups, but their emergence as a significant force in political life cannot be ruled out. The ANC has relentlessly promoted non-racialism as an ideology and as a guide to practice, regulating internal discussion of ethnicity and preventing 'factional' competition for office. Ethnic balance has been a cornerstone of ANC party lists and National Executive Committee (NEC) elections, and both key ANC institutions and cabinet itself have exhibited a carefully managed diversity.

These various accomplishments would not have been possible without the movement's transition from party of exile to a mass movement. The ANC combines the hierarchy and democratic centralism of an exile movement with the mass organizational politics that once characterized domestic anti-apartheid struggle. The rigorous organization and discipline of exile have proved useful traits for effective electoral competition. Members continue to voice their demands for participation, and committed activists bewail any dilution of the party's ideological character in the pursuit of wider electoral support. As an electoral party, however, the ANC has predictably become 'catch-all' in character.

The diversity of interests and voices that the movement accommodates dictate that both central discipline and wider deliberation are necessary to maintain political unity. A wide activist base remains essential for the ANC to mobilize electors at registration and voting time, and to enhance the legitimacy and understanding of the movement's programme of government. The ANC's system of alliances allows diverse class and ideological interests to be represented. The key relationship is the 'tripartite alliance' with the COSATU and the SACP. The SACP is essentially a faction within the liberation movement, although it possesses residual independence and periodically makes symbolic threats to leave the alliance. COSATU operates in a competitive environment that limits its leaders' ability to strike lasting deals with the ANC. COSATU activists are generally ANC supporters, however, and often important opinion formers and branch leaders.

The ANC's wider allies include the South African National Civics Organization (SANCO), the decayed residual shell of a once an important tradition of community level organization. The ANC has also engaged in relationships of varying depth and endurance with Africanist and black consciousness competitors, the IFP, and the New NP (which the ANC ultimately swallowed).

Three major challenges have been posed for the ANC in recent years. First, a growing proportion of the ANC's active membership has no direct experience of the struggle for liberation, and no intrinsic respect for conventions of authority in the movement. Many older ANC supporters are uncertain whether their tradition of reconciling diverse interests in the pursuit of 'national democratic revolution' will survive generational change and the fading of the morality of the struggle.

Second the ANC has been suffering from 'careerism' – the use of the movement by its members as a stepping stone to political office or public positions that can be abused for personal gain. The senior leadership has been hampered in its efforts to address this growing scourge by its own open pursuit of wealth and its own ethically dubious behaviour.

Third, internal politics of the ANC has been marked by tumultuous conflict in recent years. Thabo Mbeki's faction tried to suppress competition for senior ANC offices in order to prolong its hold on power. Mbeki's intention appeared to be to remain the most powerful national political leader, retaining the presidency of the liberation movement and controlling the outcome of the succession to the state presidency. This effort backfired dramatically when Mbeki's competitor Jacob Zuma swept to the ANC presidency in December 2007. Zuma was the figurehead for a wider revolt by the SACP and COSATU, the KwaZulu-Natal (KZN) ANC, and a wide range of other malcontents victimized by Mbeki or alienated by his style. Almost all Mbeki-aligned members of the ANC leadership were voted off the NEC and then in mid-2008 Mbeki was forced to stand down as state president by the new ANC leadership. Moderate veteran Kgalema Motlanthe took over the presidency in what was widely assumed to be an interim measure, pending Jacob Zuma's selection as the ANC candidate for president in advance of the 2009 elections.

The turmoil of the succession battle generated further battalions of discontented activists and political leaders. Indeed, in November of 2008, former ANC leaders Mosiuoa Lekota, Sam Shilowa, and Mluleki George launched a new party, the Congress of the People (COPE) ostensibly determined to battle the liberation movement in future elections.

Opposition Parties

We have observed that the electorate is increasingly available for capture by the opposition but that the smaller parties have so far experienced little success in building their electoral support. Instead increasing numbers of voters are opting out of elections altogether and declining to cast their ballot in favour of any of the available choices.

The strategies of opposition political parties have been the subject of much debate. On the one hand, many observers believe that the country requires a robust opposition to counter ANC dominance and to provide the possibility of an alternative government. On the other hand, other analysts suggest robust opposition will threaten the fragile stability and political co-operation that a new democracy requires.

The Democratic Alliance (DA), formerly the Democratic Party (DP), has been a consistent champion of the first view. The avowedly 'liberal' DP was formed in 1989 in a merger of four small centrist parties in the all White parliament. It served as official opposition to the NP from that year, supporting a programme of non-racial democracy, a limited state, constitutional supremacy and a market economy. It was trounced in the 1994 election by F W de Klerk's NP which almost monopolized the White vote.

Under Tony Leon, its leader for most of the post-apartheid period, the DP followed a consistent strategy of building its vote from less than 2 per cent in 1994 by bending, and occasionally sacrificing, its underlying liberal principles. Leon was a combative and skilled performer who led the party to a major milestone in 1999 by securing the second biggest vote share (9.6 per cent) and so the status of Official Opposition. This success was achieved by campaigning under a 'fight back' slogan that was widely perceived by Black citizens to be racist. Leon then negotiated an alliance with the NP to form the DA, an entity that rapidly collapsed – but primarily to the cost of the NP. The DA walked away with a bolstered membership and the prospect of securing power in the Western Cape in future elections while the NP was forced to throw itself on the mercies of its old enemy, the ANC.

Leon's successor as DA leader, Helen Zille, led the party to control of the Western Cape in 2009. This will allow the DA to demonstrate by example what it considers to be the lamentable shortcomings of the ANC as a party of government. Zille has, however, inherited the intractable challenges of the Leon era: how to build support among Black, and especially African voters; how to remain a credible liberal party with a membership and activist base heavily populated with reactionary Whites; and how to build a candidate base attractive to the full range of the country's voters. Despite its high level of organization and capacity, the DA has been unable to establish any clear line of intellectual attack against the ANC, in part because the liberation movement has adopted so centrist and largely unexceptionable a policy programme.

The NP, founded in 1914 as a vehicle for Afrikaner ethnic nationalism, was one of the twentieth century's most successful political parties.

It governed without interruption between 1948 and 1994, in which period it built and ultimately dismantled the system of apartheid. The party transformed the political landscape of South Africa, securing hegemony across the White electorate while catapulting Afrikaners to near income equality with English-speakers. Its performance since 1994 has been both unexpected and ironic. The NP gained credit alongside the ANC for its willingness to participate in negotiations, to concede a relatively bloodless transfer of power, and to participate in the Government of National Unity between 1994 and 1996.

After picking up a fifth of the vote in the 1994 election, the NP played a crucial role in convincing international markets and domestic business of the stability and fiscal rectitude of the incoming liberation movement. When it abandoned the national unity government for opposition in 1996, however, its supporters deserted in droves for the more confrontational opposition of the DP. In 1999, the NP was reduced to a regional party in the Western Cape, deriving most of its support from the Coloured South Africans it had oppressed in the apartheid era. Picking up the pieces after this reversal, its new leader Marthinus van Schalkwyk re-branded the party as the 'New' NP and embarked upon opportunistic alliances with the DP and then with the ANC. The ANC's false friendship, however, was motivated by a desire to seize control of the Western Cape, and its embrace proved to be fatal to the NP. Western Cape electors abandoned it in 2004 and the party was quickly and ignominiously absorbed into the ANC.

The IFP is not only South Africa's most prominent vehicle for ethnic mobilization but also the personal instrument of its leader Mangosuthu Buthelezi. It has historically campaigned on a Zulu nationalist platform – today toned down for wider public consumption – and its electorate is drawn predominantly from the rural population of the most populous province, KZN. The IFP's support base has been inexorably eroded by the ANC as the Zulu-speaking population of the province has become increasingly urbanized. The key significance of the movement has been in its now intermittent challenges to ANC provincial hegemony in KZN, and in its ability to use violence as a veto on political change in the province.

Three smaller parties, the PAC, the United Democratic Movement (UDM), and the Independent Democrats (ID) continue to enjoy influence greater than their tiny vote shares would lead one to expect. As parties led by and primarily supported by Black South Africans, their voices have disproportionate weight in a country in which Whites' attacks on government can be trivialized as racially motivated. The PAC, longstanding historical rival to the ANC, has been bedevilled by the infighting that comes with a sense of electoral hopelessness. Even as its share of the vote has collapsed beyond recovery, the party has continued to tear itself apart with internal factionalism.

The UDM was created by the former Transkei homeland leader Bantu Holomisa and NP constitutional negotiator Roelf Meyer. Its limited support base is concentrated in the Eastern Cape and depends on the charismatic authority of Holomisa – a man who had been very popular in the ANC after 1994 but who had been expelled for levelling highly plausible allegations of corruption against a cabinet Minster. The ID is a recent creation of feisty politician Patricia de Lille, herself a former PAC activist. It has an ostensibly non-racial approach but has an overwhelmingly Coloured and Western Cape based membership. All of these smaller parties have been hit hard by effective ANC campaigning and until recently by 'floor-crossing' legislation that allowed the ANC to poach their electorally vulnerable representatives.

The significant new player in South African electoral politics is COPE, a party formed by a breakaway faction of ANC leaders in November 2008. The long-term prospects of this party remain uncertain and its character has been interpreted in a number of quite different ways. Some analysts have seen it as offering a fresh start for South Africa's democracy because of what they see as the direct threat COPE poses to the electoral dominance of the ANC.

Others argue that COPE's key organizational strengths lie among Xhosa-speakers in the Eastern and Western Cape and that it is therefore destined to become a regional party – or even an ethnic formation akin to KZN's IFP. Finally, some cynics view the new party as a vehicle designed to save the skins of members of Thabo Mbeki's defeated faction of the ANC. Threatened with a complete loss of authority within the liberation movement, these Mbeki-supporters always intended COPE as an externalized faction of the ANC rather than as an autonomous political party. If COPE is viewed in this light, it is probable that it will determinedly exploit opportunities for provincial coalition government with the ANC, and that over the longer term it will seek a reintegration with the mother body.

Civil Society

It is often remarked that South Africa possesses a 'vibrant civil society' but the political significance – and even the truth – of this claim is in fact difficult to establish. The varied associational life of the country is exemplified by the churches and sporting associations that dominate recreational activity at weekends. In the 1980s heyday of the anti-apartheid struggle, the United Democratic Front (UDF) brought together a variety of religious, student, labour, cultural, and civic associations in the battle against state oppression. When it comes to political engagement today, however, only a relatively narrow range of pressure groups and social movements continue to exercise much impact.

Pressure or interest groups – associations of people with shared goals or values that try to influence the policy process – are in some respects distinct from political parties. They do not seek directly to govern, they have a narrow membership, they typically focus on a number of specific issues, and they escape accountability to the wider electorate. The most powerful groups of this kind in today's South Africa are producer groups: trade unions and businesses, and the representative bodies that speak and campaign on their behalf.

Some analysts have viewed South Africa as a 'corporatist' state, in which the interests of labour and business have been formally incorporated into the policy making process. However the country's quasi-corporatist bargaining forum, the National Economic Development and Labour Council (NEDLAC), has become a talking shop in recent years, its chambers increasingly bypassed by powerful business and labour interests who seek to exert more direct influence over the state. Both trade unions and business federations suffer from organizational fragmentation that makes it difficult for them to engage in productive corporatist bargaining. The most powerful union federation COSATU has used its relationship with the ANC to secure and protect gains in industrial relations legislation and public sector job protection. Where conflict has escalated between COSATU and the government, notably over privatization policy, the union federation has resorted to campaigns, strikes, and political mobilization within the alliance to get its way, rather than depending on NEDLAC structures.

Business has also bypassed corporatist structures. The South African private economy has been dominated historically by a small number of very large resources groups with operations across mining, manufacturing, services, and the financial sector. Such big businesses possess the political weight to demand an audience with government on their own terms. ANC leaders have had to remain extremely sensitive to the demands of domestic and international big business, and direct channels of communication between business and the presidency remain open for lobbies such as the National Business Institute and Business

Leadership South Africa. Smaller business groups, still prone to faction-alism and paralysed for a decade by racial divisions between the South African Chamber of Business (SACOB) and National African Chamber of Commerce (NAFCOC), have been far less effective at campaigning for influence. However, the Black Economic Empowerment (BEE) pro-cess has deepened the political connectivity of established business and created a new awareness of mutual dependency in board-rooms and gov-ernment corridors alike.

As we have seen, this process of deepening relationships between government and business has been progressing unevenly and fitfully. Many ministers remain (or claim to remain) emotionally or ideologically aligned with labour and continue to be suspicious of the intentions of big business. BEE has itself sparked furious conflicts over the slow pace of change in the situations of individual Black business people and as a result of the glacially slow shift in the extent of overall Black ownership in the economy.

Civil society associations and organisations that proclaim universal goals or declare that they act on behalf on humanity as a whole are almost always weaker than their sectional cousins. However, South Africa has historically possessed large numbers of active non-governmental organ-izations (NGOs), churches, and campaign groups. Before 1994, the vast majority of these groups were aligned with the ANC through the UDF, or at least strongly opposed to apartheid, but the post-1994 period has seen most of them struggling to retain influence in a less indulgent donor environment.

Voluntary campaign groups have suffered from shortages of resources and limited access to the media. Most importantly, perhaps, these crea-tures of the anti-apartheid struggle have remained unwilling to confront and criticize the ANC they once championed. Many activists have moved into government as officials or as politicians. The past seven or eight years, however, have seen a renaissance in localized political campaign-ing through the creation of networks of community-based mass move-ments. Such campaign groups, often strongly opposed to government policy and practice, have taken to the streets in defiance of erstwhile ANC allies, and often with the support of the ANC-aligned trade unions. For some years, Thabo Mbeki's government characterized them as 'ultra-leftists' and portrayed them as disloyal to the liberation struggle.

The rebirth of oppositional civil society after a decade of transitional quiescence is certainly not an unequivocal triumph. Some of the new social movements are led by anti-democratic ideologues. Others take too idealistic an approach to the perceived evils of globalization and international capitalism and condemn as imperfect government programmes that are bringing real advances to disadvantaged citizens. Many of the new campaign networks began as issue-based movements. The most visible and long established of the campaign groups has been the Treatment Action Campaign (TAC), campaigning effectively and creatively since 1998 against the government's policies on the treatment and support of those living with HIV/AIDS. The TAC's primary public focus has been on the public provision anti-retroviral treatments, in the first instance to prevent the transmission of HIV from pregnant mother to child and then for the rollout of a 'universal' public treatment programme for all infected South African residents. The TAC has used a variety of campaigning instruments: public protest, constitutional challenges, and, from 2003, a mass programme of non-violent civil disobedience. The larger National Association of People Living with HIV/AIDS (NAPWA) has pursued its avowed goals of de-stigmatization and safe sex with far less energy, and it has adopted a highly conciliatory approach towards government.

Another prominent group, the National Land Committee (NLC), was established in 1987 through the countrywide affiliation of land reform organizations. Over time it became an increasingly vehement (and perhaps decreasingly coherent) critic of government policy on rural and urban land redistribution. A far more fluid and anti-hierarchical mass movement closely aligned with the NLC, the Landless People's Movement, has since taken up assertive positions on farm labourers' rights and the need for a more ambitions land reform strategy.

Perhaps the most famous new social movement, the Soweto Electricity Crisis Committee (SECC), was established in 2000 to protest against electricity disconnections of payment defaulters by the parastatal Eskom. It has conducted illegal reconnections through its 'Operation Khanyisa' (light). More recently it has diversified into protesting against water cut-offs and the eviction of rent or bond (housing loan) defaulters. SECC appears to have among its executive leadership both community activists, union activists, and leftist intellectuals, and it has relationships with wider 'anti-privatisation' networks.

Similar umbrella organizations now exist in major urban areas across South Africa. In Cape Town, for example, a vigorous Anti-Eviction Campaign which emerged in 2000 around the issue of township bond-default evictions today includes water and electricity campaigning in its portfolio. The most militant and ambitious leftist grouping, formed in 2000, is the Anti-Privatization Forum (APF). The APF is dominated by organized labour and by members of the radical left disenchanted with the ANC's priorities and performance in power. Organized initially against privatization and public-private partnerships for the provision of municipal infrastructure, the APF has become an umbrella for more than a dozen other campaign groups, including SECC. At the bottom of these hierarchies of groups, there are many thousands of small community groups organized in opposition to local drug dealers and corrupt municipal politicians, or in support of myriad local economic projects and developmental initiatives. Such groups are themselves often formed around or out of savings associations, burial societies, or local civic associations.

The significance of these protest movements is widely debated. A lively dialogue continues within the liberation movement, in particular, about the proper role of pressure groups and citizens' protests. Against the backdrop of increasing irritation on the part of official and ministers with anti-privatization, landless people's, and HIV/AIDS campaigns, government has sought to increase central control over donor funds to bring the NGO sector into line with its strategic priorities. Some ANC leaders are growing increasingly sceptical that pressure group activity is conducive to democracy – while they are themselves accused by radicals of being in the pockets of business interests. Favouring integrated executive-driven policy, they do not welcome opposition to specific parts of a manifesto or an increased responsiveness of the political system to minorities.

Many liberation movement leaders habitually reiterate the centrality of majority rule to democracy, and stress the dangers of allowing undue minority influence on policy. Sectional interest groups, they claim, may impose very heavy costs on non-members through their actions – and especially through their self-serving investment decisions, the improper influence they can exert on policy makers and officials and the disruption they can cause to non-members.

Of all of the potential abusers of organizational power, it would seem to be businesses that pose the greatest threat to the integrity of the policy process and the rights of citizens. However, business people appear to have neutralized their once-vocal antagonists in the ANC. Instead it is the social movements and campaigning NGOs representing the poor and dispossessed that have been the targets of the greatest hostility. ANC leaders often darkly remark that groups like TAC are the recipients of foreign funding. On occasion, the same critics (and notably, on one very public occasion in 2003, the then Health Minister Manto Tshabalala-Msimang) have referred to the disproportionate influence of White intellectuals and activists within new social movements and campaign groups. The weak and the poor who support the ANC in elections, on this view, cannot organize as effectively as the White or ultra-leftist leaders of these atypical and 'unpatriotic' social movements.

More acceptable to the ANC has been the notion that civil society actors can provide the government with vital information and knowledge and act as partners in delivery of public services. In particular, such partners can inform the government about the issues that trouble particular sections of the community, highlight implementation failures, and provide suggestions for policy improvement. This role is once again significant in South Africa where government capacity is stretched, and the government is showing new willingness to work on 'delivery issues' with NGO partners. Some NGOs perform valuable knowledge generating and political oversight functions, with Institute for Democracy in South Africa (IDASA) and Electoral Institute of Southern Africa (EISA) at one time especially noteworthy in this regard. Such organizations have trodden a fine line in their relationships with a government that has not been indulgent of open criticism. Other NGOs have been drawn into extended consulting for government on policy, and into acting primarily as its implementing agents.

South Africa has yet to reach any national consensus on the proper role of voluntary associations – a debate that is part of the political process in any democracy. South Africans' sometimes moralizing approach to politics does not much leave space for the pluralist notion that individuals acting together, self-interestedly, and in furtherance of their particular goals, can unintentionally create better outcomes for all.

One Party Dominance

The central focus of contemporary South African political analysis has been the future and quality of its democracy. Comparative social scientists sometimes claim that the performance of new democracies elsewhere can shed light on South Africa's prospects, and on the conditions it must meet if its democracy is to be 'consolidated'. Yet using comparative political analysis to predict or improve the future is not easy. It is difficult at the best of times to generalize about complex processes on the basis of a small number of cases, but well-nigh impossible when the comparative framework is based on wholly inappropriate categories. Models used to understand democracy in Africa originated in quite different circumstances and have been shaped by historical experiences in other regions. The southern European democratic blossoming of 1974–76, influenced by the death of autocrats and colonial wars, helped to undermine what had been highly determinist assumptions about democratisation. The spill over of these changes into Latin American liberalization further emphasized the significance of human agency and historical contingency in overturning authoritarian rule. The rapid and bunched east and central European transitions, with their 'contagion effects' and external precipitation in Moscow, resulted in a further productive intellectual reconfiguration. African 'democratisation', by contrast, generated no fundamental theoretical innovations, and its distinct causal dynamic of post Cold War external engineering and imposed good governance continue to be treated as anomalous. The fallacy advanced by democracy promotion and protection experts everywhere – that if specific features of enduring democracies are absent in a particular country then they must be introduced forthwith – is at its least credible in Africa.

Systematic cross-national analysis has identified broad sets of factors – economic growth, stable political institutions, and an appropriate political culture – that have elsewhere and in the past been associated with measures of democratic persistence. Yet each of these sets of factors in South Africa, according to one lucid analysis, presents a 'paradox' rather than any clear basis for judgement (Mattes 2002). Macro-economic stability sits uneasily alongside low investment and extreme unemployment; state-of-the-art mechanisms of accountability are vitiated by one-party dominance; and a diverse civil society accompanies uneven commitment to democracy and participation.

Most domestic political authors treat 'consolidation' as little more than a semantic issue, believing that the key formal attributes of liberal polyarchy are entrenched for the next decade or more, while ANC electoral domination precludes any transfer of power. The focus of local investigation has therefore been on the quality of political life under a period of extended 'one-party dominance', and on the implications of such dominance for the longer-term future of the political system.

The common expectation of protracted ANC electoral dominance is probably well-founded. Intermittent proposals to bring the major opposition parties together promise to muster only a third of the vote, and obstacles to opposition coalition-building remain formidable. A split in the ruling alliance and the enduring desertion of a substantial body of its followers appear to be necessary conditions for the emergence of an alternative government. A shift to the left at the ANC's 2007 national conference has demonstrated once again the movement's ability to reinvent itself through internal realignments and so to retain an overarching unity.

South Africa's constitutional framework enables an electorally dominant party to achieve a preponderance of political power in the executive and legislature very directly. The 1996 constitution perpetuates the country's traditionally centralized system of executive authority. Despite certain 'concurrent powers' and a language of 'co-operative governance', the state is essentially unitary and almost no revenue-raising or legislative authority is delegated to the provinces. Parliament is a bloated and largely reactive policy-influencing legislature on the Westminster model in which party discipline is reinforced by a party-list proportional system that permits the 'redeployment' of disloyal legislators.

The ANC's overwhelming political power under this system has been greeted both positively and negatively. On the one hand, many analysts consider that only an extended period of political stability can establish the preconditions for the longer-term entrenchment of democracy. Like most new democracies, South Africa faces immense political and developmental challenges in a context of profound inequality, poverty, and social division. Any threat to ANC dominance, on this view, is also a threat to political stability and to the creation of legitimate political institutions. The ANC's widely shared self-conception as a national liberation movement helps it to contain conflict and to defuse racial or ethnic polarization, and its consensual mechanisms help it to socialise and control potentially anti-democratic leaders (Butler 2007).

As Schrire (2001) has emphasized, however, even on this positive account the ANC cannot absorb the many strains of transition on its own. Political competition is currently structured around historical (and therefore, he argues, ethnic or racial) affiliations, with no compelling ideological or policy conflicts setting the government against the opposition parties. For this reason, adversarial opposition – such as the (primarily White supported) DA's 1999 campaign on a 'fight back' manifesto – must inevitably be interpreted in polarising racial or ethnic terms. Co-operative politics – as exhibited by the NP when it helped stave off economic crisis by means of participation in the 1994–96 government of national unity – is purportedly necessary to sustain democracy. Anti-ANC coalition building, on this view, undermines the benefits of co-operation and courts a dangerous ANC counter-reaction.

Not all commentators have greeted ANC dominance and the incorporation of the opposition as either necessary or positive developments. Critics on the right and radical left have each argued that the ANC has been progressively closing down opposition and building the foundations of a new authoritarianism. 'Democracy', according to rightist critics Giliomee and Simkins, 'rests on countervailing power able to check tendencies towards authoritarian domination. The best counter is undoubtedly the presence of a strong opposition party that can guard against the erosion of the autonomy of democratic institutions and can replace a governing party that has outstayed its welcome.' Such sceptics argue that the ruling party is representing itself as the state rather than as a temporary incumbent, while other groups are losing the autonomy they require to compete. Ultimately the ANC's 'sheer preponderance of political power' will allow it to rule unilaterally and to abuse 'the advantages of incumbency and the state media to get re-elected time and again' (Giliomee and Simkins 1999: 337, 340).

These cogent positive and negative reflections on ANC dominance are considered mutually exclusive by partisans and opponents of the government. Taken together, they have posed a stark dilemma. While South Africa seemingly cannot afford robust opposition, or a fragmentation of the liberation movement, neither can it afford the consequences of deepening ANC domination. South Africa's democracy is not robust enough to cope with fluidity and party system reconstruction because of the need to build sound, legitimate, and trusted institutions. Yet the longer the ANC remains dominant, both electorally and in the executive, the more harm may be caused by state-party integration, patronage politics, opposition de-legitimation, and the abuse of incumbency.

Such circumstances have suggested only one attractive scenario. An extended period of ANC electoral dominance, over perhaps ten or fifteen years, will entrench the legitimacy of democratic institutions. At the same time, the government will face a real, but unrealised, threat of opposition defeat. It is latent opposition and non-electoral mechanisms, on this view, that will hold the government to account and check the abuse of concentrated power. Recent events, and the emergence of a new opposition party in 2008 out of the post-Polokwane ANC, will test hypotheses about the dangers of party competition and political fluidity and claims about the benefits of robust partisan competition.

Holding a Dominant Party to Account

While there is an Anglo-American expectation that party opposition plays the central role in democratic accountability, the workings of non-electoral mechanisms are emphasized in contemporary international scholarship. Even within relatively stable multi-party systems, voting cannot be used in a graduated or targeted way to punish individuals or factions for their misdeeds. Electors face massive informational and collective action problems, and it is rarely clear even to the best informed voter just which politician is responsible for which specific transgression. Even when multiple parties vigorously contest numerous elections across decades, as the history of post-war Italy demonstrates, this does not preclude entrenched collusion between the rulers at the expense of the ruled.

'Alternative government' is rare because there are so few genuine two-party or routine coalition-alternating systems. Western Europe is mostly governed by dominant-bloc coalitions which oblige smaller opposition parties to act 'responsibly' in order to keep open the door to their participation in future coalitions. New democracies, especially those with presidential systems, have often lacked party system stability altogether. On many occasions, however, single parties have established themselves in positions of long-term dominance. In some cases, such as Mexico over decades of stable one-party control, the dominant party has proven a highly imperfect vehicle for holding political leaders to account (at least to the people). In other cases, notably post-independence India, the internal pluralism of the dominant party, and the influence of opposition 'parties of pressure' aligning themselves with governing party factions, helped to secure extended if vulnerable periods of far wider accountability (Southall 2001; Reddy 2005).

ANC equivocation about the crude manipulation of Zimbabwean elections by Robert Mugabe's Zanu-PF in recent years indicates that the ANC's commitment to democratic transfers of power is questionable. Until 2008, the ANC leadership and a substantial body of opinion within the movement moved rapidly to applaud Zanu-PF's dubious victories, and the South African parliament declared 'credible' polls as farcical as that in 2002. While there have been clear diplomatic motives for President Thabo Mbeki's equivocation, the degree of genuine rather than merely tactical support for Zanu-PF among senior party figures and parliamentarians has suggested that the ANC might not consent lightly to its own expulsion by the electorate.

South Africa possesses an array of constitutionally-mandated checks to concentrated power, including a system of legislative oversight through portfolio and select committees, certain designated provincial powers, and oversight institutions partially shielded from political control: the auditor general, the public protector, human rights and gender commissions, an 'independent' reserve bank, a public broadcasting authority and an electoral commission. The government is also constrained by a supreme constitution containing a bill of rights.

Box 6.1   Thabo Mbeki

Thabo Mbeki was born in Idutywa, Transkei, in June 1942, the child of ANC activists. Mbeki joined the ANC Youth League at 14, and quickly entered student politics. After his schooling at Lovedale was interrupted by a strike in 1959, he moved to Johannesburg, where he fell under the guidance of Walter Sisulu, and he was elected secretary of the African Students' Association. Mbeki's father Govan was arrested at Rivonia and sentenced to life imprisonment on Robben Island where he became an implacable critic and rival of Nelson Mandela. Thabo left the country in 1962 for Britain where he completed a Masters degree in economics at Sussex University. Remaining active in student politics, he helped build the youth and student sections of the ANC in exile. After a period in military training in the USSR, he served in a variety of capacities in Zambia, Botswana, Swaziland, and Nigeria. During the 1980s he rose in the department of information and publicity, heading the ANC's Department of International Affairs from 1989, and thereafter became a key figure in negotiations with the NP. Mbeki became Deputy President of the new Government of National Unity. In December 1997, he became President of the ANC and in 1999 succeeded Mandela as state President. He completed two controversial terms as state president – during which time his contributions to HIV/AIDS policy and the crisis in Zimbabwe were subject to intense criticism. His campaign for re-election to a third term as ANC president ended ignominiously at the Polokwane conference of the movement in December 2007 when he was defeated by his deputy Jacob Zuma. In late 2008 he was humiliatingly forced by the ANC to resign from the state presidency.

The vulnerability of these checks to executive power became increasingly clear over the years of Thabo Mbeki's rule (see Box 6.1). The government's major arms procurement programme (see Chapter 8) has been the principal precipitant of crisis. The package has been controversial for its scale, for the naivety of its 'offset'-based financing, and for procedural irregularities including the incomplete briefing of cabinet. Elements of high-level impropriety have come to light in a series of drip-feed media revelations that have detailed the acceptance of discounted luxury cars by politicians and civil servants, insufficiently rigorous checks on involved parties' relations with subcontractors, the payment of bribes by European arms manufacturers to senior politicians and to the ANC itself, and finally a cover-up of irregularities that compromised the integrity of a large portion of the political elite.

A wide range of actors mobilized to raise and investigate these allegations, in what was in comparative terms an unusually public investigation of arms procurement corruption. The government's determination to control potential fallout from the investigations and to protect senior politicians and officials, however, led it to undermine the select committee on public accounts, the legislature's key and formerly non-partisan oversight institution. It then took steps that, in the eyes of many, compromised the integrity of the offices of the auditor general and public protector. Already criticized for starving oversight bodies of resources, the ANC leadership seemed at times to be castigating opponents for investigating impropriety. Rather than building the legitimacy of democratic institutions, these actions served to reiterate the movement's commitment to party over state mechanisms of accountability. Ultimately the implications of the arms deal have become so troubling for the movement and embroiled so many of its senior leaders in impropriety that a wider process of 'forgiveness' accompanied by amnesty seems likely to occur.

The rapidity with which most formal checks to the executive were subdued during the arms scandal has thrown the role of the judiciary into relief. The constitution licenses an activist bench, and entrenches a degree of judicial independence by means of a Judicial Services Commission (JSC) that partly insulates appointments from party manipulation. An activist bench, however, poses special problems in South Africa. The constitution sets out a number of socio-economic rights – to adequate health care, housing, education, water, and so on – which the executive is responsible for 'progressively' realising. There have already been high-profile challenges to government legislation and action in areas such as housing policy and HIV-AIDS treatment, and trench warfare may set in between the judiciary, acting on behalf of specific complainants, and an executive committed to sectorally co-ordinated and incremental policy change. The judiciary is exceptionally vulnerable to a campaign of delegitimization, especially because of its historically White composition, persistent racism in lower level court judgements, limited popular support for constitutional supremacy, and the lack of experience among the senior judiciary in making legal activism palatable to the political elite. Where the courts have found against the government, for example over the treatment to HIV-positive pregnant women, ministers have equivocated in public as to whether court judgements must be obeyed. Ministers and officials already demonstrate a talent for quasi-compliance with judicial instructions. At the height of the arms deal corruption scandal surrounding ANC president Jacob Zuma in 2008, the legitimacy of adverse constitutional court judgements was questioned by a powerful coalition of ANC and tripartite alliance leaders. Just as the relationship between government and opposition parties cannot survive endless adversarial posturing, so judges and politicians alike will need carefully to moderate open conflict while they negotiate together and entrench boundaries between policy, politics, and the law.

Internal Pluralism

The opposition and the judiciary must clearly act with a degree of sensitivity in their negotiation with ANC power. The liberation movement, for its part, can entrench the legitimacy of democratic institutions only through willing compliance with judicial review and tolerance for adversarial opposition. Currently, however, the ANC represents a parallel political order, its external relations with the formal political system shaped by its need to accommodate its own internal conflict. An effective internal pluralism – an ability to encourage and respond to political and policy disagreement within its own organizational structures – is a prerequisite for accountability in a dominant party system.

Understanding the ANC is made difficult by the absence of systematic analysis of its political dynamics and processes of leadership recruitment. The ANC's 'broad church' character combines histories and practices associated with exile, military organization, domestic struggle, trade unionism, communism, and imprisonment, which together help explain its complex behaviour. It displays both democratic and hierarchical aspects, and its style of conflict resolution is sometimes described as consensual. This conventional and largely rosy assessment of the movement has been undermined by escalating conflict and centralization – traced by his critics to Thabo Mbeki's ascension to the presidency – and then by the watershed 2007 conference at Polokwane at which the political faction loyal to Mbeki was evicted from powerful ANC positions by an alliance of forces around former deputy president Jacob Zuma (see Box 6.2)

A product of exile, primarily surrounded by fellow exiles, Mbeki rose to unexpected prominence as Oliver Tambo's protégé and the son of a brilliant Robben Island-imprisoned ANC grandee. Hostile to the politics of the provinces – the level at which the movement primarily exists for its mass membership – Mbeki used national institutions to assert his faction's authority increasingly widely and aggressively. The exile ANC leadership adopted 'democratic centralism' from its SACP ally, which in the early 1990s famously abandoned such Stalinist techniques while retaining a long-range commitment to Marxism. The ANC

Box 6.2   Jacob Gedleyihlekisa Zuma

Jacob Zuma was born on 12 April 1942 in Nkandla, in what is today KZN, the child of a domestic worker. He received little formal education as a result of his need to supplement his family's income. He joined the ANC in 1959 and after the banning of the movement in 1960 he joined its armed wing MK. He was captured and sentenced to 10 years on Robben Island and on his release he worked underground for two years before leaving for exile in Swaziland, Mozambique and finally the ANC's head office in Zambia where he became head of the intelligence department. At the ANC's 1991 conference he was elected deputy secretary general, in 1994 he became a minister in the KZN provincial government and in 1999 he became Thabo Mbeki's deputy president.

Zuma has been a controversial figure, rising as a close ally of Thabo Mbeki with whom he initiated negotiations with the apartheid government. Gifted with immense charm he played an important role in minimizing conflict in KZN during and after the political transition. Implicated in corruption charges that he and his supporters viewed as a politically inspired attempt to end his run for the ANC and state presidencies, he demonstrated enormous political resilience in fighting off legal and political challenges in 2006 and 2007. Although often viewed as an ally of the left, Zuma is a social conservative who seems likely to bolster the influence of traditionalism and patriarchy in particular in South Africa's rural areas. He was elected South African President in May 2009.

---

leadership, by contrast, was obliged to embrace capitalism, but retained democratic centralism as an instrument of political management. After 1999 the centre tightened control over 'cadre deployment' at all levels of the state and elaborated its ideology of primary accountability to the liberation movement. The NEC and the National Working Committee (NWC) that runs the party's day-to-day operations have selected parliamentary caucus officers and parliamentary committee chairs and dissolved undisciplined regional structures. Thabo Mbeki made a point of personally appointing provincial premiers, often overriding the wishes of provincial ANC activists. Although the rebellion under Jacob Zuma was premised on a return of power to the regions, there is every likelihood that the pattern of growing centralization will be re-established in future.

Centralization, of course, is hardly unique to South Africa, and should not be read as a reliable indicator of an increasingly imperial presidency. It is in part compensatory, a reaction to the emergence of refractory new fiefdoms in national and provincial government, but especially in the new integrated 'unicities' which enjoy a high and growing degree of autonomy. Centralization also reflects the growing professionalism of the ANC, its determination to contain corruption and politicking in the provinces and municipalities, and the desire of the NEC to control ethnic and 'populist' mobilization in the provinces. The idea of 'the struggle' once bound a diverse movement together, but new generations of career-minded activists are increasingly immune to traditional discipline. Given the movement's poorly institutionalized systems of officer election and internal debate, a degree of enhanced control was perhaps inevitable. Such struggles are part of the stabilising role that champions of ANC dominance consider its greatest strength, especially given the continuing presence in its ranks of independent-minded and forceful political entrepreneurs such as Winnie Mandela (see Box 6.3). It is indeed hard to see how conflicts of interest and opinion between trade union organisers and rural traditional leaders, for example, might be reconciled through any other conceivable set of institutions.

Box 6.3   Nomzamo Nobandla Winnifred 'Winnie' Madikizela-Mandela

Famous initially for her marriage to Nelson Mandela across his 26 year incarceration, political activist Winnie Madikizela-Mandela was born on 26 September 1936, child of a minister of the Forestry and Agriculture Department of the Transkei government. Educated at Shawbury school and University of the Witwatersrand, where she studied political science and international relations, Madikizela went on to work as a medical social worker at Baragwanath Hospital, conducting research into child mortality in Alexandra township that shocked her into political activism. Over three decades of political activism she was repeatedly detained, with a period of 18 months in solitary confinement in Pretoria Central prison and nine years of 'internal exile' in Brandfort where her house was twice bombed. Divorced from Nelson Mandela shortly after his release from prison, Madikizela-Mandela became an MP and member of the ANC's National Working Committee. Widely supported by activists, and possessing a popular touch that escapes the ageing and exile dominated leadership, Madikizela-Mandela's conflicts with senior figures in the movement and infringements of parliamentary protocol have been accompanied by frequent brushes with the law. Her conviction in April 2003 on multiple counts of fraud and theft set back but did not end her maverick political career. In 2007 she received more votes in the NEC elections than any other candidate.

Under Mbeki's leadership the ANC drifted perilously close to suppressing internal pluralism. Mbeki's faction sanctioned the abuse of internal and external opponents as 'unpatriotic' or 'ultra-leftist'. Potential challengers to Mbeki's authority and position – such as Cyril Ramaphosa, Mathews Phosa, and Tokyo Sexwale, struggle leaders already 'redeployed' to the private sector – were investigated by the safety and security minister in 2001 for purportedly placing the life of the president in danger. Jacob Zuma, Thabo Mbeki's number two and long-time ally, argued that his prosecution on charges of fraud and corruption was part of a conspiracy to prevent any challenge to the Mbeki's authority.

The movement's pluralist energies and unwillingness to succumb to Mbeki's attempts to perpetuate his factional and personal rule were demonstrated in 2007, however, when the national conference elected Jacob Zuma as its president by a landslide vote. SACP leaders and COSATU activist long castigated by Mbeki's supporters suddenly came into their own as a major power in the leadership.

In the midst of this relentless political infighting, doubts have begun to be raised about the oft-presumed robustness of the ANC's voter base. Four important cautions are in order for those who view the movement's dominance as inevitable. First, a growing number of voters express themselves dissatisfied with the performance of the government, and indicate that they might be available to an appropriate opposition party. The ANC is therefore not insulated against effective challenge should its performance deteriorate further. Only the absence of credible opposition parties reflecting the interests of the discontented has secured ANC electoral dominance.

Second, the ANC enjoyed a uniquely favourable economic environment under Thabo Mbeki, buoyed up by rapid international growth and a commodity boom that raised demand for South African mineral exports. As the world economy has slumped after 2008, it has become increasingly difficult to predict the social and political consequences of slower economic growth, exceptionally high levels of unemployment, and changing patterns of income and wealth distribution.

Third, while analysts have explored the potential for urban populist opposition, we do not know very much about the too-easily assumed control of the ANC over the political allegiance of the rural poor. The social forces that can destroy or sustain democracy often lie in the countryside, a fact overlooked by most contemporary democratization scholars (Yashar 1997). While the Black middle class and organized labour each has a strong voice in the movement, the far larger constituencies of the rural unemployed, the informally employed, the old, and – increasingly – AIDS-victims, have little leverage. Macro-economic conservatism precludes large-scale rural patronage, public service delivery has run aground beyond the towns, rural job-creation is a lost cause, land redistribution policy is in disarray, and the political fallout of the AIDS pandemic remains difficult to predict. The unusual political sophistication of South Africa's rural areas at the same time militates strongly against the effectiveness of consolatory populist racial appeals. As the centre is merely forced to shore up its support beyond the cities, this will in itself further strain the ANC's labour and urban alliances.

Finally, we do not yet know how to interpret the longer term prospects of the political opposition in South Africa, buoyed as they may be by a potentially fragmenting liberation movement and the emergence of new parties such as the COPE that appeal to former ANC members.

External and Economic Constraints

Many sceptics of the durability of checks and balances and internal pluralism nonetheless believe that wider, and often international, political, and economic forces will help contain ANC power. The government is vulnerable to the exit of capital and skills, it depends on business confidence to encourage investment, and it has been responsive to pressure exerted by the countries of the OECD zone. The ANC leadership has carefully avoided economic populism, and demonstrated sensitivity to international perceptions.

External influences, however, cannot reliably prevent any government from taking bad decisions under pressure of domestic circumstances. In the area of corruption, for example, international indices suggest South Africa is both major source and recipient of improper payments. The ANC faces powerful incentives to deal with allegations within party structures, especially since corrupt behaviour is hard to bring to court, and so many cadres are implicated in questionable if not illegal activities. Unwillingness to permit high-profile prosecutions, and allegations of obstruction to investigation at the highest level, suggest that party leaders harbour the illusion that the problem can be politically managed. If corruption becomes further entrenched, and passes certain thresholds into normality, only then will an external constraint come into play, as South Africa becomes regarded as 'just another African country', its international business credibility permanently compromised.

Potential capital flight has also preoccupied and constrained the government; but this sword is double-edged. The exaggerated conservatism of macro-economic policy under Mandela and Mbeki, itself in part a reaction to the fears of external actors, may have entrenched structural obstacles to faster growth. In this way it has ultimately deepened investors' concerns that sustained inequality must bring an eventual political counter-reaction. Because investors' perceptions are elusive and complex, government remains vulnerable to vicious circles of collapsing credibility and confidence.

The threat of accelerating emigration of skilled workers provides a similarly unreliable limit to government freedom of action. Emigration by those possessing scarce skills is difficult to measure but it runs into the tens of thousands every year. Émigrés, usually beneficiaries of South Africa's highly unequal educational provision, often bewail the limitations of the new South Africa in order to ease the guilt of exile. Rampant official xenophobia has meanwhile limited legal in-migration of those with scarce skills to a few thousand per year and recognition of the economic benefits of a more open immigration skills-based policy have yet to produce changes in the practices of state officials (Crush et al 2000).

The greatest danger these external constraints pose is that while they are advertised as non-negotiable, they are easily reinterpreted as 'western' impositions. Conservative macro-economic policy is viewed by many South African intellectuals and activists as merely a redefined form of African subjugation to structural adjustment policies. While a growing number of skilled Black workers are now joining White émigrés overseas, emigration is still sometimes welcomed as creating space for Black advancement (while excessive sensitivity to the interests and fears of potential emigrants justly generates resentment). The failure of international business to invest heavily in post-apartheid South Africa is widely attributed to racism and Afro-pessimism. For 'economic reality' to serve as a check on government actions it will need to be interpreted in a less politically charged way.

Conclusions

South Africa's fundamental political dilemma is that liberation movement domination is a necessary condition for the entrenchment of democratic practices and institutions, but it is also and at the same time a threat to them. Electoral defeat at the best of times represents a poorly calibrated and ineffective reaction to governing party misrule, and in contemporary South African conditions it would represent a cure worse than almost any conceivable disease. Many other mechanisms – formal checks and balances, internal pluralism within the ANC, and the external impositions of capital – continue to constrain the actions of the executive, but each has fundamental drawbacks. The centre is progressively colonising independent checks on executive power, in the legislature, provinces, and independent oversight offices. The ANC's assorted alliances are becoming increasingly conflict-ridden and cannot be relied upon to absorb societal antagonisms. Capital and skills flight set dangerously unpredictable limits to action. In each case, there is a threat of counter reaction should political entrepreneurs abuse racial polarization to defend poor governance, cadre corruption, or perverse policy.

This complex but precarious structure of accountability now faces a series of blunt political challenges, each following its particular logic, but causally interconnected in complex ways. AIDS is reducing growth, damaging business confidence and investment, and accelerating skills flight. One may speculate that it might further destabilize the tripartite alliance, foster opposition in the countryside, and hamper the battle against corruption and financial mismanagement. Corruption, if it should escalate still further, will reduce the state's capacity to manage AIDS, and provide a rationale for destabilizing opposition alliances. Skill and capital flight themselves may precipitate a further counter-reaction against business. Such potential relations between complex processes help explain the variety and uncertainty of prognoses for the country's future.

President Mbeki proved unable to steer his country safely through these rough waters. His rule was dependent on increasingly resented organizational manipulation and an abuse of racial and national liberation rhetoric. The office of state president, to be sure, demands an almost impossible combination of qualities from its incumbent, and it is unclear whether Mbeki's successor will fare any better than he has done.

A state with so little autonomy from capital as South Africa's, unable to control crime, extract service payments, or monitor its borders, is unlikely to pose any immediate threat to the opposition supporters and ANC critics who control the country's wealth. Indeed, it may be that they pose far too slight an immediate threat, and that the complacency of South Africa's wealth holders may one day generate a dangerous counter-reaction.

The ANC's capacity for rational deliberation has come under question for two quite different reasons in recent years. Under Mbeki, restrictions on ANC internal debate allowed inappropriate decisions to be taken unquestioned, a problem highlighted by government's HIV/AIDS policy. Although an alliance between leftists and provincial barons has removed Mbeki from power, it is quite possible that his successor will adopt a similar style of presidentialist leadership. It is sometimes observed that natural and social science flourish because they are open systems of knowledge-creation in which conventions of contestability and the power of evidence are sustained by powerful scientists' willingness to accept correction. Successful political leadership in the same way may depend on policy contestation, non-compliance among followers, and the timely correction of leaders' inevitable errors (Grint 2000). The growing tendency among ANC supporters to identify the person of the president with the cause of national liberation itself makes rational policy making and constructive political criticism difficult to sustain, whatever the personal character of the incumbent.

Those who understand democracy as a system of free elections, underpinned by political liberty and the rule of law, have reason to doubt the ANC's commitment to a democratic future. ANC leaders' project begins from an alternative understanding of freedom and democracy, however, rather than from an antagonism towards those values.

ANC veterans' experience of apartheid – and their extended immersion in socialist and developmental traditions – has convinced them of the limitations of the liberal ideal. Constraints on freedom, they observe, need not be external and personal, and so the protection of rights and liberties is never enough to guarantee that these constraints will be lifted. Rather than celebrating democratic elections, constitutionalism and political rights as triumphs in themselves, the ANC views these as instruments in a larger struggle: the 'national democratic revolution' towards 'the creation of a non-racial, non-sexist, democratic and united SA'.

The ANC's championing of national democratic revolution has produced clear gains, driving its relentless efforts to promote universal public services and helping to create a wider national project to realize socioeconomic rights. However, some ANC heavyweights' open contempt for Parliament and a more general distrust of pluralist pressure-group politics indicate the failure of liberal ideas to establish their authority. Understanding the 'bourgeois democracy' of parliaments and constitutions to be a provisional accomplishment, activists often still idealize a participatory democracy in which the mobilized masses directly drive transformation.

Party veterans are often less concerned with whether important decisions are actually taken by the citizenry than with whether those decisions advance what the ANC understands as the real interests of the people. Under their tutelage, a new generation of activists already chafes against the perceived constraints that liberal institutions impose.

It is an inescapable conclusion, unwelcome to those who fear protracted one-party dominance, that a cohesive tripartite alliance, enjoying sustained and co-operative relations with opposition parties, offers South Africa the best hope of entrenching its highly imperfect democracy. The movement's popular reach and legitimacy help to render the majority's dire circumstances politically supportable, and its institutions ameliorate and contain the society's diverse conflicts. However, if the advertised benefits of a collaborative political order, marked by consensus and compromise within and between parties and institutions, are to be realized, this will require a more open and democratic-spirited politics that the ANC is currently able to muster.

The real testing of liberal institutions will come when the ruling party finally faces a genuine electoral challenge – a threat that may emerge far sooner than most observers have anticipated. Suddenly the incentives to obstruct free political activity, stifle editorial independence and curtail political freedoms will escalate. In such circumstances the lack of genuine enthusiasm for liberal democratic ideas and institutions, instilled across generations of revolutionary equivocation, could prove liberal democracy's undoing.

7

Culture, Ideas, and Issues

In this chapter we explore South Africans' popular and high cultures, their intellectual preoccupations, and their everyday arguments and debates. We investigate the country's traditions of music, theatre, dance, film, and art; the character of everyday social interaction in cities, suburbs, and townships; and the most lively elements of national intellectual life. Finally we address some of the most highly charged issues in popular debate and the media: racism, crime, corruption, racism, HIV/AIDS, sport, and the 2010 soccer world cup.

Professional Cultural Production

The seemingly innocent word 'culture' evades easy definition. Social scientists sometimes talk of cultures to refer to the 'maps of meaning' through which people make sense of their world. A practice that is quite accepted in one culture may not 'make sense' in another, and a traveller may experience 'culture shock' upon encountering unfamiliar experiences that do not correspond to cultural expectations.

More everyday use of the term is also contested. In its western European lands of origin, the idea of 'high' culture refers to the artistic, expressive, and aesthetic practices and performances of a society: its poetry, literature, painting, and sculpture. 'Low' culture, by contrast, refers to the ways in which people live their daily lives – their sports and pastimes, their practices of sociability and friendship, their popular music, recreational drugs, and styles of dress. This distinction between high and low culture, and the identification of the former with a set of professional artistic practices, is the product of particular (western) historical circumstances, and it carries with it an assumption that the artist, poet, or composer stands at some distance from everyday society. This understanding can be quite misleading in societies like South Africa in which oral traditions, dance, religious practice, music, and other cultural artefacts are deeply woven into and make meaningful everyday social activity.

South African intellectuals have been wrestling with only limited success to reconcile their conflicting conceptions of the cultural. The 'intercultural dialogue' that a post-apartheid nation so requires is inhibited by distinct historical experiences and understandings of the realm of culture. In particular, 'culture' was used in the apartheid period as a vehicle for promoting racial and ethnic identities, to justify a discriminatory allocation of resources to Europeans, and as an ideological weapon in the propagation of the naturalness of culturally distinct 'communities'.

Like other colonial populations, European settlers in Southern Africa used their economic and political power to enforce their conception of cultural value. Typically, 'high' cultural practice was understood as an attainment of Whites, and it was believed to give expression to the cultural superiority of European civilization. European forms – such as classical music, ballet, opera, theatre, and fine art – were used to reiterate and reinforce White settlers' relationship to the colonial heartlands, and to celebrate the higher civilization they supposedly exemplified. State funded provincial arts councils were used to channel monies towards these cultural productions for the benefit of primarily White audiences. The Afrikaner nationalist project reinforced these tendencies while successfully achieving for Afrikaans a status of formal parity with English in education, the media, and the arts.

The aesthetic traditions and practices of Africans were treated by official cultural professionals as the products of static native cultures, significant primarily for their role in perpetuating tribal distinctiveness and division. Even many highly educated Africans, who were usually the children and grandchildren of mission-school educated elites, embraced a European conception of cultural hierarchy that denigrated African history and culture. Ironically, however, apartheid destroyed the cultural infrastructure that had allowed an African elite to aspire to proficiency in the ways of western cultural practice. As cinemas, theatres, galleries, and museums were segregated fully from the 1950s, and the centres of urban African culture were bulldozed and their communities dispersed, African intellectuals were forced to look again at the virtues of cultural products rooted in Africa. Their necessarily inconclusive investigations were sometimes couched in terms of a search for 'authenticity' or the 'traditional'.

Under later apartheid, debates around tradition became ever more sharp and double-edged, because the state was determined to create new ethnocentric cultural practices for 're-tribalised' Africans in order to reinforce the Bantustan system. The notion that there must exist a fundamental division between (superior) European and (inferior) African culture was supplanted by the high apartheid agenda of 'separate development', which was premised on the fundamentally conflictual relations between cultures and ethnic groups.

Anti-apartheid politics also influenced cultural production. 'The struggle' worked its way into almost all sites of public expression – church services, sports events, funerals, and almost any form of community meeting – as well as the political rallies that became an opportunity for new forms of dance, music, and poetry. This broader resistance culture helped to neutralize the effects of retribalisation, and to prevent a new class of official African cultural practitioners and traditionalists from advancing the regime's agenda of ethnic distinctiveness. A minority of professional cultural practitioners from the White community developed their own ways of subverting the assumptions of the apartheid order, and artists' or performers' collectives sometimes participated in African National Congress (ANC)-aligned political networks such as the United Democratic Front (UDF).

The end of 'the struggle' had a variety of repercussions for cultural professionals and practitioners. For White and historically advantaged professionals, non-racial democracy brought upheaval and soul-searching. Foreign funding for protest culture largely evaporated, and domestic anti-apartheid artistic coalitions were not well-regarded by the primarily exile ANC department of arts and culture which was determined to assert its 'vanguard role'. After an extensive process of consultation with artists, educators, and administrators in 1994, a new National Arts Council was created whose function has been progressively to redirect resources away from the traditionally Eurocentric arts councils towards historically unrecognized and undervalued forms of creativity in music, dance, crafts, and community performance.

Largely insulated from these developments, English- and Afrikaans-language writing have continued on their respective pre-1994 trajectories. However, those writing primarily in Afrikaans, and especially a new generation of women authors, demonstrate openness to international influences and an ability to embrace a rapidly changing social reality.

If the fine arts and English literature have not flourished since 1994, it is in the traditional theatre that resources and self-confidence have been most undermined by the end of the struggle. The 'protest theatre' of the 1980s was primarily a self-celebratory preoccupation of Gauteng's urban middle-class Whites. As apartheid and broader colonial themes have gradually fallen away in favour of more introspective and complex dramatic productions, the theatre has not managed to broaden its audience beyond its traditional middle class base. While Black and women performers are now commonplace, moreover, directors continue to be almost always male and disproportionately White, although a new generation of Black directors is emerging.

The transformation of dance and opera has been strikingly more successful. While western 'theatre' has stagnated, African theatrical dance has achieved unexpected economic viability. South African dance has been one of the country's few major cultural exports, with local companies performing to acclaim in the United States and Europe. As in many other areas of cultural production, South Africa's strength has developed from the abandonment of conservative conceptions of the traditional (be it European or African) and through moves towards fusions of style and choreography. In opera, classically trained Black performers have been equally successful internationally – and belatedly among domestic audiences – since 1994.

Music has been undergoing a period of more general and rapid innovation and development. The apartheid period saw a progressive racial segregation of musical output as the cosmopolitan communities that sustained non-racialism were destroyed and their populations relocated. Towards the end of the apartheid era there was an international cultural boycott that isolated musical artists and audiences from international interaction. At the same time, however, music was an instrument of resistance and opposition to apartheid, and the onset of democracy created a vacuum or a loss of purpose among the country's artistic and cultural communities as well as presenting to them new opportunities.

Choral music, which has played an especially important role in South Africa across the past century, has been least affected by these changes. South African choral music achieved international prominence after the participation of isicathamiya performers Ladysmith Black Mambazo in Paul Simon's 1986 Graceland album. Church, school, and adult choirs remain the major popular musical activity in the country. This music is often based around an early twentieth century fusion between four-part choral singing – which originated in Victorian British hymnal – and American minstrelsy, which was acquired from late nineteenth century vaudeville tours, and provided greater opportunity for social critique. 'Traditional' influences came later and have been less significant, as have the effects of other primarily American innovations such as rock 'n' roll and country music (Impey 2001; Erlmann 1999).

While the search for resilient authenticity in such historically complex forms has continued, younger South Africans have been drawn to more complex fusions between a range of domestic and international musical traditions. As elsewhere, popular music production has diversified and internationalized, and products such as techno-raves and house music have been introduced and reworked in urban culture. Local historical and continental influences have been important. The township jazz seemingly displaced by the forced removals of the fifties and sixties has been rediscovered and is being reconfigured, partly under the influence of historically more developed and innovative West African jazz and blues traditions.

Popular music, however, has been dominated by 'kwaito', a Johannesburg township genre that was the product of a great post-1994 collision of international influences. In kwaito young South Africans have succeeded in making something uniquely their own, although the form has been derided by heartless critics as 'slowed down garage music' and castigated for its derivative and apolitical character.

The Culture of Everyday Life: Urbanization and Suburbanization

The progressive urbanization and suburbanization of the South African population has wrought massive changes in the nature of everyday community life. For most Africans, of course, migrant labour has been a familiar part of the life-cycle for almost a century. In the early decades of the twentieth century, legislative changes to undermine African rural societies and destroy Black farming economies made it increasingly difficult for rural Africans to survive without remittances from the core urban economy. A pattern of migrant labour was enforced through which young men and later women would pass much of their lives in and around the 'white' cities of South Africa.

Migrant labour created both generational and gender divisions. Young men and later women worked away from their families, in hostels, backyard shacks, or informal settlements close to places of work, as part of a cosmopolitan and sometimes vibrant urban and peri-urban culture. The old, disproportionate numbers of women, and young children remained in the Bantustans, heavily dependent on remittances from the towns and later upon systems of state support like the government pension.

The annual cycle of migrancy would end each December as millions travelled to the Bantustans to spend the Christmas season with relatives and children. Such a pattern of cyclical migrancy is common to developing countries as urbanization involves stalls and reversals for individuals, even as the aggregate urban population is growing. Yet South Africa was locked by apartheid into an extremely extended process of displaced and cyclical migration.

Everyday life for most South Africans is still marked by a duality of experiences and relationships, with communities, families, and individual life-cycles straddling the chasm of existence between desperately impoverished rural areas and relatively affluent urban centres. Rural areas often still fall under the partial sway of traditional modes of authority, through which hereditary male leaders have the power to allocate land and other economic resources. Much of the rural population is old, although there are many young children undergoing their schooling away from the crime of the townships in the care of grandparents or other relatives.

Rural areas are dependent on savings, urban remittances from the more affluent and younger population living in the towns or peri-urban settlements, and state transfer payments such as the old age pension and child support grant, all supplemented by a desperate survivalist mode of agriculture. Many of the former homelands are not 'rural' at all, but rather immense and densely populated townships located at great distance from economic opportunities. Unemployment, poor health care, limited public services, high levels of infant and child mortality, and HIV/AIDS plague these areas. Everyday life is a battle against poverty and disease, punctuated by spells of mostly fruitless pursuit of pitifully remunerated labour. Women's plight is especially severe, as they undertake backbreaking chores like water collection, firewood gathering, and agricultural work, and care for a growing number of AIDS victims who have come to the rural areas to die.

The cities, towns, peri-urban townships and urban informal settlements contain a diversity of opportunity and experience, but rarely the crushing hopelessness of most rural life. Cities remain quite sharply segregated, with the White suburbs preserved today by income inequality rather than legally enforced division. There are some long-established townships, formerly native locations, which provide relatively good public services and access to urban labour markets. But these are few in number. Most urban Black people live at considerable distances from economic opportunity in townships designed to separate them from White suburbs and city centres. The search for income dominates daily

life for most township residents. The work there is largely poorly paid
and often physically draining. Workers must be up long before the sun
to take crowded and expensive mini-bus taxis, buses, or trains tens of
kilometres to places of work (or hoped-for work). [A domestic worker,
for example, may deliver her own children to a township crèche before
undertaking an arduous journey at the end of which she prepares for
school the children of a suburban household]

Townships and informal settlements, however, are not merely places of
hardship. Everyday social interaction is marked by courtesy, and opportunities for hospitality are embraced. Both church and popular music and
sport – primarily soccer, a rare sport enjoyed by South Africans of all
races – thrive on a young population. 'Shebeens' or taverns are numerous, and alcohol and drug intake can be considerable at weekends and
during festivals such as Christmas and New Year. Township communities, however, are also marked by exceptionally close systems of moral
scrutiny. They are often genuine communities, with shared political histories (often of informal settlement and organization to demand services)
as well as clear institutions for regulating crime and deviance. Far from
undergoing moral breakdown, as some outside analysts suggested in the
early 1990s, townships continue to represent extremely dense networks
of moral relationships in which mutual obligations are strong. Indeed,
such relationships are necessary for survival in difficult and uncertain
economic circumstances. It is partly because of such expectations of
mutual respect and obligation that the scourge of crime is experienced as
so intolerable and inexplicable a social evil.

Despite very uneven provision of tarred roads and drainage, civil
engineering standards are often relatively high in formal townships.
Households with mobile 'cell' phones, electricity for lighting and leisure,
and external running water and sanitation are now normal if by no means
universal in urban areas. Improved public service provision since 1994
has made a substantial difference to the lives of many established township residents, although urbanization brings more informal households
each year. Car ownership – an especially significant economic resource
given the location of the townships, and an important signifier of status –
is growing, as are small businesses devoted to auto maintenance. Church
halls, sports facilities, and community halls accommodate community,
musical and religious activities and there has been a flourishing of non-
political voluntary associations.

With the crucial difference of vastly greater economic opportunity,
the suburban life of White South Africans (and especially Afrikaners)
shares much in common with the township life of urban Africans. Despite

the potential alienation that suburbia can bring, Whites often maintain traditions of hospitality and politeness towards outsiders (although not necessarily towards Black South Africans). Traditional South African gender roles that situate the man by the braai and the woman in the kitchen with the children remain prevalent, as does a strong male orientation towards sports and outdoor activities. A high value automobile is for White men the most significant object of status, although the ideal of both a BMW and a four-wheel drive vehicle is beyond most families.

International and especially American cultural influences are evident everywhere in White as in Black South Africa, notably in the music, movies, shopping malls, and American suburban lifestyles that Whites have in recent decades embraced. Despite these parallels, however, the social lives of Black and White South Africans still rarely cross and their residential patterns remain largely segregated. Interaction between races is usually also interaction across classes in the workplace, with Whites typically of higher status. Africans rarely visit Whites' homes, except as workers, and few Whites ever visit an African suburb or township.

Government no longer enforces apartheid but markets continue to reproduce and sometimes to create anew patterns of racial segregation. Wealthy urban whites often work in business parks or fortress office blocks and shop in suburban malls, places from which poor black citizens are excluded by poverty and by private security forces using hidden violence. The spread of gated communities and golf estates, surrounded by electrified fences, has become a potent symbol of this new apartheid. Within these 'privatopias', the affluent and largely white residents enjoy private hospitals, gyms, shops, and restaurants. Home entertainment, internet banking, and new work-from-home technologies allow whites further opportunities to escape cross-class and inter-race interaction. Even political activity has been privatized, as residents debate their rights and responsibilities, haggle over the wages of their gardeners and security guards, and negotiate annual golf fees.

Most Black citizens continue to live in monoracial townships or rural areas. Black South Africans who have made their way into the new middle class find their asset-poverty continues to count against them. They struggle harder than their asset-rich White peers to support dependants, pay school fees, and service housing bonds. When they seek out a new home in a formerly white neighbourhood, close to places of work, where their children might grow up in safety and learn in a leafy suburban school, they find that prices have risen inexorably beyond their reach.

Broadcasting

The privatization of apartheid is also to some degree visible in the sphere of broadcasting. Wealthier citizens increasingly make use of private subscription services to access the dramatic productions and news services of Western Europe and America. Nevertheless the South African Broadcasting Corporation (SABC) remains a very significant provider of television and radio programming for all South Africans. A staunch supporter of apartheid oppression in the 1980s, SABC relaunched itself as a public service broadcaster immediately before the ANC's accession to power in 1994, so averting what might have been a fundamental overhaul at the hands of the new government. Under the regulatory control of an Independent Broadcasting Authority (IBA), the SABC is formally committed to independence from government and private sector interests, to the promotion of diversity, and to the pursuit of the public interest.

The most visible outcome of the SABC's new mission was a reconfiguration of television channels in 1996, through which formerly English and Afrikaans channels were allocated primarily to Nguni and Sotho languages, with only one channel devoted to domestic English-language programming (although cheap American and British imports fill the schedules of all three channels). In radio, a medium especially important for many rural South Africans, commercialization and regional licenses have increased choice and diversity, including in local languages.

The SABC, however, has many critics, who highlight its unfair competitive advantage (as a result of license fee revenues and direct transfers from the fiscus) and the continuing predominance of English in its programming. As with broadcasters elsewhere, the SABC has come under pressure from changing technologies and the internationalization of the media, which has brought new channels – both cable and free to air – and a diversity of outside voices and influences.

SABC executives and editorial teams have found themselves under heavy and persistent pressure from the ANC and from the broadcaster's parliament-appointed board over news and current affairs reporting. Senior editorial positions have been increasingly controlled by ruling party apparatchiks. In a return to apartheid-era convention, the SABC has been unwilling to affront senior ministers by aggressively reporting high level corruption, maladministration, or foreign policy failure. Despite the fact that public interest broadcaster principles are quite widely understood within the SABC, they have been defended with decreasing frequency and little enthusiasm.

The broadcaster's vulnerability to political interference was high-lighted in 2008 when the parliamentary committee that had chosen a pro-Mbeki board on the instructions of the presidency tried to reverse its decision after Mbeki's Polokwane defeat at the hands of Jacob Zuma. In the ensuing fiasco, parliamentarians, board members, and the chief executive himself became embroiled in a series of widely ridiculed legal actions in what appeared to be a battle to curry favour with competing factions in the ANC leadership. The once fanciful idea that the SABC might become a fully fledged state broadcaster, dependent on public funds and disseminating politically inspired propaganda in place of news and current affairs, would appear to be becoming a possibility.

Ideas

South Africa's history has been shaped by the overarching intellectual systems associated with White Supremacy, Social Darwinism, segregation, and apartheid. Apartheid's opponents, for their part, often embraced abstract and totalising intellectual traditions such as Marxism and Black Consciousness. Professional academic scholarship has been racialized and prone to formalism and functionalism. Given these historical weaknesses and oppositions, perhaps the most astonishing feature of the country's current intellectual life is the high degree of conformity and consensus it often seems to embody.

The collapse of apartheid ideology and the 'triumph of democracy' were elements in the wider international intellectual reconfiguration of the past two decades. The collapse of the Soviet economy and the end of the Cold War marked the demise of the only viable alternative to capitalism and undermined socialist and social democratic doctrines. A 'Washington consensus' elaborated in some detail new expectations of trade liberalization, market deregulation, and fiscal conservatism. At the same time, the project of universal liberal market capitalism advanced through a wave of democratization and market-opening between the mid-1970s and the turn of the millennium.

South Africa's professional political class capitulated in the face of these international ideological forces. A broad national consensus emerged in the early 1990s negotiations in favour of macro-economic stability, fiscal prudence, liberalization of trade, the rule of law, and representative democracy. Socialism and the public ownership of the means of production fell away rapidly as credible alternatives to market capitalism even in the eyes of avowed leftists. Recent conflict between the

ANC-aligned trade union movement and the government over privatization has, in fact, been couched in mostly non-ideological and pragmatic terms.

Africanism and modernism

Behind this seeming consensus, however, lie disagreements that are in some ways more fundamental. These differences concern the historical struggle between Africa and the West, and the relationships between African systems of ideas and those – including socialism, liberalism, and communism themselves – that originated in Europe. The notion of a distinctive African universe of ideas and values has been founded both historically and philosophically in opposition to colonialism (just as Western intellectuals have historically used their characterization of Africa to define their own 'civilisation').

One important influence on social commentary has been the fusion of Black consciousness with a distinctive Africanist field of scholarship, creating a distinctive style of intellectual discourse and political commentary. While positive and emancipatory in intention, Africanist scholarship has been confronted with the inescapable catastrophe of the failure of most of post-colonial Africa. Before the start of the latest commodity boom, African per capita incomes had stagnated or fallen for two decades, and political instability, collapsing state capacity, and rapacious political elites were widespread. Some scholars have located the origins of Africa's multiple crises in the failure of the state to fully penetrate civil society. Others argue that the continent's communities have failed to hold the African state to account, and have therefore fallen prey to it.

For one eminent scholar, Mahmood Mamdani, Africa's distinctiveness lies in mechanisms of 'indirect rule' by means of which colonial powers enforced their authority. Colonial power was exercised across Africa by means of two complementary mechanisms of native control. In the urban areas the colonial powers introduced direct rule, imposing western legal precepts and importing European models of citizenship. Away from the towns, however, they governed through indirect rule, using 'traditional' leaders and hybrid systems of legal and political authority to control rural populations, secure labour, and extract taxes. Land remained communal or 'customary', and tribal leadership was selectively imposed or reconstructed at the behest of the colonial powers. Indirect rule 'at once both reinforced ethnically bound institutions of control and led to their explosion from within. Ethnicity (tribalism) thus came to be simultaneously the form of colonial control .... and the form of revolt against it'. Free and fair elections, on Mamdani's account, cannot remove the 'decentralised despotism' that marks all post-colonial African politics (Mamdani 1996: 24, 289, 286).

White South Africans often embrace a simplified version of this dualist theory when they explain that South Africa contains both a 'first world' and a 'third world'. The first world is represented by highways and hospitals, affluent consumers and suburbs, advanced technologies and a sophisticated financial system. This world has enjoyed political rights, issue-based voting, and western political institutions, and its inhabitants (who happen to be White) are rational thinkers. The third world is characterized by poverty, subsistence agriculture, migrant labour, and devastatingly low productivity. Its social life is marked by patronage, clientelism, tribalism, and violence, and its intellectual world circumscribed by superstition, and primitive ethnic division.

Whether South Africa is really marked by such oppositions, and whether it can be understood as a product of 'indirect rule', remains highly controversial. South African intellectual life has long been notorious for 'exceptionalism', a tendency to view the country's history and politics as entirely distinct from its African neighbours. SACP theorists' exceptionalism took the form of 'colonialism of a special type', an analysis that located South Africa's uniqueness in the 'internal' character of the exploiting colonial class. Orthodox scholars said South Africa's advanced economy produced a more 'modern' form of politics than elsewhere in Africa, while the century-old cycle of labour migrancy allegedly bequeathed a substantial, anti-tribal working class.

The growing influence of broader African scholarship, however, has begun to challenge the assumption that things are different here. Exceptionalism itself is beginning to look like an apartheid-era fantasy derived from the myth that this country is the sole outpost of civilization on the 'dark continent'. Jacob Zuma's rise can be seen as drawing on the same discontents that fuelled populism elsewhere in post-colonial Africa. Economic 'indigenisation' or 'Africanisation' – the growth of the black middle class and emergence of a black bourgeoisie – invariably open up deep class divisions. A small but powerful minority of beneficiaries is pitted against a majority of losers, often using state power and nationalist rhetoric to crush the trade unions, communist parties, and smaller ethnic minority organizations who champion the poor.

Removing the distorting spectacles of exceptionalism can illuminate the character of national politics. Roger Southall (2003) has observed that southern African states otherwise as diverse as Zimbabwe, Zambia, Namibia, and South Africa have all exhibited centralized presidential power, blurred state-party boundaries, eroded parliamentary oversight, curtailed internal debate, and abuse of racial politics in an attempt to obscure emerging class divisions in the ruling party. The implication is that if we want to understand local political change we should look to wider patterns in regional politics, such as one-party dominance, growing class cleavages and inflexible liberation ideologies, rather than to the peculiarities of particular leaders, such as Thabo Mbeki or Jacob Zuma.

Exceptionalism is a curse because it is only when citizens compare their country to others that they really come to understand the wider forces that shape their history and politics. It is true that African comparisons are by no means the only illuminating ones for an industrialized society and functional democracy such as South Africa. But it is at least arguable that South Africa needs to learn lessons from other countries on this continent – and fast – if it is to avoid the pitfalls of post-colonial African government.

Issues

Some of the central issues and debates in South African politics and society emerge directly out of its history of colonialism and apartheid. Others are profoundly shaped by the racialisation that surrounds almost any area of disagreement. When asked to identify the most pressing problems facing the country, there is a high degree of agreement across racial barriers that the 'big five' issues are jobs, housing, crime, HIV/ AIDS, and poverty (see Table 7.1).

Citizens are not surprisingly preoccupied with economic issues and with poverty. As we have seen (Chapter 3), work is a practical problem for the majority of South Africans for whom employment is unavailable or does not meet their needs. Although Whites tend to complain that affirmative action is making their employment prospects impossible, for most South Africans jobs are simply scarce and their pursuit is a constant preoccupation. It is in crime and corruption, HIV/AIDS and racism that the particular preoccupations of South Africa's citizens emerge.

Crime and corruption

Crime, and especially violent crime, has an impact on almost everyone in the society, although it is undeniably at its most relentless for poor urban communities, for women, and for children. For many years identified

Table 7.1   The changing public agenda 2002 and 2006

Most important problems facing the country	% raising the issue 2006*	% raising the issue 2002
Unemployment	63	84
Housing	28	22
Poverty	27	28
HIV/AIDS	25	26
Crime	23	35
Education	12	15

*Up to 3 issues (unprompted) per respondent
Sources: Idasa 2002a, Afrobarometer 2006.

as the second most important problem facing citizens, crime has fallen behind housing and poverty in the eyes of most South Africans, perhaps as a result of declines in most categories of crime in recent years (see Table 7.2). Crime statistics are notoriously unreliable, and in South Africa the government has intermittently imposed moratoriums while attempting to revise data collection and crime classification practices. Violent crimes such as murder, attempted murder, rape, and assault remain at exceptionally high levels. Aggravated assaults and violent property crimes – including car hijackings and armed burglaries of residential properties – continue to increase. Reported property crime, however, is relatively modest given the extreme levels of inequality in the society, although security is achieved by means of expensive investments in physical barriers, private security services, and community vigilantism. There are strikingly higher rates of crime in the wealthier provinces such as Gauteng and Western Cape.

Attitudes towards crime have been shaped by a history in which the police were the instruments of popular oppression, and politically motivated violence was widespread. Other societies in transition have suffered growing levels of crime, especially where constitutional changes have, like South Africa's, obliged the police to abandon conviction through routine forced confessions and to move towards evidence-based prosecutions. Today communities participate in a wide variety of anti-crime initiatives, and the moral opprobrium heaped upon criminals has intensified. The 120,000 strong South African Police Service (SAPS), moreover, may be moving towards greater effectiveness in its criminal policing practices. Levels of training have improved. New approaches, such as 'sector' policing, which bring police officers into

Table 7.2   Changes in annual crime rates, per 100,000 people

	1995/6	1998/9	2001/2	2004/5	2007/8
Property crimes	1,693	1,685	1,623	1,282	1,090
Contact crimes	1,656	1,675	1,874	1,810	1,404
Theft and commercial	1,293	1,356	1,570	1,404	1,103
Damage to property/ arson	352	331	344	341	302
Firearms, alcohol, drugs	183	189	207	278	357
Total crimes	5,178	5,236	5,618	5,116	4,255

Source: Presidency of RSA 2008.

closer contact with communities, are being introduced. SAPS has been working with other departments in a National Crime Prevention Strategy to disrupt the cycle of violence within communities, and to remove some the conditions (such as poor street lighting) that allow criminals to flourish.

The success of these strategies is likely to be quite limited. Changes in wider social conditions, such as unemployment and persisting inequality, are not conducive to a radical reduction in crime. Violent crimes such as rape and murder, committed largely by family members or aggressors known to the victim, are especially difficult for police to inhibit and have complex and poorly understood psychosocial origins. Crime by unknown parties is disproportionally committed by young men and youths, and South Africa, already a young society, is experiencing a growth in this age cohort. A substantial proportion of young people, moreover, will grow up without one or both parents as a result of HIV/AIDS. These orphaned children – perhaps suffering from social rejection, shame, loss of education, and limited economic opportunities – may be more likely to engage in and to fall victim to criminal activity than their non-orphaned peers (Fourie and Schonteich 2001).

The criminal justice system presents a range of further obstacles to the war on crime. Relations between crime and national intelligence agencies have been poor. The prosecution service has not worked harmoniously with the detective branch, although reforms to this system have been put in place to ensure that evidence that can support prosecution will be more reliably collected in future (Steinberg 2001). The prison population of around 161,000, kept in accommodation designed for less than 100,000, includes almost 50,000 detainees awaiting trial or sentencing, a high proportion of whom are unsentenced juveniles. Attempts to reduce unnecessary incarceration have brought the prison population down from a peak of more than 185,000, but increased arrests, longer sentences, and the large awaiting-trial population contribute to severe overcrowding. The prevalence of rape and gang organization within hostel-type accommodation, moreover, has fuelled an especially severe HIV epidemic among prisoners.

Corruption has been an increasingly prominent issue in public debate in the past two or three years as a result of major scandals surrounding the arms deal, a drip feed of revelations about tender irregularities and government procurement practices, and citizens' own experiences of corruption at the hands of police officers and officials in home affairs, housing, and social welfare departments. A little under half of South Africans believe their local councillors and municipal officials are corrupt, and a third to a quarter believe the same is true of national government officials and parliamentarians. Half of South Africans believe that most police officers are corrupt, and substantial percentages believe that the same applies to health workers, tax officials, judges, teachers, and other state employees (Afrobarometer 2006b). A broader erosion of public confidence in political leaders and officials probably lies behind these deepening perceptions of endemic corruption.

White racism

The direct instruments through which the government is attempting to create a Black middle class and to reduce racial inequality in the distribution of wealth – affirmative action and BEE – are not matters of great public debate at present. They have proven relatively uncontroversial over the longer term because it is widely accepted that the injustices they are designed to ameliorate are indefensible. In everyday interaction across races, South Africans tend to drift towards issues that are relatively uncontroversial within the society.

Racialised argument flares most quickly around seemingly tangential issues that expose fundamentally different assumptions. Many Black South Africans, for example, intuitively suspect that Whites' criticisms of political leaders in neighbouring African states are racially motivated (and some critics of Robert Mugabe have certainly demonstrated that their sympathies lie with Zimbabwe's White farmers only). White South Africans almost always reflect negatively on employment equity policy – and especially on racial quotas in nationally representative sports teams – despite Whites' low unemployment rates and the history of apartheid-era destruction of Black sporting traditions.

Indeed, it is only around sport that it is easy to engage many Whites in open debate. As a group, they have been the principal beneficiaries of the post-1994 settlement. The new politics of private space has allowed them to retreat into office blocks, suburban entertainment complexes, and gated communities, where armed mercenaries can shield them from the world outside. Their near-monopoly of access to quality education has meanwhile allowed them to dominate well-paid employment in the knowledge economy.

Whites are understandably unconcerned about the quality of public services they do not very much use, and their political interventions sometimes veer towards self-parody in complaints about deteriorating public services in the white suburbs and the threat that aspirant black school pupils supposedly pose to the 'language rights' of Afrikaners. Afrikaner philosopher Dan Roodt exaggerates, but also illuminates, the irrational persecution complex that afflicts some Whites when he comments that they are 'on the receiving end of ethnic and racial persecution as bad as that suffered by the Jews in 1930s Germany'.

As a result of failures in their political leadership, Whites have drifted into historical amnesia about the apartheid era. English-speakers dismiss apartheid as a product of Afrikaner racism that had nothing to do with them. For their part, Afrikaners rely on a selective memory that embraces British scientific racism and the confinement of Afrikaners in concentration camps, but recalls more or less nothing at all about the 100 years that followed.

South Africa is heavily dependent upon its White population. It is the very privileges that they have enjoyed as a result of their history that make them irreplaceable national assets. They have skills and capacities that result from many generations of public investment in their education, and their privileged upbringing gives many of them a boundless self-confidence that makes them excellent managers and innovators.

It is all too easy for such citizens, who know they are indispensable, to slip unthinkingly into implicit blackmail: if you do not value me and praise me, I will leave these African shores, taking my skills and assets with me. White exclusion in this way becomes a self-fulfilling prophecy, because black political leaders – who have more profoundly deprived constituencies to consider – cannot easily invite hostile Whites to participate fully in national political life.

Whites continue to place a great burden of expectation upon the shoulders of what they see as 'respectable' blacks. Given that black poverty has remained widespread, even while Whites have enjoyed a post-apartheid windfall, the new middle class has been charged with demonstrating that political change can bring real economic advance for Black citizens.

Any small black step forwards, however, has been also greeted as a justification for continuing White privilege. Since one in five children in elite suburban public schools is now Black, white pupils' vast hidden subsidy is supposedly now legitimate. Black citizens' alleged consumerism is likewise used to cast many Whites' obscene materialism in a more favourable light. It was perhaps always optimistic to expect the presumptions and delusions of White and Black citizens to melt away in some post-apartheid paradise, but it is already apparent that a fuller transformation in social and racial attitude will have to wait for the next generation of so-called 'born-frees' who reached maturity after the watershed 1994 election.

Environmental degradation

Despite a flurry of interest while Johannesburg was hosting the 2002 'Rio-plus-10' World Summit on Sustainable Development, environmental issues have a fluctuating but generally low political profile. Signatory to a number of key international conventions – including the 'Montreal' convention on ozone, 'Basel' on cross-border waste, 'Stockholm' on Persistent Organic Pollutants, and 'Kyoto' on global warming – South Africa nonetheless has an exceptionally poor environmental record. It is a major greenhouse gas emitter, and the world's sixth largest producer of carbon dioxide. South Durban, the Vaal Triangle, and the North of Cape Town suffer extreme problems with organic compounds, sulphur dioxide, and particularite pollution. The country combines the urban problems characteristic of an emerging economy – vehicle and ground water pollution, hazardous industrial and medical wastes, illegal landfills, and noise pollution – with rural soil degradation, overgrazing, poor quality and limited availability of water, and agricultural pollutants. Both inshore waterways and offshore marine habitats are also heavily degraded.

Many of South Africa's most substantial environmental impacts can be traced to the historical strength of primary extractive activities, minerals processing, and associated heavy industries. This sector is a major polluter in its own right through the dumping solid wastes from gold ore separation, liquid waste pits, radon gas and silicon dust releases, and acid and chemical disposals. In addition, these energy intensive activities are supported by an electricity generation sector that relies predominantly on coal and that does not scrub emissions for sulphur. Household energy consumption continues to be dominated by polluting sources such as coal, wood, and paraffin.

The constitution states that everyone has a right to an environment that is not harmful to their health or well-being and to have the environment protected for future generations. Government policy is likewise attractively premised on three key ideas: that people should live in harmony with nature; that clean water, air, and land should be made available; and that green spaces should be a part of every citizen's immediate environment. Using the concept of 'sustainable development' (development which meets the needs of the present without comprising the ability of future generations to meet their own needs) the government has elaborated a legislative framework for managing the impacts of public sector pollution. The government is also moving cautiously towards an integrated pollution and waste management strategy – aimed at prevention rather than treatment – for the private sector. Whether these initiatives will be able to overcome the entrenched opposition of South Africa's many established polluters – including the state itself – is an open question.

HIV/AIDS

South Africa has around 5.7 million people living with HIV out of a population of 48 million. The adult prevalence (ages 15–49) is around 18 per cent, there are perhaps 1.4 million AIDS orphans, and the annual number of deaths attributable to AIDS has risen to around 350,000 (UNAIDS 2008).

Southern Africa's poverty, war-driven population movements, and hostel-based migrant labour system, have provided ideal conditions for the spread of the HIV. Spread by sexual contact, AIDS impacts most heavily on the working age population, raising dependency ratios, reducing productivity and generating knock-on effects (such as the loss of a family home) when a breadwinner dies. Moreover, AIDS will also severely undermine the human capital in the public service, business, and the professions that will be required to address the pandemic's consequences.

Divisions within the ANC have led to a fiasco of policy inconsistency and intellectual confusion around HIV/AIDS policy. The institutions set up to spearhead the battle against the disease have been virtually inoperative for most of the past decade, while stigma and confusion have continued to undermine efforts at prevention. Some have attributed this grim picture to President Mbeki's 'dissident' or 'denialist' position on AIDS as a result of his 2001 claims that the causal relationship between HIV and AIDS is merely a 'thesis', that anti-retroviral treatments are more toxic than HIV itself, and that AIDS advisory panels should contain a balance of orthodox and dissident voices.

A second and related explanation for government confusion highlights the long-standing role of race and sexuality in African nationalist discourse over HIV/AIDS elsewhere on the continent. Attributing AIDS to western degeneracy, and especially to homosexuality, some conservative nationalists as early as the 1980s castigated theories of the African origins of HIV as racist scapegoating. In March of 2002, an unofficial and unattributed paper entitled 'Castro Hlongwane, Caravans, Cats, Geese, Foot and Mouth and Statistics: HIV/AIDS and the struggle for the humanisation of the African', was circulated to the ANC's National Executive by Mbeki-confidant and election strategist the late Peter Mokaba (Mokaba et al 2002). This discussion document, which Mbeki almost certainly co-authored, interpreted HIV/AIDS as a creation of the continent's enemies, described findings that the virus originated in Africa as 'insulting', and echoed the president's late 2001 claim that conventional AIDS science views Africans as 'promiscuous carriers of germs...doomed to a mortal end because of an unconquerable devotion to the sin of lust'.

A third speculation about the causes of ANC equivocation turns on the historical significance of the liberation movement in the eyes of some of its leaders. The ANC's 1994 triumph represented the culmination of a century of anti-colonial struggle on the continent, and signalled the start of an African renaissance. On this interpretation, a proud national liberation movement assuming history to be on its side collided too violently with the intolerable reality of an AIDS catastrophe, and it is the truth that had to give way.

Explanations based on Thabo Mbeki's 'denialism', however, are broadly unpersuasive (Butler 2005b), not least because his views are more complex than have been presented and they are widely shared in the liberation movement. Denial might simply be a convenient cloak. Behind it may lay a calculated approach to government's AIDS policy dilemmas.

There is one inescapable truth about HIV/AIDS treatment that government's critics tend to evade: shortages of health workers mean that antiretrovirals will not reach more than a minority, probably a small minority, of those who need them. The drugs are now cheap, but treatment is complex, demanding clinical, psychosocial, and nutritional expertise. Meanwhile, health workers are emigrating, drifting from the public to the private sector, and moving from rural to urban areas. While the AIDS treatment plan proposes tens of thousands of new posts, tens of thousands of unfilled vacancies already strain hospitals and clinics. There is much that can be done to recruit, train, and retain health practitioners, but more money cannot suddenly precipitate new human resources.

Whatever government does – and there is no question it should do much more – the grim fact remains that most HIV-positive citizens will die of AIDS-related illnesses without receiving antiretrovirals. Far from the turning away 'denial' suggests, government has been active across a wide front with ameliorative measures. It has emphasized nutrition and built alliances with traditional healers, who dominate rural palliative care, and overseen a huge social welfare expansion to support families and communities living with HIV/AIDS.

Yet senior politicians continue to send out confusing messages about how HIV is spread and the value of condom use, refuse to mobilize society in a crusade against the pandemic and continue to condone stigmatization. It appears that equivocation and obfuscation may be part of a wider attempt to defuse the consequences of unequal access to treatment.

Government is exploiting stigmatization and confusion to encourage the notion that AIDS victims have no automatic right to treatment – while moving quietly ahead with publicly funded treatment for social groups seen as economically or politically essential. The rich and the political elite have access to privately financed antiretrovirals, and we can soon expect government to make access for health professionals a priority. Business has been slow to address the effect of HIV/AIDS on productivity and skills, but is waking up. AIDS kills skilled workers in their 20s and 30s. Extending their productive life is essential if a fiscal and productive crisis is to be avoided. Organized workers are politically powerful, propelling them towards the front of any anti-retroviral queue.

AIDS also undermines the state's coercive capacity, its ability to collect taxes and provide services, and the commitment of the new middle classes to democracy is crucial to its survival. Bureaucrats, skilled military personnel, the police, and other public servants vital to the functioning of the state have also moved up the state-funded anti-retroviral queue.

As the pandemic progresses, the ANC's most loyal constituency – the rural poor – is the group most certain to be shut out from any anti-retroviral programme. Government has forged a new alliance with traditional leaders, presumably in part with the intention of reinforcing social cohesion in the areas hardest hit by the pandemic.

The rationing dilemma helps to explain government's hostility to the language of entitlement. South Africa's extensive social welfare system creates expectations of assistance. If antiretrovirals are a right, a discriminatory and rationed antiretrovirals programme must arouse anger.

Formal sector workers would demand treatment for relatives and friends. New social movements would arise, dwarfing today's water and electricity protest groups. Inability to deliver rural antiretrovirals would result in movement to the cities, overwhelming health facilities and worsening public service backlogs.

The carrot of social grants is not enough: government also needs the stick of stigmatization. Ministers have refused to accept ownership of the AIDS problem, the 'Castro Hlongwane', document rejecting 'as fundamentally incorrect and antidemocratic the attempts to transfer the responsibility to look after oneself to the state ... Each one of our citizens has a responsibility to take all necessary measures to protect his or her health.'

Such a shift of responsibility for HIV/AIDS to its victims promotes shame and encourages stigma. Perhaps ministers fear that only shame can limit open defiance, curtail protest against the injustice of selective treatment, and inhibit the urge to seek treatment in the urban health system.

The government, however, cannot expect that poor, unskilled, and stigmatized AIDS sufferers will continue to lie down and die quietly in the former homelands. An unusually sophisticated rural population, with extended historical experiences and networks in urban areas, will migrate or return to the towns and cities in search of treatment and hope, and stigmatization is unlikely for long to inhibit the political organization of those affected by HIV/AIDS.

Conflict over HIV/AIDS has also created political and institutional precedents favourable to the entrenchment of democratic politics: that it is legitimate to use courts against government; that the president can be wrong, and cabinet can correct him; and that ordinary citizens, including ANC members, can legitimately disagree with the party (Butler 2005a).

Sport and the 2010 FIFA World Cup

There have been moments when sport has seemed to offer to South Africans a tantalizing glimpse of a society united across racial and ethnic divisions. The Rugby World Cup victory on home soil in 1995 brought thousands of citizens onto the streets in celebration, and the announcement in 2004 that the country would host the 2010 FIFA World Cup sent a wave of excitement and national pride across the country as a whole. More routinely, however, sport continues to divide as much as it unites, and to symbolize the unaddressed legacies of a century of racism and dispossession.

As in other colonial societies, indigenous sports became increasingly confined to older citizens in rural areas while the major European sporting codes established themselves in urban areas. Middle-class English-speaking Whites brought with them the major team sports rugby and cricket but also less competitive and less male-oriented leisure activities such as tennis, golf, swimming, and bowls (Beinart 1994: 177–78).

White South African teams in rugby and cricket established themselves as among the best in the World during the second half of the twentieth century. Rugby had special appeal to men in Xhosa and Coloured as well as Afrikaner societies. While the Black rugby traditions were starved of resources, Afrikaner schools and universities became nurseries for a particular style of rugby that emphasized physical engagement and forward power. As Afrikaners moved into the middle class and the suburbs, they also adopted the suburban leisure activities of English-speakers. Women were confined to the lower status team sports such as netball and hockey. Wealth, climate, and environment however allowed a wide swathe of White South African society, men and women, to engage in sports of affluence such as swimming, surfing, tennis, and golf. In part because of the centrality that sport assumed in White South African life, international sports boycotts of apartheid South Africa that started in the 1960s eventually had a quite substantial impact on White public opinion about the character and sustainability of apartheid.

After 1994, desegregation of the traditionally White sports occurred quite rapidly at an institutional level but most codes demonstrated a very slow pace of integration in the highest representative teams. This has ensured that sport remains highly politicized, with the selection of national teams and coaches in cricket and rugby being particular bones of contention. In other sports, Black South African participation in golf (the game of business), cycling, gym attendance, and long distance running – including wildly popular ultra-marathons – has increased rapidly, but the same institutional and economic barriers to equality of opportunity have so far prevented the emergence of racial representivity at the highest level.

The high visibility of the major bourgeois and colonial sports has tended to obscure changes in patterns of sporting activity and integration in mass based codes and leisure activities, in particular those linked to gambling. Boxing is a sport that has thrived in White urban areas and Black townships alike. The umbrella body Boxing South Africa enjoys significant government funding to promote the sport and it has enjoyed financial stability as well as a growing support base among women fighters and fans. In the post-segregationist era, racial attitudes are perpetuated in an integrated system in the particular fascination that fights between Black and White fighters sometimes seem to generate.

The major sporting activity enjoyed by South Africans of all kinds is association football or soccer. As in almost every other society, football has widespread appeal and professional teams enjoy significant followings. White, Indian, Bantu, and Coloured football associations were formed in the forty years commencing 1892, and participated in energetic league structures. Football remained the major White working class sport as well as the most popular support in Black communities round the country.

Strict prohibitions on racial mixing, however, made international football the earliest significant sporting casualty of apartheid. South Africa was constitutionally obliged to send either all-White or all-Black teams to international events, a restriction that the Confederation of African Football rejected in principle from its founding in 1957. Race also created controversy in relationships with FIFA although formal expulsion from the international body did not occur until 1976. It was only in 1991 that a multiracial South African Football Association (SAFA) could be formed and 1992 that an integrated team was able to play its first match, and the team went on to an astonishing win in the African Nations Cup in 1996.

National enthusiasm in 2004 about securing the right to stage the 2010 World Cup coincided, however, with a massive collapse in the fortunes of the team, and it has repeatedly failed in recent years in both continental and global competitions. Despite a flood of sponsorship monies into the local professional game, the performance of national team Bafana Bafana (the lads) has trailed that of Banyana Banyana (the girls) in recent years, with the women's team consistently among the continent's top three performers.

The World Cup is a matter for widespread discussion. Sceptics have continued to complain that the stadiums will not be ready, that crime and HIV/AIDS will deter spectators and that the logistical complexity of the world's second most important sporting spectacle (after the Olympics) will be beyond the South African government's capacities.

These fears are almost certainly misplaced. Stadium construction and the preparation of communications infrastructure for the Cup are well in hand. Improvements in the country's transport infrastructure are underway, including the expansion of airports and the construction of mass transit systems. The greatest problems concern bus and mini-bus taxi provision in larger host cities, and the general mobility of visitors between and after matches. Visitors' security is inevitably a concern in South Africa but the country is a low terrorism risk, has a good safety record for major sporting events, and will enjoy the support of an army of citizen volunteers during the weeks of the competition.

A beneficial legacy from the competition is by no means assured. Nevertheless, international sporting events have the potential to open up a country to international tourism and to sweep away the misconceptions of potential investors. They can also bring a population together in a shared project that has lasting value in building a shared national identity.

8

South Africa and the World

South Africa bears the imprint of a history of domination by external forces. The modern South African state was created at the turn of the twentieth century by the world's then greatest empire. Its peoples are a product of continental migratory drift, cross-oceanic slavery, and colonial aggression. Its more recent history was profoundly influenced by the Cold War, and today it is enmeshed in the dynamic of a new period of economic globalization.

The most powerful 'realist' tradition in the study of international relations identifies the state, in rational pursuit of the national interest, as the central actor of international politics. Foreign policy choices, however, tend to advance the interests of some domestic actors while retarding those of others, and South Africa's apartheid governments mostly failed to define let alone to pursue a national interest. Pretoria was a key actor in its region in the apartheid era, building and undermining institutions to promote the immediate goals of its governments and the narrow interests they represented. The republic used military and economic muscle to prevail over weaker neighbours, while also making use of a conventional variety of co-operative instruments, including multilateral institutions, treaties, and diplomatic agreements. Even in its immediate neighbourhood, however, military, business, and parastatal relationships, rather than intergovernmental ones, have dominated interstate conflict and co-operation.

Beyond the immediate Southern African region, the state has enjoyed only limited ability to impose itself in the face of powerful international economic and political forces. International strategy in the apartheid era was driven by a relatively small elite within the ruling National Party (NP), serving the perceived interests of a minority of the country's people. The NP's strategic goals were contested by a parallel international African National Congress (ANC) diplomatic and military system, which managed increasingly to isolate Pretoria in the international community and to secure a right to be heard as the legitimate voice of the South African people in international forums.

Today the ANC can claim to represent the people of South Africa, and it has fashioned a realistic strategy of multilateral international, continental, and regional diplomacy. However, it has not embarked upon any genuine exercise to build national consensus around what would seem to be appropriate and realistic foreign policy goals.

Modern South African International Relations

In the first half of the twentieth century, South Africa's international relations were framed by its position in the British Empire. Notwithstanding domestic division, she participated in the Great War and was rewarded in 1919 with the former German possession of South West Africa, today Namibia, which became her protectorate. South Africa's domestic economy was thereafter closely but perversely tied to the fortunes of the international economy. From the abandonment of the Gold Standard to turmoil in the contemporary Middle East, tumult in international affairs has often raised demand for the 'safe haven' of gold, boosting South Africa's foreign exchange earnings and raising domestic demand. The global industrial wars have also benefited South Africa, as a marginal participant in fighting, yet one with the ability to export into the war economy of its allies. The period of international despair, commencing with the great depression of the 1930s and culminating in the devastation of World War II, was for these reasons an era of great prosperity for South Africa. Her primary commodity gold appreciated dramatically in value in the 1930s.

As the World War II approached, the economies of the industrial powers turned to re-armament leaving open markets for primary and manufactured outputs. From 1940, there was a major expansion in the defence industry as, with British assistance, major investments were made in the manufacture of military hardware for the Allies' war effort. South Africa ended the war a manufacturing economy for the first time, with a rapidly urbanizing population – the latter's predominantly Black composition being one of the precipitants of the electoral triumph of the NP under the apartheid slogan in 1948. Thereafter South African foreign policy moved rapidly into line with the racial priorities of the NP, and the relationship to British imperial interests was severed.

These developments occurred in the context of two great structural changes in the international system, and in how it was understood. The first was the emergence of the Cold War, a four decades long struggle in which the Soviet Union and its satellites and proxies faced off against an alliance of capitalist powers, led by the United States but supported by all of the world's major market economies. The second development was the idea and the reality of the 'Third World', as European powers ceded their colonies, and Asia, Africa, and Latin America entered an era of partial political autonomy but continued economic dependency.

South African external policy was trapped between the contradictory logics of these twin processes. In the 1950s, White South Africa was committed to racial supremacy and segregation in a continental context increasingly marked by African nationalist assertion and colonial withdrawal. The claims of inherent White supremacy and the need to civilize the native were becoming internationally unacceptable as justifications for White domination. At the same time, the Cold War allowed the South African government to elaborate a rhetoric of pro-Western anti-communism, and a conception of natural alliance with the United States and Europe. This rhetoric found echoes in the West in an age of uneasy decolonization and the nascent era of Cold War by proxy. While the 1960's deepening of the Cold War in this way strengthened Pretoria's hand in Washington, the decade also saw the emergence of civil rights movements in the United States, and a constituency opposed to the racialisation of the state under apartheid. South African foreign policy was increasingly a matter of playing off the country's fairly limited strategic significance against its growing unpopularity.

The creation of the Bantustans in the 1960s, and the elaboration of the doctrine of 'separate development', tried to align racial domination with the growing movement of post-colonial independence. The homelands, the government indicated, were to be independent African states – as viable and natural as Lesotho, Swaziland, or Botswana – that would permit African 'nationals' to fulfil themselves through their own systems of government. In part because of intense diplomatic lobbying and public campaigning by the exile ANC and an international anti-apartheid movement, none of them was ever to secure international recognition.

Pretoria's position was nonetheless buttressed until the mid-1970s by a number of strategic advantages. The first was the existence of a substantial White dominated power bloc in the region, which shared common interests in the maintenance of the status quo. For Pretoria, the collapse of authoritarianism in Portugal, and the hasty consequent withdrawal of that power from Angola and Mozambique in 1975, had very significant repercussions. Former 'buffer states' were replaced by the self-characterized 'Front Line States', with an avowedly common agenda of displacing the apartheid regime. South Africa, however, could still rely on the fraternal support of Rhodesia, which had pursued its own policy of White domination after unilaterally withdrawing from British control in 1965. South Africa, moreover, had extended its control over South West Africa (Namibia), which had become a virtual province and in which apartheid had been instituted from 1964.

Pretoria had further significant foreign policy resources at its disposal. South Africa remained the predominant economy in the region. Even front line states vociferously opposed to the apartheid regime had to accommodate themselves to the reality of their dependence on its transport infrastructure, technical skills, the remittances foreign workers sent home from its mining economy, its key exports, and its role as a market for their products. Smaller and landlocked states, in particular, suffered an extreme dependence. The 'liberated' states to the north thus found it impossible to exert a continuous and unequivocal pressure on the apartheid regime.

At the same time the military capacity of South Africa was unrivalled. The national defence force had only 20,000 members at the start of the 1960s, but this had grown to 80,000 by the end of the 1970s. A defence industry built upon wartime production was bolstered in the 1950s through the nurturing of domestic research and development capability. In 1963, the United Nations (UN) introduced a voluntary ban on arms sales to Pretoria. While this was to become mandatory only in 1977, important states, including the United States in 1964, introduced voluntary prohibition early on. Pretoria's response was to redouble domestic capacity-building, creating Armscor (Armaments Development and Production Corporation, later Armaments Corporation of South Africa) in 1968. Armscor rationalized and consolidated private and public sector capacity, developed domestic self-reliance in pivotal technologies, and built the foundations upon which a major export industry arose in the 1980s (Smaldone 1997: 350–54).

The 1978 ascension of former Defence Minister PW Botha to the prime ministership signalled an escalation in the role of the military in politics. Externally, South Africa became more exposed after Rhodesia reached independence as Zimbabwe in 1980. Botha's multifaceted strategy involved alliances or accommodation with smaller and weaker foes, covert aid to rebels in neighbouring states to destabilize their unfriendly regimes, and the creation of increasingly fearsome deterrence and counter threat capabilities – including sometimes the use of pre-emptive strikes in episodes of open aggression. The regime attacked the forward bases of the ANC in the front line states, abducting and assassinating ANC cadres and destroying military assets. Major attacks took place in Mozambique (1980, 1981, 1983, 1987), Lesotho (1982, 1985), Botswana (1985, 1986, 1988), Zambia (1986, 1987), and Zimbabwe (1982, 1986) (see Smaldone 1997: 339–46).

Domestically, under the rubric of 'total strategy', the regime committed itself to a counter-insurgency approach. Botha reconfigured the executive to create a 'state within a state' dominated by military and intelligence interests. A National Security Management System brought some order to the security and intelligence apparatus. One cabinet committee – the State Security Council (SSC) – secured ascendancy over other parts of the state, implementing 'total strategy' with the support of its own extensive secretariat and administrative capacity. The SSC brought together ministers of defence, foreign affairs, justice and law and order with senior military, police, and intelligence chiefs. At the same time, the military-industrial complex developed in scale and intensity, with the workforce of Armscor, for example, growing from 10,000 in 1974 to around 33,000 a decade later. Despite the UN ban on arms exports, South Africa exported to more than 50 countries in the 1980s, including African states Zaire, Gabon, Morocco, and Malawi, and insatiable consumers Iran and Iraq. The 1980s also saw the culmination of South Africa's nuclear, chemical, and biological weapons programmes, with at least six nuclear warheads built out of domestically enriched uranium by the mid-1980s. These weapons were dismantled in 1991 under US pressure, and Pretoria signed the Nuclear Non-Proliferation Treaty.

The ascendancy of the military establishment, however, was always partial. Despite progressive militarization, 1989 South Africa was in just forty-fourth place in the world in terms of military spending as a proportion of Gross National Product (GNP) and just forty-ninth in terms of the size of its forces (Smaldone 1997). The security establishment was politically vulnerable to a White electorate dissatisfied with NP strategy, and the 1989 unravelling of the Soviet empire undercut the power of its anti-Communist rhetoric. A falling away of Soviet arms shipments into the region fundamentally changed the balance of forces and the incentives facing actors. The US pressured regional powers to accept Namibian independence in 1990, together with a joint South African, Soviet, and Cuban withdrawal from the conflict in Angola. In the early 1990s, as the region faced climate-induced drought and famine, South Africa even mobilized its technical and financial resources to assist its neighbours, signalling a fresh conception of relations between former adversaries.

The year 1989 also transformed the relationship between the South African state and its foreign sponsors. In the 1980s, US policy was driven by a desire to ameliorate Soviet influence in the region and to entrench the NP regime as a bulwark against communist ideology and practice. The significance of South Africa, otherwise a small state in an area of very limited strategic importance to the United States, was enhanced by the country's minerals wealth, and particularly by the abundance of platinum, gold, and uranium. In compensation for the reduced strategic salience of the Cape sea routes, South Africa had emerged as a producer of many of the scarce metals vital to the technologies and industries of the future, and remained geographically within striking distance of the major resource reserves of Angola and Congo.

While the United States enforced the UN voluntary arms embargo, and refused to recognize independent homelands, successive administrations continued a policy of 'constructive engagement' with Pretoria. This stance was justified for the US executive by the purported need to maintain influence over an otherwise obdurate regime and by the costs that sanctions would bring to the poor in South Africa. However, congressional opinion is also important in the making of US foreign policy and anti-apartheid politics played a special role in congressional-presidential branch conflict in the 1980s. Reagan's hawkish White House was widely criticized by leaders in the federal legislature. The fractious congressional black caucus, in particular, found in apartheid an issue around which it could sustain its internal coherence. One consequence was the passing over a presidential veto in 1986 of the Comprehensive Anti-Apartheid Act, which laid down a complex system of disincentives and sanctions to US investment in South Africa, prohibited loans, and curtailed existing economic contacts. Two thirds of US firms active in the Republic sold all or part of their holdings (Byrnes 1997).

South Africa's relations with its more significant trading partner, the European Union, were still more complex. By 1992, the European Union (EU) accounted for more than half of all foreign direct investment in South Africa, and was the market for more than 40 per cent of South African exports, as well as the source of a variety of loans, grants, and aid monies. Of the two key trading partners within the EU, German companies continued their operations in South Africa with little disruption. The United Kingdom meanwhile shadowed Ronald Reagan's policy of constructive engagement under Margaret Thatcher, and through the mechanism of the Commonwealth, in which the United Kingdom was a

major force, fought off efforts to construct a more aggressive programme
of sanctions against Pretoria.

By 1989, a variety of domestic actors were converging upon a negotiated settlement (see Chapter 1), and the collapse of the USSR added
fresh momentum to this process. The ANC's allies in the South African
Communist Party were undergoing a far-reaching overhaul of their orthodox Cold War pro-Moscow stance. Moderates within the Afrikaner establishment and business were promising a negotiated settlement, and their
opponents no longer had the external justification of anti-Communist
defiance to fall back on. Apartheid's fundamental mechanisms of population control had turned out to be unsustainable, and the political foundations of NP dominance were crumbling. After 1989, regime change in
South Africa was almost inescapable.

Foreign and Defence Policy from Mandela to Mbeki

The early 1990s brought an unwinding of the relationships between the
security state and the establishment, and a new focus on the practical
problems that would come with any political settlement between the NP
and the ANC. For the next decade, the longer-term strategic priorities
of the new South Africa jostled for attention with the more immediate
imperatives of remaking the military and creating a stable and coherent
state. Within the ANC, idealist and pragmatic schools of thought battled
for supremacy.

Practical imperatives were legion. First, the transition to democratic
rule had to be managed in a context of immense suspicion on both sides,
but especially ANC concern about the willingness and capacity of the
military to protect an ANC government threatened with ethnic conflict
or even civil war. The military and intelligence establishments had to
be discreetly brought on side and into the negotiated settlement. At the
same time, the armed forces had to be unwound from the state, a process
that had commenced under FW de Klerk. While the defence force had
no real escape from this change, its co-operation was bought at considerable cost. A swathe of promotions, early retirements, sunset clauses, and
other incentives were offered by the incoming government. More pain-
fully for many, the ANC effectively abandoned any systematic attempt
to identify and punish those in the military and intelligence responsible
for apartheid era atrocities.

Second, the various military and intelligence structures of the ANC
and the government had to be integrated as quickly and effectively

as possible. On the military front, this involved the incorporation of not just the ANC's armed wing, Umkhonto we Sizwe (MK), into the defence force, but also the Pan Africanist Congress's (PAC's) military arm the Azanian People's Liberation Army (APLA). Both MK and APLA forces were unevenly trained in traditions quite different to those prevailing in the South African Defence Force. In addition, the homelands' military forces had to be absorbed. The merger process was accomplished but at great human cost to many of the younger generation of MK volunteers who did not find a permanent place in the defence force and represent a potential source of political difficulty for the government in the future.

A third set of problems concerned the industrial complex attached to the military, especially the Denel offshoot of Armscor. As domestic and international military spending fell across the late 1980s and into the 1990s, Denel shed labour alarmingly, and with it skills, foreign exchange, and technological and other comparative advantage. In 1994, weapons exports were still over a billion Rand and employment in the sector over 50,000. One of the incoming ANC government's earliest decisions was to maintain manufacturing capacity in this sector and to continue to promote military exports – even though many ANC supporters believed this ran counter to the disarmament agenda advanced prior to 1994. Proponents of an industrial adjustment strategy to reconfigure South Africa's weapons-building capacity for less malign uses were vetoed by the pragmatists who saw this sector as essential for jobs and exports.

The uncertain relationship between the pragmatic and moral dimensions of foreign policy was evident in a watershed article on the ANC's likely post-apartheid foreign policy agenda that appeared in 1993 under the name of Nelson Mandela (1993) in *Foreign Affairs.* This article set out broad principles to guide South Africa's post-1994 external relations, including the promotion of human rights and democracy, the encouragement of peace through negotiation and arms control agreements, the integration of African concerns into foreign policy, further co-operation through the Southern African Development Community (SADC), and integration into global trading relationships. In practice, almost all of the benign intentions behind this agenda were under attack from the moment the ANC came to power in 1994.

As Mandela's presidency got under way, with the uninspiring figure of Alfred Nzo at the helm in Department of Foreign Affairs (DFA), the ANC's lofty moral ambition repeatedly ran aground on the rocks of realpolitik. The honeymoon between Mandela and Clinton's New Democrats did not survive the first few month's of ANC rule. Mandela harangued the United States for failing to deliver on what he believed were promises of massive aid and investment. The United States for its part bewailed the ANC's refusal to abandon ties with what it characterized as rogue states or terrorist regimes – in Cuba, Iran, Libya, and Syria. Mandela developed a doctrine of universality through which the republic suspended judgement on the behaviour of other states, a position which sat uneasily with the commitment to high morality with which it had commenced its rule. Its attempts to lobby against the US trade boycott of key ANC ally Cuba played especially badly in the United States , as did its later support for the Palestinian cause and for Zanu-PF in Zimbabwe.

Mandela's universality hit the hard wall of reality in the form of the People's Republic of China, when South Africa tried to finesse the conflict between the authoritarian behemoth and the newly democratic Republic of China (Taiwan) with which South Africa had very significant trade and investment relations. After a poorly managed attempt to satisfy Beijing that South Africa was an exception to the usual rules of diplomatic recognition, Pretoria was forced to sever full diplomatic relations with Taiwan in full glare of international publicity.

Closer to home, Mandela then tried to intervene in a human rights crisis in Nigeria, in order to prevent the arbitrary execution of human rights activists including poet Ken Saro-Wiwa in 1995. Mandela severed diplomatic relations, only to be condemned by other African leaders for high handiness and interference, and by domestic liberation movement critics for acting on behalf of the West against a fellow African regime. Inflated rhetoric about the common interests of Africa's peoples was exposed by the violence and xenophobia that marked (and continues to mark) treatment of immigrants in a region beset by population displacements. There are several million illegal immigrants in South Africa, popularly viewed as competitors for work as well as scapegoated for disease and crime. (The ANC in government has maintained much of the internal policing apparatus of apartheid and uses it aggressively to curtail the opportunities of migrants to South Africa or to expel them.)

Alongside what critics viewed as the moralizing aspect of South Africa's foreign policy under Mandela, there was a tendency to embark upon grandiose projects and to overstretch the nation's limited human and organizational resources. This failing worsened under his realist successor Thabo Mbeki. The prominence of South Africa in global policy forums policy has not been purely a product of ambition. In the heady immediate aftermath of the 1994 election, South Africa rapidly acquired important executive roles in the international institutions from which it had been excluded under apartheid, including the United Conference on Trade and Development, the G77, the Commonwealth, the Non-Aligned Movement (NAM), the SADC, and the Organisation for African Unity (OAU), later the African Union (AU) (Hughes 2004). Western powers were keen for South Africa to assume responsibility for peace-keeping and brokering operations in Africa where they themselves lacked the credibility to act.

The country could look back to a long history as a self-conceived intermediary between potentially conflicting forces. In the early decades of the twentieth century, South Africa's leaders conceived of their role as mediators between the Great Powers of Europe and the complex systems of indigenous authority that persisted in Africa. The period of apartheid-era isolation has left it slow to condemn, while its remarkable political transition bolstered its self-conception as a state with a unique capacity to mediate, build peace, and broker new agreements between entrenched combatants.

At times this self-conception has been delusional. Peace in Africa is in the interest of South Africa, but the ANC's ongoing preoccupation with conflicts elsewhere, including in Ireland and the Middle East, has not always been endearing to potential allies. South Africa's leaders some-times exaggerate the uniqueness of the society's transition to democracy, and overestimate the lessons it can teach other societies whose problems are more overarching than those Mandela and de Klerk surmounted in 1993 and 1994.

A lack of realism and proportion bedevils some of government's other ambitions. Among the 'new' foreign policy issues that the ANC has championed since 1994 are sustainable development and anti-pollution initiatives, population control, mechanisms for dealing with communicable diseases, arms proliferation, migration issues, democratization, and human rights concerns. Yet South Africa itself has a record that is questionable at best with regard to almost all of these issues: it is a major polluter, one of the world's leading greenhouse gas emitters, a substantial arms exporter, and an intolerant host to migrants which is losing key skills through out-migration. It has, moreover, questionable status in the field of public health. There has consequently been little international tolerance for South Africa's claims to speak with authority in these areas.

Many domestic commentators have echoed the accepted wisdom that South Africa contains first and third worlds, or the developed and the undeveloped world, and so claimed that its leaders have some special place as interlocutor between North and South (Barber and Vickers

2001: 343–44. Yet, as we saw in Chapters 3 and 4, South Africa is a fairly wealthy developing country with an appalling record of violence and inequality. Far from indicating any special capacity to ameliorate inequalities and consequent social conflicts, this reality may demonstrate that the society is quite exceptionally poor at coping with such challenges.

Of equal significance is the ANC's own composition as a movement, embracing as it does a variety of conceptions of the character of international power politics. Many prominent policy makers in government emerged out of Eastern Communist traditions, and the South African Communist Party (SACP) of which most leading ANC cadres were members was highly sympathetic to the Soviet Union's self-serving interpretation of the global order. Others, however, shared Western European conceptions of the improvability of political institutions, the benign role of multilateral institutions, and the desirability of regulated market economies and representative democracy. In developing means of functioning in the face of its own internal contradictions, the ANC became adept at managing ambiguity and negotiating differences between others.

Foreign Policy for the Twenty-first Century

South African diplomacy and external strategy during the four decades after 1948 were driven by the desire to defend and advance the domestic agenda of White domination. The ANC's honourable initial instincts from 1994 were to shake the very foundations of realpolitik and to advance an international agenda worthy of a 'New' South Africa. Critics claim that despite the failure of this approach, the government lacks any clear sense of priorities in foreign affairs and that there has been too little debate about the nature or content of national strategic interest. Certainly, little effort has been made to forge a national consensus through debate, and government has pursued many contradictory objectives – including the mollification of domestic constituencies – simultaneously and sometimes uncertainly.

During his two terms as state president, Thabo Mbeki emphasized that a central external problem facing all African states is their progressive marginalization in the international economy. Economic development elsewhere has lifted hundreds of millions out of the despair of poverty in the past two decades, and may continue to improve the lots of still more numerous millions in China, India, and Latin America in coming decades. Africa has been largely excluded from these momentous developments (see Table 8.1). The key question for African leaders is how to participate

Table 8.1   Global annual per capita income growth 1975–99

Region	% world population	% growth per capita income
East Asia and the Pacific	31	6
South Asia	23	2.3
OECD	19	2
Latin America & Caribbean	8	0.7
Arab states	4	0.3
Sub-Saharan Africa	10	-1

Source: UNDP 2002.

in this economic order, to attract investment, to trade, and to become part of the value adding supply chains that make up the international economy. Africa has suffered severely from volatile commodity prices, uncertain investor interest, spiralling debt burdens, and policy prescriptions that have hindered rather than promoted economic development.

The Mbeki government registered this priority and its actions suggested that it had embraced the fundamental role of foreign policy in advancing business interests. Early ANC cabinets allowed moral ambition and the pragmatics of doing business to come into conflict, creating unproductive stand-offs and embarrassment for South African and foreign representatives. Conflict with the European Union and the United States in trade negotiations rapidly disabused them of the notion that leverage is best exerted from the moral high ground. Today, the central role of diplomatic representation overseas is unashamedly to secure export markets, business partners, and foreign direct investment for South Africa. Moreover, Mbeki created an International Investment Council designed to pick the brains of prominent international business people, and under its guidance launched an International Marketing Council in the attempt to improve international perceptions of the country as an investment and tourism destination.

If the primacy of economic affairs is now widely appreciated, the content of the national interest in this area is still poorly defined. One difficulty is that South Africa's currently important economic relationships are not aligned with liberation movement theology. Western Europe and the United States remain South Africa's key trading partners and sources of investment, skills, and technology, while important constituencies within the ANC consider that its destiny lies within Africa and elsewhere in the South. The liberation movement, some Africanists claim, can catalyse continental renaissance and bring the continent towards a new relationship of equality with the West. The density of diplomatic, trading and other ties with Western Europe and the United States is for them a cause for concern rather than for celebration.

Both international financial institutions such as the World Bank and International Monetary Fund (IMF) (which demand that prudent fiscal and monetary policy and liberalized markets are preconditions for loan finance) and trans-national corporations are viewed with huge suspicion by many ANC intellectuals. Some liberation movement thinkers, moreover, seek not merely a pro-African agenda, but an anti-Western one, and the DFA has come under some pressure from the ANC parliamentary caucus to build its diplomatic infrastructure around such ideological rather than economic imperatives.

One major external policy scandal concerns the highly controversial 1999 Strategic Defence Procurement Package (widely known as 'the arms deal'). The government had conducted a national defence review in 1995 with a view to determining the future role and structure of the military. Its findings were endorsed by parliament in 1998, and government moved remarkably rapidly into a procurement phase, with cabinet announcing as early as September 1999 that technical analysis, affordability studies, tendering, and selection processes were complete. The package was intended to amount in total to more than R20 billion over 8 years (or R30 billion over 12 years if an option to procure additional equipment was exercised). Its rationale included supposed 'industrial offsets', or counter-trade agreements, in terms of which the suppliers undertook to carry out procurement or other economic activities within South Africa to a value of more than R100 billion.

Controversy surrounded the deal almost from the moment it was signed. It brought allegations of corruption in the procurement process and demands from the legislature's public accounts oversight committee for the clarification of unexplained irregularities in procurement and potential conflicts of interest. The package has become increasingly controversial for its scale, for the naivety of its 'offset'-based financing, for procedural irregularities that included the incomplete briefing of cabinet, and for a seemingly endless escalation of costs. Elements of high-level impropriety – discounted luxury cars for politicians and civil servants and insufficiently rigorous checks on involved parties' relations with subcontractors – brought increasingly vociferous criticism.

A wide range of actors mobilized to raise and investigate these allegations, in what was in comparative terms an unusually public investigation of arms procurement corruption. The government's determination to control potential fallout from the investigations and to protect senior politicians and officials, however, led it to undermine the select committee on public accounts, the legislature's key and formerly non-partisan oversight institution. It then took steps that, in the eyes of many, compromised the integrity of the offices of the auditor general and public protector. Already criticized for starving oversight bodies of resources, the ANC leadership seemed at times to be castigating opponents for investigating impropriety. A drip feed of revelations continued across the Mbeki years and these ultimately implicated the president himself and his deputy Jacob Zuma in alleged impropriety. The struggle between these political leaders and others to escape prosecution had substantial negative consequences for parliament, independent oversight institutions, and the courts, as well as creating immense tensions within the ruling party.

The African Union, Nepad, and Zimbabwe

Thabo Mbeki's presidency brought milestones in the diplomatic history of the continent, including the launch in 2002 of two significant and related initiatives, the African Union (AU) and the New Partnership for Africa's Development (NEPAD). The AU is successor to the ill-starred Organization of African Unity, a divided and latterly inertial body, which failed in the context of postcolonial economic and political crisis to identify or prosecute continent-wide goals and interests. The AU proposes an immensely ambitious framework for co-operation between states, ultimately moving towards a quasi-federal relationship on the model of the European Union. Its institutional innovations include an African parliament, the evolution of a common African judicial system, and closer economic relationships to be secured by means of customs unions and free trade agreements. The AU project has wide emotional appeal, because it promises to end decades of subjugation of Africans to foreign economic, cultural, and political domination. It proclaims that Africans, through their own collective efforts, will achieve a cultural and intellectual equality with their peers in the West.

While South Africa came late to the AU process, the philosophical underpinnings of its ambitious agenda were spelled out by Thabo Mbeki in a speech to the US Corporate Council on Africa in 1997, when he astonished his audience with the claim that 'the African Renaissance is upon us!' The notion of continental renaissance flies in the face of conventional western assumptions about the stagnation of Africa's economies and the failure of its political leaders to develop sustainable pathways to prosperity. Dismissing such 'Afro-pessimism', proponents of African renaissance claim that a new kind of inter-state relationship can be built out of the unhappy heritage of conflict in Africa. Sceptics counter with the claim that the architecture of the AU cannot function in today's Africa, and serves only to place still more power in the hands of a cross-national clique of venal and corrupt leaders.

The second major initiative that emerged in 2002, the NEPAD, was in its heyday described by its proponents as the AU's economic blueprint. NEPAD was the most significant effort to assemble a strategic approach to Africa's overall developmental challenges. It was scarcely a programme for concrete advance, so diverse and diffuse were its goals, and so ambiguously worded its proposals for action. But it did assemble a series of priorities for the continent that might have provided the basis of concerted action by governments, donors, and private investors. Among the central pillars of NEPAD was the notion that it should act to co-ordinate the economic relations between African states collectively and the developed world. Thus it aimed to forge common continental positions in multilateral trade negotiations, a common strategy with regard to development aid, a single debt reduction policy, as well as dealing on a collective basis with the promotion of foreign investment in Africa, conflict resolution, and infrastructural investment. More problematically, NEPAD was also ostensibly informed by respect for an open society and for democracy.

NEPAD was an immensely ambitious institution that depended on South Africa's capacity to unify African states behind it and to persuade European and North American partners of its viability, while at the same time avoiding the perception that it sought to railroad fellow African states into an agreement designed to advance its own interests and values.

Western critics of NEPAD immediately highlighted weaknesses in voluntary 'peer review' governance mechanisms designed to promote good governance, and pointed to the failure of African states to rationalize their own chaotic systems of regional economic communities (of which there are some 14) before demanding access to developed country markets. NEPAD's ability to flourish within the AU was also immediately questioned, and over time criticism of South African hegemony, ineliminable Anglo-French tensions, and conflicts of interest and opinion surrounding key competitors such as Nigeria and Libya took their steady toll on the initiative. The growth of Chinese influence in Africa over the past decade, moreover, has offered an alternative conception of international partnership to those regimes unwilling to conform to Nepad's (fairly minimal) governance imperatives. It seems likely that NEPAD will eventually integrate into the AU in a relatively modest form as an agency through which international and regional trade negotiations will be conducted and as a mechanism for co-ordination of cross-country infrastructural and other investment projects.

Some of the more ambitious continental programmes conceived for NEPAD may eventually be implemented at regional level, perhaps through a re-energized SADC. The SADC is a more coherent and potentially manageable group of states than the AU and it would be less riven by the rivalries that threaten any continental body. Good governance mechanisms and trade liberalization might in future be advanced hand in hand in South Africa's more immediate neighbourhood. At the same time, however, South Africa's immediate neighbours include Zimbabwe. This country's recent dismaying descent into economic and political chaos has provided an object lesson in the limits of South African power even in the heart of the SADC region.

Zimbabwe's economy was relatively small in comparison to South Africa's before the onset of the current crisis but it was a very significant neighbour nevertheless. The implosion of the Zimbabwean economy undermined external confidence in the region and set back the project of creating a vital regional economy. The two countries share a common and permeable border and as the crisis in Zimbabwe deepened the flow of cross-border economic and later political migrants turned to a flood, with ultimately dangerous consequences for the fabric of urban township communities in Gauteng that had to absorb the migrants.

Despite the importance of Zimbabwe to South Africa, Thabo Mbeki's government found it difficult to exert any real influence over president Robert Mugabe's degenerating and increasingly military dominated Zanu-PF regime. ANC leaders remained sceptical that the opposition Movement for Democratic Change (MDC) represented an authentic alternative to its fellow liberation movement, and expressed further doubt about allowing the electoral eviction of a liberation movement by a 'foreign sponsored' and union-based party with no liberation legitimacy to its credit. The diplomacy that was required to steer Zimbabwe towards the government of national unity that the ANC leadership favoured, and away from respecting the outcome of a decisive national election, proved for many years to be beyond the reach of the South African government and inadvertently threw into question its commitment to abiding by the outcomes of democratic elections at home.

Mechanisms for Foreign Policy Making

The creation of a coherent machinery for making and implementing foreign policy after 1994 threw up a number of challenges. The incoming Mandela government had to manage the integration of apartheid-era and liberation movement personnel and traditions in diplomacy and intelligence, while simultaneously transforming the content of external policy. Officials of the DFA were inevitably regarded with distrust and hostility by the incoming elite, and the Defence Ministry was unavoidably preoccupied with structural reviews, procurement policy, and the creation of an integrated defence force. The Department of Trade and Industry and the Treasury have secured ascendancy in foreign trade, investment, and economic relationships. Even more markedly, the Presidency has dominated the cluster of International Relations Peace and Security (IRPS), intervening sometimes heavy-handedly in foreign investment promotion, the creation of the AU, the Zimbabwe crisis, and NEPAD, among others. The Presidency has also worked hand-in-glove with actors such as the African Renaissance Institute and the parastatal Eskom to shape the content of external policy.

The 'presidentialisation' of foreign policy is not unique to South Africa, but it has been accompanied by a sometimes alarming deterioration in the morale and capacity of the DFA. Strained by the country's participation in a rapidly expanded range of multilateral commitments, the DFA has struggled to retain the personnel and organizational coherence required to make South Africa a credible international actor.

Parliament has remained a weak actor in foreign affairs. The ANC caucus has limited members to ritual affirmations of leadership-driven policy. Members of the foreign affairs oversight committee are often briefed on policy change but none of them can claim an active role in shaping it. While there is a parliamentary committee dealing with African foreign policy issues, it is almost inoperative and defers to the Foreign Affairs committee on issues of potential sensitivity in which the presidency is involved, such as NEPAD and human rights in Africa.

The international relations subcommittee of the ANC's National Executive Committee plays a role in shaping foreign policy priorities and in communicating these to the caucus and to ministers and officials. However, successive ANC presidents have been able to seize this area as their own and personally to influence the character of South Africa's external profile and strategy.

Opposition parliamentarians have been more vocal about foreign policy than the ANC, especially with regard to the crisis in Zimbabwe and the conflicts in Palestine and Iraq. However, the primarily White and English-speaking leadership of the official opposition Democratic Alliance (DA) deprives it of popular legitimacy when commenting on the behaviour of liberation movements such as Zanu-PF, and this lack of authority is shared by think tanks like the South African Institute for International Affairs. Indeed, DA attempts to steer a course closer to the United States and Israel on middle east conflicts were exploited by the ANC to portray it as sympathetic to imperialism and a 'new apartheid' in Palestine. ANC leaders have used these more distant international crises quite skilfully to promote the ANC as a leader within the international non-aligned movement, to build upon existing relationships and sympathies in the Arab world, and to defuse domestic tensions over more local policy with regard to Zimbabwe.

The influence of the Presidency in foreign policy making has been controversial. While Presidents Mandela and Mbeki unmistakably offered leadership and sometimes moved decisively across a complex diplomatic terrain, presidential leadership has often alienated officials and antagonized stakeholders in the state, business, and civil society. These problems have not entirely detracted from the emergence of South Africa as a middle power of some weight and significance. South Africa has also marked out a position for itself in the current rethinking of the international political architecture. It does not merely mediate between the states of the South and the North, it is engaged in debates about the desirability of reform of international institutions themselves, including the United Nations Security Council, the G7, the World Trade Organization (WTO) and the IMF. As new intergovernmental formations have emerged across the South, moreover, and in new alliances between the emerging powers of Brazil, Russia, India, and China, South Africa has become positioned as Africa's North–South and South–South interlocutor.

As part of this wider ambition, South Africa secured a non-permanent seat on the United Nations Security Council from January 2007 to December 2008, an achievement that officials believed would assist Pretoria's campaign for a permanent seat in a reformed UN. During its tenure, however, South Africa controversially found itself aligned with authoritarian regimes over issues as diverse as repression and democratic reforms in Burma, human rights abuses in Uzbekistan and Belarus, sanctions against Iran, Kosovo's independence bid, and the condemnation of rape as a weapon of war – as well, more predictably, as the imposition of targeted sanctions against the Zimbabwean regime. While these actions do not demonstrate that Pretoria's commitments to human rights and democracy are spurious, they do demonstrate the limitations of the initially idealist approach that the ANC brought to foreign affairs in 1994.

9

South Africa in the Twenty-First Century

The struggle against apartheid propelled South Africa to an unhappy international prominence. The country continues to carry a weight of expectation for those who hope for a more prosperous and less conflict-ridden future for the world's developing countries. South Africa is now at the heart of an emerging project to remake Africa's political life and transform its economic prospects. She is also at the centre of the struggles of the countries of the South for more representative global institutions and for a more equitable international trading order.

The practical significance of these attempts to remake the international order is hard to assess. The new economic giants of Asia threaten to become not friends but rather new imperial powers, and the complexity and depth of Africa's multiple crises almost defy comprehension. South Africa's economy, moreover, is too small for her to be a major global actor, yet it is big enough to make her an inadvertent regional bully and to stir the animosity of political rivals elsewhere on the continent.

Pretoria has plenty of problems of her own closer to home. The country's triumphant 1994 election signalled the start of a new era of uncertainty for all South Africans. The increasingly desperate and violent struggle of the National Party (NP) establishment to maintain minority political domination was thankfully over. The task of creating a less divided and more equal society still lay ahead. This chapter offers a preliminary assessment of the liberation movement's achievements after a decade and a half of rule. It goes on more tentatively to predict what the future will hold for a society that, more than almost any other, has divided scholars and surprised political analysts.

214

The Economy, Human Development, and Welfare

Continued economic growth and a decline in poverty and inequality are pre-requisites for the political stability and social reconciliation to which South Africans aspire. It is through the creation and distribution of wealth that the many conflicts of this democracy will be ameliorated or exacerbated. The record of the ANC on this score deserves credit. In the early post-war period, a golden era for the economies of many nations, South Africa grew at between four and six per cent per year for two full decades. In the years that followed, however, falling commodity prices, political conflict, and structural rigidities in the economy all played a part in a lamentable legacy of low and erratic growth. The NP tossed aside fiscal responsibility in its desperate efforts to cling to power.

When the African National Congress (ANC) swept into office in 1994, it inherited a dangerous budget deficit and an escalating national debt. The movement's achievement in abandoning socialism and presiding over a decade of deficit reduction that culminated in budget surpluses is considerable. ANC leaders have inculcated an awareness that good public services require not more but better public spending. Yet the liberation movement has had to draw heavily on its reserves of popular trust, as it has presided over a stagnation of formal sector employment. Perhaps 40 per cent of those who desire work are denied it. Inequality and poverty initially deepened dangerously during the first years of ANC rule, and the (effective) use of social grants to alleviate poverty remains a highly unsatisfactory substitute for a thriving market economy.

Government has made most progress in making available water, sanitation, electricity, decent schooling, housing and healthcare, basic public services that were previously a near-preserve of whites. The obstacles valiantly overcome and the improvements in quality of life that have often resulted cannot be overemphasized. A wide swathe of Black South African society today lives in households with basic services and amenities unthinkable ten years ago. Yet the very poor are still denied the dignity of access to 'universal' public services by user charges and economic insecurity. Like other developing countries, South Africa has to run simply to stand still, as the demands thrown up by urbanization, rural decay, and social dislocation accumulate day in and day out.

The private sector has experienced mixed fortunes in this new era, with private investment picking up on the back of liberalization and increased business confidence. Growth for a time reached the 5 per cent per annum level at which it began to dent unemployment, but such a rate of growth is not currently sustainable. Businesspeople complain that profound skills deficiencies and labour market regulation militate against the employ-ment creation the government seeks. Small and informal businesses will not create sufficient jobs to absorb the army of young unemployed. The devastation wrought by unemployment is set to continue.

Black economic empowerment (BEE) remains another priority given South Africa's history of racial division. Yet while empowerment will release entrepreneurial and intellectual energy in the longer term, it is costly now. ANC strategy has mostly steered a prudent course, balancing the costs of empowerment against the dangers of delay.

The challenge of HIV/AIDS casts a shadow over the society. In the economy the pandemic is increasing employee turnover and reducing productivity. It is testing the social fabric of the poorest communities, where it places an intolerable burden upon the women who are society's carers and providers. The pandemic is an exceptional challenge that requires a new level of co-operation between government, business, and citizens – and better political leadership – if its worst potential implica-tions are to be mitigated.

Reconciliation, Nation-building, and Democracy

Apartheid left a residue of bitterness and suspicion. While some indi-viduals transcended the segregation that blighted the twentieth century, generations will have to pass before race is no longer an impediment to trust. Policy makers have rightly given priority to reducing the profound inequalities of status and wealth that continue to stoke the fires of racial conflict. However, equally taxing political challenges must be faced con-cerning the limited entrenchment of democracy and the failure to estab-lish a robustly open and plural society.

On the surface democracy is South Africans' preferred form of rule. Open debate and political competition seem essential if conflicts of interest and opinion are to be accommodated. However, the language of democracy is complex and carries different meanings to different ears. Only a minority of (mostly White) beneficiaries of apartheid celebrate democracy for its promotion of political opposition and human rights (including the right to property). Most South Africans understand democracy primarily in instrumental terms, as a political form through which inequality is curtailed and basic public services, such as hous-ing, water, and food, are made available to the people as a whole. The gulf between these interpretations of its meaning leaves South Africa's democracy vulnerable should economic injustice persist.

The ANC dominates the South African political landscape, although challenges to its electoral power are already on the horizon. The movement's strength has helped to cushion fragile and awkward new institutions against the repercussions of conflict and inequality. South Africa's democracy may still be too weak to cope with party fragmentation or racial polarization, because it lacks sound, legitimate, and trusted institutions. However, the longer the ANC continues unchallenged both electorally and in the executive, the more harm may be caused by state-party integration, patronage politics, opposition de-legitimation, and the abuse of incumbency.

Even the benefits of ANC dominance – should it persist – are far from assured. Its leadership sometimes places other former liberation movements above the rules of the democratic game, and it privileges internal mechanisms of accountability over the constitution. Can it be relied upon to bolster the legitimacy of the new political order and to entrench constitutional government? If this vast, sprawling, and ideologically diverse movement is unlikely to fall under the effective control of an authoritarian leadership, disenchanted activists may nevertheless abandon the ANC for new rivals and voters may decide in increasing numbers to stay at home.

The brightest and best of the new generation are already turning their backs on politics and the public service. The ANC, if this continues, may progressively become the fiefdom of crude political entrepreneurs, the corrupt, and the cynically ambitious. An ANC weakened in this way would be unlikely to bring about a more equitable and benevolent distribution of the country's wealth and productive assets. Indeed, it might be responsible for a collapse in the capacity of the state to provide public services, and ultimately for a ruinous counter-reaction against entrenched injustice. This die is by no means cast. South Africa's plurality and political energy are already reasserting themselves. ANC leaders may succeed in sustaining their government as the engine of the country's social and economic transformation, and they might yet render the liberation movement a force for a more open and democratic politics.

Recommended Reading

1   Historical Context

There is a wealth of popular and academic writing on modern South African history. Excellent general histories include Beinart 2001, Worden 2000, Thompson 1990, Davenport 1991 and Saunders 2001. Sparks 1995 offers a lively survey of the transition process. On pre-twentieth century history, see Beinart and Bundy 1987, Bundy 1988, and Wilson and Thompson 1982. On segregation and apartheid, see the collection of seminal essays in Beinart and Dubow 1995, and the contrasting viewpoints of Davies 1979, Wolpe 1988, and Lipton 1985. The internal strains of the apartheid project are explored in Posel 1991, Price 1991, and Greenberg 1987, and its black politics in Lodge 1985 and in the four volumes of Karis and Carter 1972–7. The demise of apartheid is analysed in Etherington 1994 and Stedman 1994. For elegant studies of the emergence of the Witwatersrand see Van Onselen 1982a and 1982b, and for a magical account of a twentieth century sharecropper, see Van Onselen 1996.

2   A Rainbow Nation?

On climate, ecology, and geography see Preston-Whyte and Tyson 1989, Haldenwang 1997, and Fox and Rowntree 2000. The meanings and significance of 'tribalism' and ethnicity in Southern Africa are explored in Bekker 1993, Mare 1992, and most illuminatingly Vail 1989. On Coloured and Indian South Africans, see Du Pre 1994, James and Simons 1989, Desai 1997, and Freund 1995.

3   The South African Economy

For overviews of macro-economic policy challenges, see Nattrass 2000; for an insider's perspective of economic policy under Mandela and Mbeki see Hirsch 2005; and for a leftist perspective see Marais 1999. A range of orthodox perspectives on achievements and failings since 1994 can be found in a special issue of *Journal of African Economies*, 16:5, August 2007. Black economic empowerment is analysed in Ramaphosa 2004, Southall 2005, and Butler 2006.

4 Social Structure and Social Policy

Class, social structure, and employment are explored in Seekings and Nattrass 2005. For social welfare see Taylor 2002, and for overviews of poverty challenges see Bhorat and Kanbur 2006 and Seekings 2007. Critical analysis of housing, urban social infrastructure, and privatization policy can be found in Smith 2000, Hemson 2004, Bond 2000, and Makgetla 2001. Government's own macro-social report RSA 2006 is informative and well organized. On education, see Chisholm 2004 for an overview, Fiske and Ladd 2005 for an incisive recent contribution, and Kallaway 2002 for history.

5 Government

Picard 2005 offers a sober assessment of the post-apartheid state. Venter 2001 offers a readable introduction to South Africa's post-1996 system of government. On intergovernmental relations, see Levy and Tapscott 2001b, Murray 2001 and Levy 2001. For discussion of the role of local government, see Parnell et al 2002, and Cameron 1999 and 2000.

6 Political Life

On the evolution of post-1994 politics, Lodge 1999 and 2002, and Schrire 2001, are essential. A gloomy but coherent view of one-party dominance is advanced in Giliomee and Simkins 1999. For briefer overviews see Mattes 2002 and Butler 2003. On political attitudes and democracy, see Mattes 2007, and on the African National Congress (ANC) see Butler 2005c and 2007b, Reddy 2005, Suttner 2003, and Lodge 2004 and 2005. South Africa's regional context is explored in Southall 2003 and Melber 2003. Contemporary politics can also be explored by means of autobiographies (De Klerk 1999, Feinstein 2007, Kasrils 1998) and political biographies, Gevisser 2007 (Thabo Mbeki), Butler 2007a (Cyril Ramaphosa), Lodge 2006 (Nelson Mandela), and O'Malley 2007 (Mac Maharaj).

7 Culture, Ideas, and Issues

For a fascinating overview of South Africa post-1994 culture, see Kriger and Zegeye 2001 (upon which Chapter 7 drew heavily). On music, see Erlmann 1999, and on religion Chidester 1992. For investigation of emerging lifestyles and consumption patterns see Burgess 2002. Issues in intercultural dialogue are explored illuminatingly in Kaschula and Anthonissen 1995. Steinberg 2001 offers an eye-opening introduction on the crime and policing in South Africa.

On HIV/AIDS policy, see Whiteside and Sunter 2000, Mattes 2003, Nattrass 2004, and Butler 2005a and 2005b.

8   South Africa and the World

For historical overviews see Barber and Barrett 1990, Geldenhuys 1990, and Olivier and Geldenhuys 1997. On the security state and the military, see the luminous Seegers 1996, together with Alden 1995, Hanlon 1986, and Grundy 1986. Exile diplomacy is detailed in Thomas 1996 and contemporary developments can be followed in SAIIA 2008. The contemporary policy process is explored in Hughes 2004, the significance of policy change in Cilliers 1999, and South Africa's corporate expansion in Africa in Daniel et al 2004.

South Africa on the Internet

A government yearbook and a pocket guide to South Africa, both updated annually, can be downloaded free from the government communications service <www.gcis.gov.za>.

1 Historical Context

The history of modern South Africa can be explored through South African History Online <www.sahistory.org.za> which offers timelines, biographies, and graphics as well as access to the country's national history curriculum. Digital Innovation South Africa (DISA) <www.disa.ukzn.ac.za> is an online scholarly resource focusing on South Africa's socio-political history during the freedom struggle.

2 A Rainbow Nation?

Issues concerning the land can be approached through government departments for the environment, land affairs, agriculture, and water and forestry, <www.deat.gov.za>, <www.land.pwv.gov.za>, www.nda.gov.za, and <www.dwaf.gov.za>. The Department of Arts and Culture is at <www.dac.gov.za>.

3 The South African Economy

The most useful official site is the Treasury <www.treasury.gov.za> and data can also be accessed at the official statistics agency <www.statssa.gov.za> and the Reserve Bank <www.reservebank.co.za>. Academic analysis can be accessed through <www.ber.sun.ac.za>, or Economic Research Southern Africa <www.econrsa.org>. Development-related sites include Development Bank of Southern Africa <www.dbsa.org.za> and country-specific information can be accessed through international organizations such as the World Bank and United Nations Development Programme <www.worldbank.org> and <www.undp.org>. Major business organizations include Business Unity South Africa <www.busa.org.za> and Business Leadership South Africa <www.businessleadership.org.za>.

4   Social Structure and Social Policy

The best place to access current empirical social research is University of Cape Town's Centre for Social Science Research <www.cssr.uct.ac.za>. Other useful sites include <www.sairr.org.za>, <www.cps.org.za>, the business-sponsored Centre for Development and Enterprise <www.cde.org.za>, and the Department of Social Development <www.dsd.gov.za>. The Centre for Civil Society offers leftist analysis <www.ukzn.ac.za/ccs>. The Human Sciences Research Council <www.hsrc.gov.za> has a wide range of social research available online.

5   Government

The system of government is explained at <www.gov.za> where there are links to the national constitution, national and provincial departments, traditional authorities, public administration systems, and state institutions supporting constitutional democracy. Parliament is at <www.parliament.gov.za>.

6   Political Life

Key political party sites include the ANC <www.anc.org.za> and its labour and communist allies <www.cosatu.org.za> and <www.sacp.org.za>. The official opposition Democratic Alliance can be found at <www.da.org.za> and the Inkatha Freedom Party (IFP) at <www.ifp.org.za>. Useful sites include Institute for a Democratic South Africa <www.idasa.org.za>, Electoral Institute of Southern Africa <www.eisa.org.za> and policy and legislation updates can be found at <www.polity.org.za>. Rich interview transcripts with many of the country's political leaders can be found on Padraig O'Malley's site at <www.omalley.co.za>.

7   Culture, Ideas, and Issues

Media sites include business newspaper *Business Day* <www.bday.co.za>, the Sowetan <www.sowetan.co.za>, the *Mail and Guardian* <www.mg.co.za> and the *Sunday Times* <www.suntimes.co.za>. The Universities of Cape Town

<www.uct.ac.za>, Witwatersrand <www.wits.ac.za>, and Stellenbosch <www. sun.ac.za> have interesting sites and links. For HIV/AIDS, see international sites <www.who.org>, <www.unaids.org> and <www.aegis.com> (which has an excellent search facility). Campaign group Treatment Action Campaign <www. tac.org.za> has analysis and links. Projections of the impact of HIV/AIDS can be found at the Actuarial Society of South Africa <www.actuarialsociety.org.za>.

8   South Africa and the World

For international relations, see the official sites of the Department of Foreign Affairs <www.dfa.gov.za>, the New Partnership for Africa's Development <www.nepad.org>, and the African Union <www.africa-union.org> together with Non-government Organizations (NGOs) <www.saiia.org.za> and <www. igd.org.za>.

A range of contact lists for politics, government, the media, and other sites can be found at <www.gcis.gov.za/docs/directories/index.html>. Popular South African blogs can be accessed through <www.amatomu.com>.

All listed sites were accessible 30 August 2008.

Bibliography

Adam, H. et al (1997), *Comrades in Business* (Cape Town: Tafelberg).

Afrobarometer (2006a), 'The Public Agenda: Change and Stability in South Africans' Ratings of National Priorities'. *Briefing Paper #45* (Cape Town: Afrobarometer).

Afrobarometer (2006b), 'Resurgent Perceptions of Corruption in South Africa.' *Briefing Paper #43* (Cape Town: Afrobarometer).

Alden, C. (1995), *Apartheid's Last Stand: The Rise and Fall of the South African Security State, 1978–90* (London: Macmillan).

Alexander, N. and K. Heugh (2001), 'Language policy in the New South Africa', in Kriger and Zegeye 2001, 15–39.

Arndt, C. and Lewis, J. (2000), 'The macro-economic implications of HIV/AIDS in South Africa: A preliminary assessment', *Journal of South African Economics*, 68:5, 856–7.

Asmal, K. (1995), 'The making of a constitution', *Southern African Review of Books*, No. 36.

ASSA (2002), *Actuarial Society of South Africa AIDS model* (Cape Town: Actuarial Society of South Africa).

Barber J. and B. Vickers (2001), 'South Africa's foreign policy', in Venter 2001, 312–44.

Barber, J. and J. Barratt (1990), *South Africa's Foreign Policy: The Search for Status and Security 1945–88* (Cambridge: Cambridge University Press).

Barkan, J. (2005), 'Emerging Legislature or Rubber Stamp? The South African National Assembly after Ten Years of Democracy', *CSSR Working Paper No. 134* (Cape Town, University of Cape Town Centre for Social Science Research).

Beinart, W. and C. Bundy (1987), *Hidden Struggles in Rural South Africa: The Politics and Popular Movements in the Transkei and Eastern Cape, 1890–1930* (Johannesburg: Ravan).

Beinart, W. (1994), *Twentieth Century South Africa* (Oxford: Oxford University Press).

Beinart, W. (2001), *Twentieth Century South Africa*, 2nd edition (Oxford: Oxford University Press).

Beinart, W. and S. Dubow (1995) (eds), *Segregation and Apartheid in 20th Century South Africa* (London: Routledge).

Bekker, S. (1993), *Ethnicity in Focus: The South African Case* (Durban: Indicator South Africa).

Bell C., Devarajan S. and Gersback H. (2003), 'Long-run economic costs of AIDS', *Policy Research Working Paper WPS 3152* (Washington: World Bank).

BER (2001), *The Macro-Economic Impact of HIV/AIDS in South Africa* (Stellenbosch: Bureau for Economic Research).

Bhinda, N., S. Griffiths-Jones, J. Leape, and M. Martin (1999), *Private Capital Flows to Africa: Perception and Reality* (The Hague: FONDAD).

Bhorat, H. and R. Kanbur (2006) (eds), *Poverty and Policy in Post-Apartheid South Africa* (Cape Town: Human Sciences Research Council Press).

Bhorat H., P. Naidoo, and C. van der Westhuizen (2006), 'Shifts in Non-Income Welfare in South Africa: 1993–2004', *DPRU Working Paper 06/108* (Cape Town, Development Policy Research Unit, University of Cape Town).

Bond, P. (2000), *Cities of Gold: Townships of Coal* (Trenton: Africa World Press).

Bonner, P. et al (1993) (eds), *Apartheid's Genesis 1935–1962* (Johannesburg: Witwatersrand University Press).

Bundy, C. (1988), *The Rise and Fall of the South Africa Peasantry*, 2nd edition (London: James Currey).

Burgess, S. M. (2002), *SA Tribes: Who We are, How We Live and What We Want from Life in the New South Africa* (Cape Town: David Philip).

Butler, A. (2003), 'South Africa's political futures', *Government and Opposition*, 38:1, 93–112.

Butler, A. (2005a), 'The negative and positive impacts of HIV/AIDS on democracy in South Africa', *Journal of Contemporary African Studies*, 23:1, 3–26.

Butler, A. (2005b), 'South Africa's HIV/AIDS policy, 1994–2004: How can it be explained?', *African Affairs*, 104:41, 591–614.

Butler, A. (2005c), 'How democratic is the African National Congress?', *Journal of Southern African Studies*, 31:4, 719–36.

Butler, A. (2006), 'Black economic empowerment: An overview', *New Agenda*, 22, June.

Butler, A. (2007a), *Cyril Ramaphosa* (Oxford: James Currey, and Johannesburg: Jacana).

Butler, A. (2007b), 'The state of the African National Congress', in S. Buhlungu, J. Daniel, R. Southall, and J. Lutchman (eds), *State of the Nation: South Africa 2007* (Cape Town: Human Sciences Research Council Press) 35–52.

Byrnes, R. (1997) (ed.), *South Africa: A Country Study* (Washington: Library of Congress).

Cameron, R. (1999), *The Democratisation of South African Local Government: A Tale of Three Cities* (Pretoria: Van Schaik).

Cameron, R. (2000), 'Megacities in South Africa: A solution for the new millennium?' *Public Administration and Development* 20, 155–65.

CGD (2008), *The Growth Report: Strategies for Sustained Growth and Inclusive Development,* Conference Edition (Washington: Commission on Growth and Development).

Chidester, D. (1992), *Religions of South Africa* (London: Routledge).

Chisholm, L. (2004) (ed.), *Changing Class: Education and Social Class in Post-apartheid South Africa* (Cape Town: HSRC Press).

Christopher, A. J. (2001) *The Atlas of Changing South Africa,* 2nd edition (London: Routledge).

Cilliers, J. (1999), 'An emerging South African foreign policy?', *Africa Quarterly*, 39:1, 41–68.

Coetzee, J. et al (2001) (eds), *Development: Theory, Policy and Practice* (Cape Town: Oxford University Press).

Cooper, F. (1996), *Decolonisation and African Society: The Labour Question in French and British Africa* (Cambridge: Cambridge University Press).

Crafts, N. (1996), 'Post neo-classical endogenous growth theory', *Oxford Review of Economic Policy,* 12:2, 30-47.

Crankshaw, O. (1997), *Race, Class and the Changing Division of Labour under Apartheid* (London: Routledge).

Crocker, C. R. (1992), *High Noon in Southern Africa: Making Peace in a Rough Neighbourhood* (New York: Norton).

Crush, J. et al (2000), *Losing Our Minds: Migration and the 'brain drain' from South Africa* (Cape Town: Southern African Migration Project).

Crush, J. and V. Williams (2001), *Making Up the Numbers: Measuring Illegal Immigration to South Africa,* Migration Policy Brief 3 (Cape Town: Southern African Migration Project).

Daniel, J., J. Lutchman, and S. Naidu, (2004), 'Post-apartheid South Africa's corporate expansion into Africa', *Review of African Political Economy,* 100, 343–48.

Davenport, T. R. H. (1991), *South Africa: A Modern History, 4th edition* (London: Macmillan).

Davies, R. (1979), *Capital, State and White Labour in South Africa in 1900–1960: An Historical Materialist Analysis of Class Formation and Class Relations* (Brighton: Harvester).

De Klerk, F. W. (1999), *The Last Trek: A New Beginning* (London: Pan Macmillan).

De Waal, A. (2003) 'How will HIV/AIDS transform African governance?' *African Affairs,* 102:406, 1–23.

Desai, A. (1997), *Arise ye Coolies: Apartheid and the Indian, 1960–1995* (Johannesburg: Impact Africa).

DFID (2001), *Meeting the Challenge of Poverty in Urban Areas* (London: UK Department for International Development).

DME (1998), *White Paper on the Energy Policy of the Republic of South Africa* (Pretoria: Department of Minerals and Energy Affairs).

DSD (2001), *The Road to Social Development* (Pretoria: Department for Social Development).

Du Plessis, S. and B. Smit, 'South Africa's growth revival after 1994', *Journal of African Economies* 16:5, 668–704.

Du Pre, R. H. (1994), *Separate but Unequal: The 'Coloured' People of South Africa* (Johannesburg: Jonathan Ball).

Elster, J. (1993), 'Rebuilding the Boat in the Open Sea: Constitution-Making in Eastern Europe'. *Discussion Paper, 24* (Oxford: Centre for European Studies).

Erlmann, V. (1999*), Music, Modernity and the Global Imagination: South Africa and the West* (Oxford: Oxford University Press).

Etherington, N. (1994), 'Is it too early to start devising historical explanations for the end of apartheid?', in Rich 1994, 101–19.

Feinstein, A. (2007), *After the Party: A Personal and Political Journey inside the ANC* (Johannesburg: Jonathan Ball).

Fine, B. and Z. Rustomjee (1996), *Political Economy of South Africa* (Johannesburg: Witwatersrand University Press).

Fiske, E. B. and H. F. Ladd, *Elusive Equity: Education Reform in Post-apartheid SA* (Cape Town: HSRC Press, 2005).

Fleishman, M. (2001), 'Unspeaking the centre', in Kriger and Zegeye 2001, 91–115.

Ford, C., Lewis, G. and Bates, B. (2002), 'The macroeconomic impact of HIV/AIDS in South Africa', in Kelly et al 2002, 10–20.

Forrest, D. and B. Streek (2001), 'Mbeki in bizarre AIDS outburst', *Weekly Mail and Guardian*, 26 October, archive availability <www.mg.co.za> [30 April 2009].

Fourie, P. and M. Schonteich (2001), 'Africa's new security threat', *African Security Review*, 10:4, 29–42.

Fox, R. and K. Rowntree (2000) (eds), *Geography of South Africa in a Changing World* (Cape Town: Oxford University Press).

Freund, W. (1995), *Insiders and Outsiders* (London: James Currey).

GCIS (2002), *South African Yearbook 2001/2* (Pretoria: Government Communications and Information Service).

Geldenhuys, D. (1990) *Isolated States: A Comparative Analysis* (Johannesburg: Jonathan Ball).

Gevisser, M. (2007), *Thabo Mbeki: The Dream Deferred* (Johannesburg: Jonathan Ball).

Giliomee, H. and C. Simkins (1999) (eds), *The Awkward Embrace: One-party Domination and Democracy* (Cape Town: Tafelberg).

Goodman, J. B. and L. W. Pauly (1993), 'The obsolescence of capital controls? Economic management in an age of global markets', *World Politics* 46, 50–82.

Greenberg, S. B. (1980), *Race and State in Capitalist Development* (Johannesburg: Ravan).

Greenberg, S. B. (1987), *Legitimating the Illegitimate: State, Markets, and Resistance in South Africa* (Berkeley: University of California).

Grint, K. (2000), *The Arts of Leadership* (Oxford: Oxford University Press).

Grundy, K. W. (1986), *The Militarization of South African Politics* (Bloomington: University of Indiana Press).

Haaker, M. 2002, 'Economic consequences of HIV/AIDS in Southern Africa', *Working Paper 38 WP/02/38* (Washington, DC: International Monetary Fund).

Haldenwang, B. (1997), *A Socio-demographic Profile of the South African Development Community Region* (Stellenbosch: University of Stellenbosch Institute for Futures Research).

Hanlon, J. (1986), *Apartheid's Second Front* (London: Penguin).

Hausmann, R. (2008), *Final Recommendations of the International Panel on Growth* (Pretoria: National Treasury).

Hemson, D. (2000), 'Policy and practice in water and sanitation', *Indicator South Africa,* 17:4, 48–53.

Hemson, D. (2004), *Beating the Backlog: Meeting Targets and Providing Free Basic Services* (Pretoria: HSRC).

Hirsch, A. (2005), *Season of Hope: Economic Reform under Mandela and Mbeki* (Natal: University of KwaZulu-Natal Press).

Hughes, T. (2004), *Composers, Conductors and Players: Harmony and Discord in South African Foreign Policy Making* (Johannesburg: Konrad Adenauer Stiftung).

Idasa (1995), *Making Affirmative Action Work* (Cape Town: Institute for Democracy in South Africa).

Idasa (2002a), 'Democratic governance in South Africa: the people's view', *Afrobarometer,* 11 December 2002 archived at <www.idasa.org.za> [7 February 2003].

Idasa (2002b), 'The changing public agenda', Afrobarometer, 11 December, archived at <www.afrobarometer.org> [30 April 2009].

Idasa (2002c), 'Political party support in South Africa', Afrobarometer, 13 December, archived at <www.afrobarometer.org> [30 April 2009].

IMF (2008), 'South Africa: Selected Issues', *Series Country Report No 08/347* (Washington: International Monetary Fund).

Impey, A. (2001), 'Re-fashioning identity in post-apartheid South African music', in Kriger and Zegeye 2001, 229–36.

ING Barings (2000), *Economic Impact of AIDS in South Africa* (Johannesburg: ING Barings).

Jacobs, S. (2000), 'An imperial presidency?', *SAIRR Regional Topic Paper* (Johannesburg: South African Institute for Race Relations).

James, W. G. and M. Simons (1989) (eds), *The Angry Divide* (Cape Town: David Philip).

Johnson, R. W. and L. Schlemmer (1996), *Launching Democracy in South Africa* (New Haven: Yale University Press).

Johnston, A. et al (1994) *Constitution-Making in the New South Africa* (London: Leicester University Press).

Kallaway, P. (2002), *History of Education under Apartheid 1948–1994* (Cape Town: Pearson).

Karis, T. and G. M. Carter (1972–77), *From Protest to Challenge: A Documentary History of African Politics in South Africa 1882–1964,* 4 volumes (Stanford: Hoover Institution Press)

Kaschula, R., and C. Anthonissen (1995), *Communicating across Cultures in South Africa* (Johannesburg: Hodder and Stoughton).

Kasrils, R. (1998), *Armed and Dangerous: From Undercover Struggle to Freedom* (Johannesburg: Jonathan Ball).

Kelly, K., Parker, W. and Gelb, S. (eds.) (2002), *HIV/AIDS, Economics and Governance in South Africa: Key Issues in Understanding Response: A Literature Review* (Johannesburg: Centre for AIDS Development, Research and Evaluation).

Kingdon, G. and J. Knight (2007), 'Unemployment in South Africa, 1995–2003: Causes, problems and policies', *Journal of African Economies,* 16:5 813–48.

Kriger, R. and A. Zegeye (2001), *Culture in the New South Africa* (Cape Town: Kwela Books).

Landau, L. B. (2006), *Discrimination and Development?* Forced Migration Working Paper No. 21 (Johannesburg, Forced Migration Studies Project, University of Witwatersrand).

Leftwich, A. (2000), *States of Development* (Cambridge: Polity Press).

Lemon, A., (1991) (ed.), *Homes Apart* (David Philip: Cape Town).

Levy, N. (2001), 'Instruments of intergovernmental relations', in Levy and Tapscott 2001a, 89–110.

Levy, N. and C. Tapscott (2001a) (eds), *Intergovernmental Relations in South Africa* (Cape Town: IDASA).

Levy, N. and C. Tapscott (2001b), 'Intergovernmental relations in South Africa', in Levy and Tapscott 2001a, 1–21.

Lipton, M. (1985), *Capitalism and Apartheid: South Africa, 1910–84* (Aldershot: Gower).

Lodge, T. (1985), *Black Politics in South Africa since 1945* (London: Longman).

Lodge, T. (1999), *Consolidating Democracy: South Africa's Second Popular Election* (Johannesburg: Witwatersrand University Press).

Lodge, T. (2002), *Politics in South Africa: From Mandela to Mbeki*, 2nd edition (Oxford: James Currey).

Lodge, T. (2004), 'The ANC and the development of party politics in modern South Africa', *Journal of Modern African Studies*, 42:2, 189–219.

Lodge, T. (2005), 'The African National Congress: There is no party like it; Ayikho Efana Nayo', in J. Piombo and L. Nizjink (eds), *Electoral Politics in South Africa: Assessing the First Democratic Decade* (New York: Palgrave Macmillan) 109–28.

Lodge, T. (2006), *Nelson Mandela: A Critical Life* (Oxford: Oxford University Press).

Lonsdale, J. (1988) (ed.), *South Africa in Question* (Cambridge: Cambridge University Press).

MacDonald, M. (1992), 'The Siren's Song: The political logic of power-sharing in South Africa', *Journal of Southern African Studies*, 18:4, 709–25.

Mahdi, P. M. (1997), *Black Economic Empowerment in the New South Africa* (Randburg: Knowledge Resources).

Makgetla, N. (2001), 'Policies and realities: The state of privatisation', *South African Labour Bulletin*, 25:4, 16–23

Mamdani, M. (1996), *Citizen and Subject: Contemporary Africa and the Legacy of Late Colonialism* (Princeton: Princeton University Press).

Mandela, N. (1993), 'South Africa's future foreign policy', *Foreign Affairs*, 72:5, 86–97.

Maphai V. and K. Gottschalk (2003), 'Parties, politics and the future of democracy', in D. Everatt and V. Maphai (eds), *The Real State of the Nation* (Johannesburg: Interfund) 51–74.

Marais, H. (1999), *South Africa: Limits to Change* (Cape Town: University of Cape Town Press).

Mare, G. (1992), *Brothers Born of Warrior Blood: Politics and Ethnicity in South Africa* (Johannesburg: Ravan).

Mattes, R. (1995), *The Election Book* (Cape Town: IDASA).

Mattes, R. (2002), 'South Africa: democracy without the people', *Journal of Democracy*, 13:1, 22–36

Mattes, R. (2003), 'Healthy democracies? The potential impact of AIDS on democracy in Southern Africa', *ISS Paper No. 71* (Pretoria: Institute for Security Studies).

Mattes, R. (2007), 'Democracy without People', *Afrobarometer Working Paper #82* (Cape Town: Afrobarometer).

May, J. (2000) (ed.), *Poverty and Inequality in South Africa* (Cape Town: David Philip).

May, J., I. Woolard, and S. Klasen (2000), 'The nature and measurement of inequality and poverty', in J. May 2000 (ed.), *Poverty and Inequality in South Africa* (Cape Town: David Philip) 18–20.

McGregor, R. (1999), *McGregor's Who Owns Whom in South Africa* (Johannesburg: Purdey Publishing).

Melber, H. (2003) (ed.), *Limits to Liberation in Southern Africa* (Cape Town: HSRC Press).

Mitchie, J. and V. Padayachee (1997) (eds), *Political Economy of South Africa's Transition: Policy Perspectives in the Late 1990s* (London: Dryden Press).

Mokaba P. et al (2002), *Castro Hlongwane, Caravans, Cats, Geese, Foot and Mouth and Statistics: HIV/AIDS and the Struggle for the Humanisation of the African* (unpublished unofficial discussion document) available at <www.virusmyth.com/aids/hiv/ancdoc.htm> [30 April 2009].

Moll, T., (1990) 'From booster to brake: apartheid and economic growth in comparative perspective', in Nattrass and Ardington 1990, 88–106.

Muradzikwa, S. (2002), *Foreign Investment in SADC* (University of Cape Town: Development Policy Research Unit, working paper 02/67).

Murray, C. (2001), 'Constitutional context of intergovernmental relations in South Africa', in Levy and Tapscott 2001a, 66–83.

National Treasury (2008), *Budget Review 2008* (Pretoria: South African National Treasury).

Nattrass, N. and E. Ardington (1990) (eds), *Political Economy of South Africa* (Cape Town: Oxford University Press).

Nattrass, N. (2000), *Macroeconomics: Theory and Policy in South Africa* (Cape Town: David Philip).

Nattrass, N. (2002), 'AIDS, Growth and Distribution in South Africa', *CSSR Working Paper 7* (University of Cape Town: Centre for Social Science Research).

Nattrass, N., (2004), *The Moral Economy of AIDS in South Africa* (Cambridge: Cambridge University Press).

Nattrass, N., and J. Seekings (2001), ' "Two Nations"? Race and economic inequality in South Africa today,' *Daedalus*, 130:1, 45–70.

Nel, P. S. (1997) (ed.), *South African Industrial Relations* (Pretoria: Van Schaik).

Olivier, G. and D. Geldenhuys (1997), 'South Africa's foreign policy: From idealism to pragmatism', *Business and the Contemporary World*, 9:2, 107–17.

O'Malley, P. (2007), *Shades of Difference: Mac Maharaj and the Struggle for South Africa* (New York: Viking Penguin).

Parnell, S., E. Pieterse, M. Swilling, and D. Wooldridge (2002) (eds), *Democratising Local Government: The South African Experiment* (Cape Town: University of Cape Town Press).

Picard L. (2005), *The State of the State: Institutional Transformation, Capacity and Political Change in South Africa* (Johannesburg: Wits University Press).

Posel, D. (1991), *The Making of Apartheid* (Oxford: Clarendon).

Presidency (2000), *Integrated Democratic Governance: A Restructured Presidency at work* (Pretoria: Presidency of the Republic of South Africa Communications Research Unit).

Preston-Whyte, R. and P. Tyson (1989), *Atmosphere and Weather of Southern Africa* (Cape Town: Oxford University Press).

Price, R. (1991), *The Apartheid State in Crisis: Political Transformation in South Africa, 1975–1990* (Oxford: Oxford University Press).

Przeworski A., M. Alvarez, J. Cheibub and F. Limongi (2000), *Democracy and Development: Political Institutions and Well-being in the World, 1950–1990* (Cambridge: Cambridge University Press).

Ramaphosa, C. (2004), 'Black empowerment: Myths and realities', in F. Sicre (ed.), *South Africa at 10* (Cape Town, Human and Rousseau) 72–84.

Reddy, T. (2005), 'The Congress Party model: South Africa's African National Congress (ANC) and India's Indian National Congress (INC) as dominant parties', *African and Asian Studies*, 4:3, 271–300.

Rich, P. B. (1994) (ed.), *The Dynamics of Change in Southern Africa* (London: Macmillan).

Roberts, B. (2008), 'Between trust and scepticism', *HSRC Review*, 6:1, 10–11.

Rodrik, D. (ed.) (2003), *In Search of Prosperity: Analytic Narratives on Economic Growth* (Princeton, NJ: Princeton University Press).

RSA (1995), *Labour Relations Act* (Pretoria: Republic of South Africa; Act No. 66 of 1995).

RSA (1996), *Constitution of the Republic of South Africa* (Pretoria: Republic of South Africa; Act No. 108 of 1996).

RSA (1997), *Basic Conditions of Employment Act* (Pretoria: Republic of South Africa; Act No. 75 of 1997).

RSA (1998a), *Employment Equity Act* (Pretoria: Republic of South Africa; Act No. 55 of 1998).

RSA (1998b), *Competition Act* (Pretoria: Republic of South Africa; Act No. 89 of 1998).

RSA (2002), *Mineral and Petroleum Resources Development Act* (Pretoria: Republic of South Africa; Act No. 28 of 2002).

RSA (2006), *A Nation in the Making: A Discussion Document on Macro Social Trends in South Africa* (Pretoria: Republic of South Africa, Policy Coordination and Advisory Services).

Sadie, Y. (2001), 'Political parties and interest groups', in Venter 2001, 261–93.

SAIIA (2008), *Yearbook of International Affairs* 2006/7 (Johannesburg: South African Institute for International Affairs).

Sangweni, S. S. and N. Mxakato-Diseko, (2008), 'It does not matter what slant or take you have on the developmental state: At the end of the day, a strong, coherent and astute public service is critical', in Ben Turok (ed.), *Wealth Doesn't Trickle Down: The Case for a Developmental State in South Africa* (Cape Town: New Agenda).

Saunders, C. (2001), *A Dictionary of South African History,* 2nd edition (Cape Town: David Philip).

Schrire, R. (1994) (ed.), *Malan to de Klerk: Leadership in the Apartheid State* (London: Hurst).

Schrire, R. (2001), 'The realities of opposition in South Africa: Legitimacy, strategies and consequences', *Democratization,* 8:1, 135–48.

Schmitz, T. (1999), 'Rethinking delivery? A review of the efforts of the Department of Water Affairs, 1994–9', *Centre for Social Studies Policy Brief No. 16* (Johannesburg: Centre for Policy Studies).

Schulz-Herzenberg, C. (2007), 'A silent revolution: South African voters, 1994–2006', in S. Buhlungu, J. Daniel, R. Southall, and J. Lutchman (eds), *State of the Nation: South Africa 2007* (Cape Town: Human Sciences Research Council Press) 114–145.

Seegers, A. (1996), *The Military in the Making of Modern South Africa* (London: Taurus).

Seekings, J. (1993), *Heroes or Villains? Youth Politics in the 1980s* (Johannesburg: Ravan).

Seekings, J, (2007), *Poverty and Inequality after Apartheid*, CSSR Working Paper No. 2000 (Cape Town: University of Cape Town Centre for Social Science Research).

Seekings, J. and N. Nattrass (2005), *Class, Race and Inequality in South Africa* (New Haven: Yale University Press).

Simkins, C. (2004), 'Employment and unemployment in South Africa', *Journal of Contemporary African Studies*, 22:2, 253–78.

Sisk, T. (1995), *Democratization in South Africa* (Princeton: Princeton University Press).

Skinner, K. and N. Mqadi (1999), 'Women and water', *Indicator South Africa*, 16:2, 55–62.

Smaldone, J. (1997), 'National security', in Byrnes 1997, Chapter 5.

Smith, D. (2000) (ed.), *The Apartheid City and Beyond* (London: Routledge).

Southall, R. (2001), 'Conclusions', in *Democratization* 8:1, 275–84.

Southall, R. (2003), *Democracy in Africa: Moving beyond a Difficult Legacy* (Cape Town: HSRC Press).

Southall, R. (2005), 'Black empowerment and present limits to a more democratic capitalism in SA', in S. Buhlungu, J. Daniel, R. Southall, and J. Lutchman (eds), *State of the Nation: South Africa 2007* (Cape Town: Human Sciences Research Council Press), 175–201.

Southall, R. (2006), 'Can SA be a developmental state?', in Buhlungu S, J. Daniel and J. Lutchman (eds), *State of the Nation: South Africa 2005–2006* (Cape Town: Human Sciences Research Council Press), xvii–xiv.

Sparks, A. (1995), *Tomorrow is Another Country* (New York: Hill and Wang).

Stadler, A. (1987), *The Political Economy of Modern South Africa* (London: Croom Helm).

Statistics South Africa (2001), *South Africa in Transition: Selected Findings from the October Household Survey of 1999 and Changes that have Occurred between 1995 and 1999* (Pretoria: Statistics South Africa).

Statistics South Africa (2002a), *Statistics in Brief 2002* (Pretoria: Statistics South Africa).

Statistics South Africa (2002b), *Earning and Spending in South Africa* (Pretoria: Statistics South Africa).

Statistics South Africa (2003), *Census 2001: Key Results* (Pretoria: Statistics South Africa).

Statistics South Africa (2006), *Income and Expenditure Survey 2005–6* (Pretoria: Statistics South Africa).

Statistics South Africa (2007a), *Mid–Year Population Estimates, South Africa (P0302)* (Pretoria: Statistics South Africa).

Statistics South Africa (2007b), *Labour Force Survey* (Pretoria: Statistics South Africa).

Statistics South Africa (2008a), *GDP First Quarter, South Africa (P0302)* (Pretoria: Statistics South Africa).

Statistics South Africa (2008b), *Labour Force Survey (P2109) September* (Pretoria: Statistics South Africa).

Stedman, S. J. (1994) (ed.), *South Africa: The Political Economy of Transformation* (London: Lynne Rienner).

Steinberg, J. (2001) (ed.), *Crimewave* (Johannesburg: Witwatersrand University Press).

Stover, J. and Bollinger, L. (1999), *Economic Impacts of AIDS in South Africa* (Connecticut: Futures Group International).

Suttner, R. (2003), 'Culture(s) of the African National Congress of South Africa: Imprint of exile experiences', in H. Melber (ed.), *Limits to Liberation in Southern Africa* (Cape Town: HSRC Press) 178–99.

Taylor, R. and M. Orkin (1995), 'The racialisation of social scientific research on South Africa', *South African Sociological Review,* 7:2, 43–69.

Taylor, V. (2002) (chairperson), *Transforming the Present – Protecting the Future: Report of the Committee of Inquiry into a Comprehensive System of SocialSecurity for South Africa* (Pretoria: Department of Social Development).

Teer-Tomaselli, R. (2001), 'Nation-building, social identity and television in a changing media landscape', in Kriger and Zegeye 2001, 85–106.

Terreblanche, S. and N. Nattrass (1990), 'A periodisation of the political economy from 1910', in Nattrass and Ardington 1990, 6–23.

Thomas, S. (1996), *Diplomacy of Liberation* (Johannesburg: Taurus).

Thompson, L. (1990), *A History of South Africa* (London: Yale University Press).

UNAIDS (2008), *Epidemiological Factsheet on HIV and AIDS: South Africa* (New York: United Nations Program on HIV and AIDS).

UNCTAD (1999), *Foreign Direct Investment in Africa: Performance and Potential* (New York and Geneva: United National Conference on Trade and Development).

UNDP (2007), *Human Development Report 2007/8* (Oxford: Oxford University Press and the United Nations Development Program).

Vail, L. (1989) (ed.), *Creation of Tribalism in Southern Africa* (London: James Currey).

Van der Berg, S. (2006), 'Public spending and the poor since the transition to democracy', in Bhorat and Kanbur 2006, 201–31.

Van Onselen, C. (1982a), *Studies in the Social and Economic History of the Witwatersrand 1886–1914: Volume I New Babylon* (Johannesburg: Ravan).

Van Onselen, C. (1982b), *Studies in the Social and Economic History of the Witwatersrand 1886–1914: Volume II New Ninevah* (Johannesburg: Ravan).

Van Onselen, C. (1996), *The Seed is Mine* (Cape Town: David Philip).

Venter, A. (2001) (ed.), *Government and Politics in the New South Africa* (Pretoria: Van Schaik).

Whiteside, A. and C. Sunter (2000), *AIDS: The Challenge for South Africa* (Cape Town: Human and Rousseau Tafelberg).

Wilson, M. and L. Thompson (1982) (eds), *A History of South Africa to 1870*, 2nd edition (London: James Currey).

Wolpe, H. (1988), *Race, Class and the Apartheid State* (London: James Currey).

Worden, N. (1994), *The Making of Modern South Africa: Conquest, Segregation and Apartheid* (Oxford: Blackwell).

Worden, N. (2000), *The Making of Modern South Africa: Conquest, Segregation and Apartheid*, 3rd edition (Oxford: Blackwell).

World Bank (1998), *World Development Report 1998-9: Knowledge for Development* (Washington, DC: World Bank).

Yashar, D. (1997) *Demanding Democracy: Reform and Reaction in Costa Rica and Guatemala, 1870s–1950s* (Stanford: Stanford University Press).

Index

ABSA Group, 72
Act of Union, 13, 110
Actuarial Society of South Africa
(ASSA), 223
affirmative action, *see* employment
equity
African Growth and Opportunity
Act, 64
African National Congress (ANC)
achievements, 2, 23, 24, 31–2,
143–7
constitution, 27–9, 110–15, 116
domination, 156–66
foreign policy, 3, 197, 198, 203–5,
206, 207, 212, 213
formation, 11, 15, 16
front line states, 199–200
government, 31–2
internal pluralism, 159, 162–5
non-racialism, 37
political organization, 143–7
Polokwane conference, 43, 135,
158, 160, 162, 180
social movements, 154–5
Umkhonto we Sizwe (MK),
24, 144, 203
women, 108, 109
Youth League, 15, 29, 143, 160
Zanu-PF, 159
African political kingdoms, 7, 8, 10, 12
African renaissance, 1, 209
African Renaissance Institute, 212
African Union, 118, 205, 209, 223
Africanism, 30, 181
Afrikaans, 14, 33, 34, 36, 37, 38–9,
40, 42, 47, 172, 173, 179

Afrikaners
boers, 7, 8, 10
Broederbond, 19, 23
frontier racism, 35
Great Trek, 9, 10
nationalism, 15, 16, 75
parastatals, 67, 92
politics, 15–18
suburbanization, 177–9, 193
vulnerability, 9, 187
see also National Party
aged person's grant, 95, 96
agriculture, *see* farming
AIDS, *see* HIV/AIDS
Alden, C., 220
Alexander, N., 40, 224
alien vegetation, 67
ANC, *see* African National Congress
Angola, 11, 24, 198, 200, 201
Anthonissen, C., 219
Anti-Eviction Campaign, 153
Anti-Privatisation Forum, 153
apartheid
collapse, 19–22
entrenchment, 5, 14–18, 19
Grand Plan, 17–18
high apartheid, 19–22
residual effects, 126, 128, 139
separate development, 19–22
armaments, 161, 199, 200, 201, 203,
205, 208
arms deal, *see* Strategic Defence
Procurement Package ⌐208
Armscor, *see* Denel
asbestos, 68
Asia, 136, 198, 207, 214

Asmal, Kader, 30, 111, 224
Auditor General, 82, 114, 159,
    161, 209
automobiles, 64, 178
Azanian People's Liberation Army
    (APLA), 203

Bantustans, 20–23, 31, 32, 35, 44, 49,
    102, 104, 106, 110, 131, 137, 173,
    175, 176, 198
Barber J., 205, 220
Barratt, J., 224
Basel Convention, 188
Basic Conditions of Employment Act,
    73, 230
Basic Income Grant (BIG), 74
Beinart W., 193, 218, 224
Bekker, S., 224
Belgium, 64
Bhinda, N., 65
Biko, Steve, 11
biological weapons, 200
Black consciousness, 113, 146,
    180, 181
Black economic empowerment,
    see economy
Boer War, *see* South African War
boers, *see* Afrikaners
Bond, P., 219, 225
Bonner, P., 18, 19, 225
Botha, P.W., 27, 43, 113, 199
Botswana, 20, 200
Brazil, 86–7
Britain
    gold, 11–12
    imperialism, 5, 8–9, 13
    migrants, 9, 39
    scientific racism, 9, 35
    Social Darwinism, 13
    Westminster model, 116–7
    see also United Kingdom
broadcasting, *see* media
Broederbond, 19, 23
Budget Council, 130
Bundy, C., 10, 218, 224, 225

Burgess, S.M., 219
bus boycotts, 15
Business Day, 222
Buthelezi, Mangosuthu, 46, 149
Butler, A., 219, 220
Byrnes, R., 201

cabinet, 43, 59, 70, 97, 108, 111, 112,
    113, 114, 116, 118, 119, 120, 121,
    122, 125, 128, 146, 160, 192
Cameron, R., 219
Cape, 6, 7, 8, 9, 10, 13, 16, 18, 19, 25,
    30, 39, 44, 45, 48, 50, 73
    see also Eastern Cape; Northern
    Cape; Western Cape
Cape Town, 6, 10, 13, 33, 73, 153, 188
Carter, G.M., 218
Centre for Development and
    Enterprise (CDE), 222
Centre for Policy Studies (CPS), 222
Chamber of Mines, 14, 69
Charterism, 30
Chidester, D., 219, 225
child mortality, 34, 88
child support grant, 95–6, 97, 98, 176
China, 62, 204, 206
chromium, 34, 68
churches, *see* religion
class, *see* social structure; inequality
climate, 4, 47–8, 193, 200, 218
Clinton, Bill, 203
coal, 49, 68, 69, 71, 99
Cold War, 156, 180, 196, 200, 202
    see also Soviet Union
colonialism, 1, 5, 6, 7, 8, 9, 10, 12, 19,
    20, 22, 37, 39, 43, 48, 79, 110,
    115, 116, 145, 156, 168, 172, 174,
    181, 182, 190, 193, 196, 198
Coloured South Africans, 15, 17, 30,
    33, 35, 36, 38, 47, 90, 93, 104,
    110, 126, 140, 149, 150, 193, 194
Commission for Gender Equality,
    see women
Community Based Public Works
    Programme, 67

Competition Act, 60
Comprehensive Anti-Apartheid
   Act, 201
Congo, 201
Congress of South African Trade
   Unions (COSATU), 2, 11, 25,
   58, 68, 70, 93, 97, 113, 142,
   145, 146,
   see also tripartite alliance
Congress of the People (COPE), 147,
   150, 158, 166, 217
Constitution, 3, 4, 11, 12, 28–30, 33,
   34, 38, 46, 53, 60, 71, 100, 108,
   109, 110–7, 118, 119, 120, 124,
   126, 127, 129, 135, 137, 138, 140,
   143, 148, 153, 157, 159, 161, 169,
   184, 189, 194
   see also rights
Constitutional Court, 28, 29, 125,
   126, 161
Convention for a Democratic South
   Africa (CODESA), 11, 28
corporatism, 117, 122
Correctional Services,
   Department of, 119, 127
corruption, 3, 4, 60, 63, 65, 66, 79, 80,
   96, 127, 131, 135, 137, 150, 161,*160,*
   163, 164, 165, 166, 168, 171, 179,
   183,⟮186⟯
Council for Conciliation, Mediation
   and Arbitration (CCMA), 74
crime, 2, 50, 52, 66, 80, 108, 136,
   168, 171, 176, 177, 183–5, 194
Crush, J., 49, 167
Cuba, 200, 204
culture, 22, 36, 171–4, 175

dance, 171–4
de Klerk, F.W., 11, 26–7, 29, 111, 113,
   148, 193, 202, 205, 219
democracy
   ANC, 126, 138, 145, 148,
   152–66, 169
   prospects, 139, 142, 148, 170
   transition, 1, 4, 23–30, 56

vulnerability, 31, 142, 145–8,
   152–5, 155–6
Democratic Alliance (DA), 30, 37,
   143, 148, 212, 222
Democratic Party (DP),
   see Democratic Alliance
Denel (Armscor), 67, 199, 200, 203
Denmark, 64
Desai, A., 218
Development Bank of Southern
   Africa, 67, 72, 221
diamonds, 34, 68
disabilities, 101
Drakensbergs, 40
Du Pre, R.H., 218
Dubow, S., 218
Durban, 34, 46, 131, 140, 188
Dutch East India Company, 6, 7, 10
Dutch Reformed Church,
   see religion

East London, 34, 131
Eastern Cape, 9, 25, 29, 34, 45, 48,
   49, 105, 150
economy
   Africa, 55–6
   Black economic empowerment
   (BEE), 71, 73, 75–80, 82, 83,
   152, 153, 186, 216
   developmental state, 60–3, 78, 82,
   97, 107, 121, 136, 137
   financial markets, 65, 72
   foreign direct investment, 64, 65,
   66, 201, 207
   growth, 24, 31, 34, 56–63, 107,
   134, 143, 156, 165, 167, 168, 215
   Growth, Employment and
   Redistribution (GEAR), 31, 58,
   59, 92, 93
   key facts, 61
   output and expenditure, 55–7
   policy, 58–62
   public sector, 67–8
   trade, 8, 63–5, 116, 118, 119, 180,
   204–7, 209, 210, 211, 213

Economy – *continued*
    see also labour relations;
        unemployment
education, 32, 49, 52, 66, 75, 80, 84,
    85, 86, 87, 90, 91, 96, 103–7, 119,
    125, 127, 129, 135, 161, 167, 184,
    187, 219
elections
electorate, 140–2
national results, 142–3
system, 139–40
    see also floor crossing
Electoral Institute of Southern Africa
    (EISA), 155, 222
electricity, 2, 57, 58, 67, 69–70,
    98–100, 132, 153, 177, 178,
    192, 215
emigration, *see* migration
employment, *see* unemployment
employment equity, 73, 76, 77, 108,
    109, 186
environment, 116, 118, 129,
    188–9, 221
Erlmann, V., 175, 219
Eskom, 61, 67, 69, 70, 71, 153, 212
Etherington, N., 218
ethnicity
    diversity, 4, 33, 36, 38
    high apartheid, 19, 20, 23, 44
    re-tribalisation, 20–23
    tribalism, 7, 22
    see also race
European Union (EU), 64, 65, 117,
    201, 207, 209
executive branch, 4, 20, 109, 111–16,
    117–21, 122, 123, 124, 125, 127,
    129, 130, 131, 135, 140, 157, 158,
    160, 161, 168
    see also cabinet; presidency
exchange controls, 60, 72

Fagan Commission, 19
farming, 7, 13, 14, 16, 17, 48, 49, 56,
    57, 72, 94, 175, 221
finance, *see* economy

Finance, Department of, *see* Treasury
Financial and Fiscal Commission,
    30, 130
First National Bank, 72
floor crossing, 140, 150
forced removals, *see* population
Foreign Affairs, Department of, 119,
    127, 200, 203, 206, 223
Forrest D., 226
Fort Hare, University of, 29, 106
Fourie, P., 185
Fox R., 218
France, 64, 115
Free State, 25, 34, 45, 48
    see also Orange Free State
Freedom Front, 143
Freund, W., 218

G8, 65
Gabon, 86, 200
Gauteng, 34, 44, 45, 46, 48, 49, 50,
    54, 105, 134, 174, 184, 211
GEAR, *see* economy
Geldenhuys, D., 220
gender, *see* women
German Democratic Republic, 144
Germany, 64, 112, 115, 116, 117,
    197, 201
Giliomee, H., 157, 158, 219
gold, 5, 11, 12, 14, 15, 34, 39, 40, 48,
    56, 63, 64, 68, 188, 197, 201
Goodman, J.B., 23
Government of National Unity, 27,
    29, 46, 47, 149
Great Trek, *see* Afrikaners
Greenberg, S.B., 218
Grint, K., 169
Griqua, 47
Group Areas Act, 11, 17
Grundy, K.W., 220

Hanlon, J., 220
health, 66, 67, 82, 87, 91, 101, 107,
    125, 127, 132, 137, 154, 161, 176,
    186, 190, 191, 192, 205, 215

Hemson, D., 219
Hinduism, 33
HIV/AIDS, 3, 4, 11, 45, 46, 50, 67,
    81–2, 88–9, 95, 101, 121, 153,
    154, 160, 168, 171, 176, 183, 184,
    185, 189, 190, 191, 192, 194, 216,
    220, 223
Holomisa, Bantu, 150
Home Affairs, Department of, 46, 50,
    104, 109, 127
homelands, *see* Bantustans
housing, 2, 61, 63, 98, 101–2, 104,
    109, 127, 161, 183, 184, 216, 219
human development, 85–9
    see also inequality
human rights, *see* rights
Human Rights Commission,
    30, 50, 114

immigration, *see* migration
Immorality Act, 17
Impey, A., 175
Independent Broadcasting
    Authority, 179
Independent Democrats (ID), 149, 150
Indian South Africans, 15, 16, 17, 30,
    33, 36, 46, 47, 90, 93, 104, 110
Industrial Development
    Corporation, 67
industrial relations, *see* labour
    relations
inequality, 68, 81, 84, 89–97, 103, 104,
    109, 157, 167, 176, 184, 185, 206
infant mortality, 34, 88
influx controls, 13, 14, 23, 24, 92
Inkatha Freedom Party, 29, 30, 37,
    46, 112, 141, 142, 143
Institute for Democracy in South
    Africa (IDASA), 155
interest groups, *see* pressure groups
International Monetary Fund, 60, 208
International relations
    Africa, 207–11
    future, 206–9
    history, 196–205

Mandela, 200–5
    see also African Union; NEPAD
Iran, 200, 204, 213
Iraq, 200, 212
Ireland, 205
Israel, 212
Italy, 64, 89

James, W.G., 218
Japan, 62, 64, 136
Johannesburg, 12, 13, 21, 26, 29, 33,
    34, 36, 40, 45, 50, 51, 106, 128,
    131, 134, 160, 175, 188
Johnston, A., 28
Judaism, 33
judiciary
    constitutional court, 28, 29, 125,
        126, 161
    functions, 4, 122, 124–7, 162
    independence, 4, 122, 124–7
    Judicial Services Commission,
        124, 161

Kalahari, 40
Karis, T., 219 218
Kaschula, R., 220
Khoisan peoples, 5, 6, 38, 47
Kriger, R., 220
KwaZulu-Natal, 31, 34, 45–7, 105,
    111, 147
Kyoto convention, 188

labour, 9, 10, 12–18, 23, 39, 40, 46,
    53, 68, 71
    see also labour relations;
        migration; unemployment
Labour Party, 14
labour relations, 73–5, 94
Labour Relations Act, 73
Ladysmith Black Mambazo, 174
land
    indirect rule, 181–2
    Landless People's Movement, 153
    reform, 75, 103, 109, 153
Land Bank of South Africa, 67, 72

landscape, 40, 217
language
    broadcast media, 179
    diversity, 22, 34, 35, 36, 38, 39
    division, 37–8, 187
    multilingualism, 173
    Pan South African Language
        Board, 37–8, 114
Latin America, 64, 156, 198, 206
legislature, *see* parliament
Lekota, Mosiuoa, 147
Lembede, Anton, 143
Leon, Tony, 148
Lesotho, 20, 34, 40, 198, 200
Levy, N., 219
Libya, 204, 210
Limpopo, 34, 42, 44, 45, 48–9, 105
Lipton, M., 218
literature, 39, 171–3
local government, *see* municipalities
Lodge, T., 219

McGregor, R., 229
Madikizela-Mandela, Winnie,
    25, 164
Mail and Guardian, 222
Makgetla N., 219
Malan, D.F., 15, 16
Malawi, 219
Malaysia, 64
Mamdani, M., 181, 182
Mandela, Nelson, 1, 2, 3, 11, 16, 25,
    27, 29, 34, 48, 76, 113, 131, 144,
    160, 164, 167, 202, 203, 204,
    205, 211, 213, 218
manganese, 34, 68
Marais, H., 218
Mare, G., 218
Marxism, 163, 180
Mattes, R. (Bob), 219
May, J., 219
Mbeki, Govan, 128
Mbeki, Thabo
    African renaissance, 1, 190, 209, 212
    critics, 152, 159

foreign policy, 159–60, 161, 202–5
    life, 128, 160, 163–4
    NEPAD, 64, 209, 210, 211, 212
    presidency, 128, 136, 147–8, 163,
        164, 168, 189–90
media, 26, 28, 38, 51, 53, 79, 116,
    120, 152, 158, 171–2, 179
Meyer, Roelf, 150
Mexico, 85, 86, 159
Middle East, 205, 213
migrant labour, 10, 13, 14, 68, 108,
    175, 182
migration, 8, 9, 14, 17, 45, 59–53, 167,
    205, 226, 228
    see also xenophobia
military, 10, 12, 14, 17, 20, 24, 27,
    29, 112, 144, 160, 196, 197,
    199–203, 208, 211
Milner, Alfred, 13
Mining, 11, 12, 13, 14, 15, 48, 56–8,
    64, 65, 68, 69, 99, 100, 151, 199
    see also diamonds; gold
Mokaba Peter, 190, 229
Moll, T., 56
monetary policy committee,
    see 'reserve bank'
Montreal Convention, 188
Motlanthe, Kgalema, 3, 128, 147
Mozambique, 11, 13, 24, 34, 49, 163,
    198, 200
Mpumalanga, 34, 45, 48, 140
Mugabe, Robert, 186
municipalities, 2, 31, 61, 70, 100–3,
    112, 114, 130, 131–4, 164
Muradzikwa, S., 65
Murray, C., 219
music, 172–5, 177, 178, 219

Namibia, 24, 34, 37, 197, 199
Natal, 8, 13, 26, 27, 30, 31, 34, 39, 44,
    45–7, 105, 111, 147, 227
National African Chamber of
    Commerce (NAFCOC), 74, 152
National Arts Council, 173
National Assembly, *see* parliament

National Association of People
 Living with HIV/AIDS,
 see HIV/AIDS
National Business Initiative, 151
National Chamber of Provinces,
 see parliament
National Economic Development and
 Labour Council (NEDLAC),
 74, 151
National Land Committee, 153
National Party, 11, 16, 19, 24, 42, 111,
 143, 146, 148–50, 160, 196, 197,
 201, 202, 214
National Security Management
 System, 200
National Treasury, *see* Treasury
National Union of Mineworkers
 (NUM), 113
Native Affairs Department, 19
Natives (Urban Areas) Act, 11
Natives Land Act, 14
Nattrass, N., 14, 81, 90, 93, 218,
 219, 220
NEDLAC, *see* National Economic
 Development and Labour
 Council
Nelson Mandela Metropole, 34, 131
New Partnership for Africa's
 Development (NEPAD), 64,
 209–10, 211, 212
Nigeria, 160, 204, 210
non-governmental organisations
 (NGOs), 96, 100, 108, 152, 154,
 155, 223
North-West Province, 34, 45, 48
Northern Cape, 34, 45, 48, 140
nuclear weapons, 200
Nzo, Alfred, 26, 203

opera, 172, 174
opposition politics, 96, 97, 120, 141,
 142, 144, 147, 148, 149, 154,
 156–68, 170, 212, 216, 217, 222
Orange Free State, 16, 18, 44
 see also Free State

Organisation for African Unity
 (OAU), 205
Organisation for Economic
 Cooperation and Development
 (OECD), 207
Orkin, M., 141

Palestine, 212, 213
Pan Africanist Congress (PAC), 30,
 144, 149, 150
Parliament, 111–8, 122, 123–4, 139,
 148, 169, 179, 208, 209, 212, 222
Parnell, S., 219
pass laws, 11, 14, 15, 18
 see also influx controls
pension, *see* aged person's grant
Phosa, Mathews, 165
platinum, 34, 64, 68, 201
poetry, 39, 171, 173
policing, *see* crime
pollution, *see* environment
population
 forced removals, 19, 20, 23, 33
 growth, 14, 18, 15, 56
 HIV/AIDS, 45
 life expectancy, 34, 35, 45
 mother tongue, 36
 Population Registration Act, 11, 17
 'race', 33, 35, 198
Portugal, 198
Posel, D., 19
poverty, *see* human development
Presidency, 3, 59, 63, 64, 85, 111, 113,
 118, 119, 120, 121, 128, 134, 160,
 163, 180
pressure groups, 151–4
Pretoria (Tshwane), 24, 34, 45, 164
prison, *see* crime
provinces, 44–8, 112–4, 116, 128–34,
 164, 168, 184
 see also individual provinces
public agenda, 184
public expenditure, 59, 121, 128
Public Protector, 30, 114, 159,
 161, 209

race, 20, 35, 36, 40, 42, 45, 84, 89, 90,
    109, 141, 178, 190, 216
    see also ethnicity
Rainbow Nation, 33, 35, 36, 37
Ramaphosa, Cyril, 75, 77, 112,
    113, 165
Rand Revolt, 14
Rand Water, 67
Reconstruction and Development
    Programme (RDP), 58, 59
Reddy, T., 159, 219, 230
refugees, 8, 51
religion
    affiliations, 40
    African independent churches, 40–2
    Christianity, 33–36, 40–2
    diversity, 33, 36, 40, 41, 42
    Dutch reformed churches, 41–2
    politics, 40
    Zion Christian Church, 41, 42,
        43, 44
republic, 11
Reservation of Separate Amenities
    Act, 17
Reserve Bank, *see* South African
    Reserve Bank
reserves, native, 13, 14, 15
rights, 15, 20, 23, 28, 30, 35, 38, 50,
    53, 71, 78, 104, 107, 108, 112,
    114, 125–6, 135, 153, 154, 159,
    161, 169, 178, 182, 187, 198, 203,
    204, 205, 212, 213, 216
Rivonia trial, 19, 144, 160
Robben Island, 29, 128, 144, 160,
    162, 163
rural South Africa, 2, 13, 14, 33, 39,
    44, 48, 55, 61, 67, 73, 84, 87, 89,
    92, 95, 96, 101, 108, 109, 131,
    138, 149, 163, 164, 166, 176, 180,
    190, 191, 192, 215, 224
Rustomjee, Z., 58

Safety and Security, Department of,
    119, 127, 165, 178
San, *see* Khoisan

Sandton, 45
Sangweni, S., 137, 231
sanitation, 67, 87, 91, 98, 100, 127,
    177, 215
Saro-Wiwa, Ken, 204
Saunders, C., 218, 231
Schlemmer, L., 141
schools, *see* education
Schrire, R., 157, 219, 231
Seegers, A., 220
Seekings, J., 90, 91, 93, 95, 96, 219
segregation, 5, 11, 13, 14–19, 32, 35,
    36, 45, 46, 76, 89, 143, 180,
    216, 218
    see also apartheid;
        White Supremacy
Select Committee on Public
    Accounts, 161, 209
separate development, *see* apartheid
separation of powers, 28, 69,
    112–5, 122
service payments, 133, 168, 215
Sesotho, 33, 34, 36, 37, 38
Setswana, 33, 34, 36, 37, 48
Sexwale, Tokyo, 79, 165
Sharpeville, 43
shebeens, 177
silver, 34, 68
Simkins, C., 32, 91, 157, 158
Simons, M., 218, 228
Sisulu, Walter, 143, 160
slavery, 8, 9, 196
Smaldone, J., 199, 200
Smuts, Jan, 16
Social Development, Department of,
    61, 95, 103, 109, 129, 135, 222
social movements, *see* pressure
    groups
social policy, 18, 84–109
social structure, 84–8
socioeconomic rights, *see* rights
Sotho, 9, 48, 79
South African Institute for
    International Affairs (SAIIA),
    220, 223

South African Broadcasting
Company, 179–80
South African Chamber of Business
(SACOB), 74, 152
South African Communist Party
(SACP), 3, 37, 58, 68, 79, 93, 97,
142, 144–7, 163, 165, 182, 206
see also tripartite alliance
South African Defence Force,
see military
South African Native National
Congress, *see* African National
Congress
South African Reserve Bank, 60, 72,
159, 221
South African Revenue Service
(SARS), 59, 82
South African War, 11, 12
South Korea, 62, 136
Southall, R., 62, 137, 159, 182
Southern African Development
Community (SADC), 64, 118,
203, 205, 211
Soviet Union, 24, 144, 180, 198, 200,
201, 206
Soweto, 11, 21, 24, 45, 76, 113
Soweto Electricity Crisis
Committee, 153
Sparks, A., 218
sport, 2, 73, 171, 177, 187, 192, 193, 194
Standard Bank, 72
State Security Council, 200
Statistics South Africa, 221
Steinberg, J., 185, 219
Stockholm convention, 188
Strategic Defence Procurement
Package, 3, 161, 186, 208
suburbanization, 175–9
sunset clauses, 29, 202
sustainable development,
see environment
Swaziland, 20, 34, 89, 160, 163, 198
Sweden, 64
Switzerland, 64
Syria, 204

Taiwan, 62, 204
Tambo, Oliver, 16, 24, 26, 29, 143
Taylor, R., 141
Taylor, V., 232
Technical Intergovernmental
Committee, 130
Teer-Tomaselli, R., 232
Telkom, 61, 67
Thatcher, Margaret, 201
theatre, 39, 171–4
Thompson, L., 7, 9, 218
titanium, 34, 68
total strategy, 200
tourism, 47, 48, 72–3, 195, 207
townships, 18, 26, 33, 45, 50–1, 73,
105, 153, 171, 176–8, 193
see also urbanization
Trade and Industry, Department of,
60, 61, 62, 73, 212
trade unions, 3, 11, 15, 25, 58, 74, 93,
113, 142, 151, 152, 182
see also COSATU
Transitional Executive Council, 28
Transnet, 67
Transvaal, 9, 11, 16, 18, 44
Treasury, 1, 2, 59, 97, 117–22, 128,
134, 212
Treatment Action Campaign,
see HIV/AIDS
trekkers, *see* Afrikaners
tribalism, *see* ethnicity
tripartite alliance, 3, 58, 145, 146,
162, 168, 170
Truth and Reconciliation
Commission, 53
Tshabalala-Msimang, Manto, 154
Tshwane *see* Pretoria
Tutu, Desmond, 4, 33

Umkhonto we Sizwe (MK),
see African National Congress
unemployment, 2, 47, 50–1, 56, 58,
67, 74, 80, 87, 89, 91–5, 108, 156,
165, 187, 215, 216
unicities, *see* municipalities

Union of South Africa, 10
United Democratic Front (UDF), 25,
    59, 152, 173
United Democratic Movement
    (UDM), 149, 150
United Kingdom, 64, 112, 116, 117,
    133, 144, 201, 202
United Nations, 199, 213, 222, 233
United Nations Development
    Program (UNDP), 85–6, 87, 88
United Party, 16
United States, 64, 112, 115, 117, 198,
    201, 204, 207, 208, 212
uranium, 34, 68, 69, 200, 201
Urban Areas Act, 11, 14
Urbanization, 2, 5, 15, 16, 17, 24, 44,
    45, 51, 102, 134, 175–7, 215
user charges, *see* service payments

Vail, L., 218
Van Onselen, C., 218
Van Skalkwyk, Martinus, 149
vermiculite, 68
Vickers, B., 224

Washington consensus, 24, 180
water, 2, 8, 67, 81, 88, 98, 100–1, 108,
    132, 153, 161, 176, 177, 189
Water Affairs and Forestry,
    Department of, 61, 67,
    100–1
Water Services Act, 100
Western Cape, 30, 38, 47, 48, 50, 73,
    148, 149, 150, 184
    see also Cape
White Supremacy, 13, 17, 19, 20, 32,
    36, 180, 198
Witwatersrand, 11, 12, 20, 40

Witwatersrand, University of, 106,
    164, 223
Wolpe, H., 218
women
    BEE, 75
    disadvantage, 52, 67, 89, 99, 100,
        107–9, 121, 126, 161, 173, 175,
        183, 193, 216
    violence, 107–8
Worden, N., 9, 218, 233
World Bank, 65, 81, 107, 208, 222
World Cup, FIFA *see* sport
World Summit on Sustainable
    Development, 45, 188
World Trade Organisation, 118, 213
World War I, 11
World War II, 11, 15, 56, 144, 197

xenophobia, 49–53, 54, 167, 197
Xhosa, 6, 8, 48, 150, 193

Yashar, D., 165
youth, 15, 24, 29, 30, 95, 121,
    160, 231
    see also unemployment

Zaire, 200
Zambia, 160, 163, 182, 200
Zanu-PF, 159, 204, 211
Zegeye, A., 219
Zimbabwe, 3, 11, 24, 37, 49, 160, 182,
    199, 200, 204, 209, 211–3
Zion Christian Church (ZCC),
    see religion
zirconium, 34, 68
Zulu, 6, 7, 8, 10, 11, 46, 112, 140, 149
Zuma, Jacob, 3, 43, 128, 147, 160–2,
    164, 165, 180, 183, 209